Fishing with Hyenas

Fishing with Hyenas

Theresa Mathews

Lighthouse Press
Roche Harbor, WA

Fishing with Hyenas
copyright © Theresa Mathews, 2016—2019
All rights reserved

This is a work of creative nonfiction. The events are portrayed to the best of the author's memory. Some names and identifying details have been changed to protect the privacy of the people involved. Without limiting the rights under copyright reserved above, no part of this publication may be reproduced, stored in, or introduced into a retrieval system, or transmitted in any form, or by any means (electronic, mechanical, photocopying, recording, or otherwise) without the prior written permission of the author except in the case of brief quotations or sample images embedded in critical articles or reviews. The scanning, uploading, and distribution of any part of this book via the Internet, or via any other means, without the permission of the author is illegal and punishable by law. Please purchase only authorized editions and do not participate in or encourage electronic piracy of copyrightable materials. Your support of the author's rights is appreciated. For permission, address your inquiry to: theresa@theresa-mathews.com. Website: **www/theresa-mathews.com**

Paperback ISBN: 978-1-796513-64-6
Library of Congress Control Number: 2016948638

Mathews, Theresa
Fishing with Hyenas
1. Memoir; 2. Commercial albacore fishing; 3. Death, bereavement, and healing.
   I. TITLE

Interior editing, design, & original production by
Carla Perry, Dancing Moon Press
Cover design & production by Kristen Ingebretson
Cover design inspired by Libbie Hawker's vision
Author photograph by *Barbara Cromwell*
Manufactured in the United States of America

Lighthouse Press
P.O. Box 4383
Roche Harbor, WA 98250

SECOND EDITION 2019
FIRST EDITION 2016

Dedication

**This book is dedicated to fishermen
and their families
everywhere.**

Acknowledgments

ALTHOUGH WRITING IS A SOLO-SPORT, I couldn't have done it without the involvement of others. My family and friends never tired of hearing me talk about the book when I hoped it would somehow write itself. From the moment I spoke about my idea, I had fans. It is an honor to acknowledge these wonderful people because without them, I would not be able to share my story with you today.

My parents, Bonnie Hendrickson and Jimmie Dorsey, have supported and believed in me my whole life. They held me up during my darkest days and stood proudly beside me as I soldiered on. My dear friend Barbara Cromwell was my first beta reader. Without her honest desire to read the final product, I might have given up on this book endeavor many years ago.

Sue Slater, whose strength, friendship, and willingness to share some of her own stories as I wrote mine, are gifts I will treasure forever. Permission to publish her daughter Megan's poem in my memoir is an honor for me, and I hope this tribute to the Slater family makes them proud.

Mike and Paulette Brown, Kami Jennings, and Wendy Seaa Brown will always be family to me. They helped me through every step of my life at sea, extensive dealings with the boat, and technicalities as I tried to recall details of my fishing days. Highlights of their lives on the ocean gave deeper insight into the amazing lifestyle and fishing community they've been part of for decades.

Wes Wickham will always be a like a brother to me. He described pieces of his life and adventures on the water, and I'm delighted to include them in this book.

I appreciate my writing mentor, Susan Wingate, who's been a

major support from day one. A huge thank you to the rest of my beta readers: Colette Landerville, Helen George, Sara Grose, and Tracy Peterson, who offered excellent suggestions and encouragement to see this project through.

Carla Perry was the perfect person to collaborate with for the publication of this book. She shared her editing talents in a way that tightened my writing without losing my voice. I'm grateful for the compassion and professional direction she provided.

A huge shout out goes to Eric Jewett, who's endless support during the final stretch gave me the push I needed to finish this project.

The numerous friends I'm lucky to have in my life have kept me inspired and motivated. My Hyena family and the Friday Harbor community rallied for me when I was completely broken, and I will forever be grateful for their generosity and love. I thank everyone who has been on this journey with me, whether from the beginning—or during the past few years.

For Bart

Contents

Introduction: The Hyenas 1
Chapter 1: The Explosion 8
Chapter 2: Bart 17
Chapter 3: Falling 25
Chapter 4: The Reunion 35
Chapter 5: Getting Ready 42
Chapter 6: The Slaters 52
Chapter 7: Death's Journey 61
Chapter 8: The Board Meeting 74
Chapter 9: The Browns 85
Chapter 10: The Detour 94
Chapter 11: Nippers 101
Chapter 12: Highs and Lows 107
Chapter 13: Walking Through Molasses 116
Chapter 14: 79th Day at Sea 129
Chapter 15: The Visitor 138
Chapter 16: The Dream 144
Chapter 17: Pago Pago 151
Chapter 18: Moving Forward 165
Chapter 19: First Watch 170
Chapter 20: Big Day 174
Chapter 21: Déjà Vu 190
Chapter 22: Power/Powerless 200
Chapter 23: Typhoon Hagibis 210
Chapter 24: Senses 217
Chapter 25: The Turnaround 224
Chapter 26: Family 234
Chapter 27: Dresses and Chain Saws 239
Chapter 28: Another Big Blow 249
Chapter 29: The Hyena Memorial 254

Chapter 30: Dead in the Water...267
Chapter 31: Wes (aka Norton)..276
Chapter 32: The Scattering..282
Epilogue: Near Extinction..290
In Memoriam 293
Special Tribute...294
About the Author..295

Introduction: The Hyenas

THE HYENAS ARE THE MOST WONDERFUL PEOPLE I've ever met. Since living at sea with them, I've added a dozen Hyenas to my extended family.

Comprised of a unique blend of personalities and lifestyle choices, many of these folks would probably not choose to be friends with each other "on the beach" if they met under different circumstances. But out there—in the middle of the ocean? Well that's another story. I should probably add that "on the beach" is a term fishermen (and others who spend time on the water) use when they describe life on land.

There are approximately 400 vessels in the U.S. albacore troll fleet based in ports up and down the West Coast of the United States.

"Trollers" are boats that fish by using a trailing baited line from behind their slow-moving vessels. These fishermen primarily fish in the North Pacific Ocean, but a handful of them fish seasonally, traveling to the South Pacific during the winter months back home.

As with every industry, there are folks driven by greed and dishonesty. But there are also people who remain competitive, yet help their brothers and sisters succeed. The Hyenas, a tight-knit group of albacore tuna boat captains, come from that cloth. As a result, all the Hyenas have become very successful fishermen. In fact, most captains not already in the Hyena group wanted in!

Let me back up a bit. The pelagic nature of albacore—the fact that they exist in open waters—makes their continuous movement difficult to figure out when you want to know where to find them.

Tuna travel along a hard edge of water temperature. A hard temperature edge forms where cool water meets warmer water—an edge difference of two to three degrees. These hard edges follow the ocean's currents and often are hundreds of miles long. There are dozens of small species that follow these edges, and albacore feed on those smaller fish.

In the early 1990s, when the fishing industry was thriving in the North Pacific, the ocean was full of tuna boats. Most boats were either jig boats or bait boats, which catch tuna via pole and line. Both methods of fishing make it possible to sustain the fishery because albacore must actually be hungry and must bite the hooks in order to be caught.

When tuna fishermen use jig fishing and pole and line methods, they harvest only when the fish are feeding and this helps control the quantities caught so that they don't destroy the entire species. When weather conditions drive tuna outside 200 miles of the United States coastlines into international waters, the fishers head west to those warmer waters offshore.

There are specific requirements for boats fishing in U.S. waters. The Jones Act separates U.S. waters from international waters by a 200-mile distance from all shores. It states that any fishing vessel with a hull built in a foreign country (even if the boat is a U.S. registered vessel and owned and/or operated by a U.S. citizen) is unable to fish inside the 200-mile limit. The Jones Act also states that if a "foreign" vessel is caught fishing inside the 200-mile limit, the owner could be fined tens of thousands of dollars and possibly lose their boat.

Not all tuna boats are large enough, or well equipped enough, to go that far offshore. And it is much easier to locate a school of fish when you have several boats looking for them. Even with today's technology, a boat can drive right by a school that's several miles wide and several miles across and not know the fish are right outside the sonar's signal.

But when multiple boats work together, as the Hyenas do, they can distance themselves anywhere from a quarter-mile to two miles wide while cruising on the same latitude. When a boat lands on a biting school (not all schools bite), they can alert fellow fishing vessels to their location. To control the fishing site, the first boat remains located on the school. When you're out there alone, on an outer edge of the school and the school moves, you can lose them in a second. Albacore tuna are one of the fastest species in the ocean and can travel up to sixty miles per hour in spurts. Even with top-of-the-line sonar equipment, the speed of albacore can get them out of range in a hurry if they change direction.

As I mentioned earlier, not all fishermen are team players. Some choose to keep their daily catch numbers to themselves, or they may disclose a lower number than what they actually caught. Those captains rarely give out their fishing location when they are "in 'em."

But birds of a feather flock together. And these cutthroats enjoy their pissing contests. The honest professionals will help each other and, in turn, help themselves. The people who understand the value in numbers while fishing out on the open seas have been grouping for years and have long-standing agreements on the rules by which they fish.

How they live at sea is a given. Without hesitation, they bail out one another during dangerous situations time and time again. Many lives have been saved by their selflessness—even by someone they might have fought with tooth-and-nail the day before. A kinship has developed between these men *and* women. The fact that they have played a part in making each other more successful fishermen, makes that kinship even deeper. To protect their group, if another fisherman wants in, they take a vote. Not every fisherman gets in. Many have been denied access.

The Hyenas all purchased radios and set them to the same frequency so the group could talk privately while on the ocean, which kept outsiders from listening in. The Hyenas would hear what the rest of the fleet was up to and, if they felt something was "fishy" with one of the other member boats, they could move in and help.

More than once, an outsider fishing an area looked up to see a row of boats cresting the horizon, moving in on their territory. "They're like a pack of frickin' hyenas!" someone once shouted. And the name stuck.

HOW THE HYENAS GOT THEIR HANDLES

Assigning (or earning) a nickname to ensure confidentiality was half the fun of becoming a member of the special group.

Bart's Hyena name was Midnite. When the group was forming, Bart was running a black boat called the *Middlepoint*. It had great big sodium lights that could be seen for miles, and sometimes he would forget to turn them off. One day, Bart was cruising in broad daylight and Jack teased him, calling to him on the radio, "What's the deal, Bart? Do you think it's midnight or something?" Bart told me his new handle made him feel like an action hero and he liked that a lot.

Jack ran the *Lady Smith* when he joined the group. The owner of the vessel creatively advertised the boat by describing it as "the ultimate fishing vessel." A few of the guys teased Jack by saying he was "the ultimate fisherman on the ultimate fishing boat." His handle became Ultimate from then on. He and his wife, Sue, began referring to their two daughters as The Little Ultimatums.

Wes had a passion for classic motorcycles and rode a Norton. Someone called him Norton one day, which Wes thought was pretty cool, and the name stuck.

Mike's Hyena name was Senior. Senior and his wife, Paulette (who they called The Admiral because she constantly told her husband what to do and how to do it), owned and operated the *Wendy Seaa*, which was also the name of their oldest daughter. A guy named Pacific—who was named after the Pacific Ocean— married Mike and Paulette's daughter, Kami. Kami and Pacific fished on their boat the *Kami M*, which they bought from Kami's parents. Addressing Mike as Senior seemed fitting since Pacific was occasionally referred to as Junior.

Miguel was an American named Mike who built his boat, the *Maverick*, in Mexico. Calling him by his Hispanic name came naturally, and minimized confusion between the two other Mikes who entered in the group.

Stephano ran the *America*. Because he served as father to the group, he became known as Pops. Pops, like most fishermen, liked his drink. He would get on the radio after having a couple and his voice would take on a slow and lazy tone, which created a second name for him: Sleepy. Pops loved the ocean and did not want to spend any more time "on the beach" than necessary. He rarely spent more than five to ten days a year on land.

Guitar Man—or G-Man for short—loved to play his guitar whether in port or at sea and always during a "board meeting." His real name was Mike and he had a boyish way about him, so the group fondly called him Mikey as well.

Barry had a nasal voice and eyes that squinted (one more than the other). He wore thick, black-rimmed glasses, and had a laugh like Popeye. Calling him Popeye was a no-brainer.

Bobby never wanted to jinx his good luck when he was on fish. When the group would congratulate him for finding a large school, he would reply, "Don't booger me! Don't booger me!" So Booger became his name.

One year, Dave and a group of boats delivered fish to a dock located in the inside passage up north. As they waited their turn to unload, they saw a deer swim from one island to another. Dave put his boat in gear, left his place in line among the other boats, and ran his boat toward the deer. He harpooned the darned thing and he and his crew ate venison for weeks! Crockett became his Hyena name because he'd acted like Davy Crockett.

Don's former fishing career in the longline business is the basis of his Hyena name: Longline. However, some members of the group fondly referred to him as Dirty Don because it was not important to him to keep his boat clean.

JB stood for John Boy. JB was a good soul of a man who liked his booze and broke a lot of rules, but would give you the shirt off his back.

There were many more respected and cherished men and women in the Hyenas, and they fished together year after year. Like the salt that runs through their veins as a current, many of the Hyenas work and play the way a tight-knit family would.

The following list of Hyenas are not characters in this story, but they have been valuable members of this group for many years— and their nicknames are fun to say—so I included them here: Sandbar, Steamer, Bandini, Mumbles, Eastwood, Slider, Tacker, Juicy Fruit, Bean, Hook, Tinman, Stretch, Cisco, Pepper, Goncho, Zulu, Diablo, Mako, and Batgaff.

Several websites describe the Pacific Coast fisheries in detail. For information about sustainability, methods used to catch albacore, various species of tuna, and much more, visit:

American Albacore Fishing Association: http://americanalbacore.com/

Seafood Watch: http://www.seafoodwatch.org/ocean-issues/fishing-and-farming-methods

Highs Seas Tuna: http://www.highseastuna.com/

Chapter 1:
The Explosion

TUESDAY, AUGUST 15, 2006 WAS THE WORST DAY OF MY LIFE. With the long hours I'd been putting in at work, and too much wine the night before, I decided to skip my workout and sleep in. The sound of the phone ringing woke me.

I leaped out of bed but thought twice about answering. The only person who would call that early in the morning was Bart, and I didn't want to get busted for sleeping in. I wonder why I would think sleeping in is a crime. The person awake and calling at that hour never cares. Bart would not have cared.

But I didn't answer the phone.

I shook my cobwebs loose and turned on my cell phone so I wouldn't miss him when he called back. At 7:06, the cell phone rang, just as I had expected. I was sure it was Bart even though the satellite phone number didn't show up on caller ID. The fishing had been great for weeks and I knew I'd be hearing from him any day to let me know he was on his way in.

"Hello!" I answered, anticipating my husband's sexy voice.

"Theresa?"

I'd know Jack's voice anywhere. The static behind his voice told me he was still out with Bart. Jack and Bart were fishing 100 miles off the coast of Astoria, Oregon.

Jack ran the *Dalena* and Bart was captain of our boat, the *Lady Barbara*. Jack was my favorite. He reminded me so much of Bart.

They were twin souls.

Jack's wife, Sue, and I were complete opposites. She was a tomboy and I was, and always have been, a girlie girl. We always said, "Between the two of us we make the perfect woman."

"Hey, Jack! How's it going?" My excitement rang through the receiver.

"Ah, Theresa… I hate to call. Uuuhhh, somethin' happened to Bart."

Jack had one of those soothing voices with a slight southern drawl that rose to a higher pitch at the end, as if he was asking a question.

"Oh God, Jack, what happened? Is he okay? He's gonna be okay, right?" I escalated to major panic mode. A million thoughts ran through my head. *Did they get hit again? Some dumb ass rammed them broadside a month earlier. I saw Bart just two weeks ago and he and the boat were fine. Did he slip and fall and hurt his back? He has such a bad back. Poor thing. He really should take better care of himself. I keep trying to encourage him to exercise, but he just puts it off. Did he break his arm or cut off his finger? Oh, dear Lord. What happened to my Bart? He'll be okay though, 'cause my Bart is always okay.*

"Oh, Theresa?" There was that question again. "I think he's gone."

"Gone? What do you mean *gone*? You *think* he's gone? Well, that means there is still a pulse then, right? No. No. No. No. He can't be gone! Dead? No. Bart's not dead! What happened? Tell me there's still a pulse, Jack! Oh, God, this can't be. This can't be. No. This is not right…."

My mumbled blathering got louder. I paced in circles.

Jack interrupted. "Please stop yelling, Theresa. You've got to calm down. I know it's hard. I'm so sorry."

"Just tell me if there's a pulse, Jack!"

"There is no pulse, Hon."

"Jack, what happened?" My pace picked up as I tried to wrap my brain around what I was hearing.

I can fix this. Jack will tell me there was a mix-up. The guys will call Jack on the radio and tell him Bart's pulse is back and he's breathing normally. It will all be fine. Jaime is Bart's first mate and he can fix this. They love Bart like family. He's in good hands. They'll be calling Jack any second. Besides, Jack said he THINKS he's gone, that means if I THINK hard enough, he won't be gone. Think. Breathe. My Bart! God, don't let this be real! It's not real. I can't be a widow. I'm only forty-two years old! Jesus God! What the fuck! You can't take my Bart. Not now! Oh please, Lord, don't take him away from me!

Jack explained what happened and I spiraled deeper into shock and disbelief. Bart had a heart attack.

I feared this day for years but never thought it would actually happen.

Not like this. Not this soon.

Yet, I knew. Deep down, I knew.

How could I have prevented this? Didn't Bart know too? How come I didn't notice the warning signs? Were there warning signs? Or was it just a fear I had of losing someone I loved so dearly?

Jack (Ultimate) spoke apologetically. "He went in to take a shower and never came out. I noticed at 6:30 he was still drifting, so I called over on the radio and said, 'It's awfully early to be drifting, Midnite. Is everything okay over there?' Then Booger came on and asked (like he thought something was wrong too), 'Why would you say that, Ultimate?' Then Jaime came on the radio, 'Mayday, mayday, mayday! Captain down!' God, Theresa, I'm so sorry. They've been working on him for over an hour." Then Jack stopped speaking.

"But they have a pulse, right, Jack?" I begged as if the more I pleaded, I'd actually be able to change the outcome. And if they were still working on him, then maybe Jack just didn't have all the facts. He was on another boat, after all.

"Please tell me there's a pulse!" I demanded. But in my gut, I knew there was no pulse. Bart took his shower at 5:30 every morning like clockwork. Jack said Bart's hair wasn't wet and the water was off. So Bart had to have died just as he stepped into the stall. He had been dead for over an hour and a half and I knew it. My husband was never coming home.

"There is no pulse. He's gone, Theresa. Oh God, I'm sorry. The Coast Guard will be calling you in a minute so we need to get off this line. They're sending out a helicopter."

Jack had to focus on the details and keep a clear head or we'd both perish. Someone had to steer this sinking ship!

"Okay," I kept saying, "Okay. Okay. Let me get a hold of myself. Ah Jesus, Jack! What am I going to do?" I started crying again. I don't know how I ended up on the floor but I peeled myself off the carpet. I'd been crawling on the floor like the house was burning and the only safe place was on the ground where I could breathe.

I had to call my mom. Her phone rang twice.

"Mama?"

She knew something was wrong by my tone and the way I addressed her.

"Yes, darling… what is it?"

"Bart's dead," I squeaked.

"No!" she screamed.

We cried together while I repeated what Jack told me. I was pacing again. My chest hurt.

"I'm on my way, Honey," she assured me. She had to come from Spokane, Washington. An entire day's travel to the island.

"Don't come all the way yet," I told her, "I have to go get Bart. I've got to get out of here. I don't know what I'm doing yet. Just get ready and I'll let you know where to go soon. Will you call Dad and Bryan? I need someone else to call everyone."

"Of course I will, Honey."

I couldn't be alone another minute, but couldn't find the next-door neighbors. So I called Cal, who lived just down the road.

Cal had been like a brother to me, and he loved Bart. Cal was one of Bart's closest buddies.

"Oh my God, Cal, Bart's dead," I whaled in a blurred screech.

"Stop yelling!" he shouted. "Who IS this?"

"It's T," I said. I settled myself and spoke clearly, but still in a faint voice. "Cal?" I said. "Bart's *dead*."

"What? Oh God, T. Want me to come over?" I could hear him choking back his tears.

"Yah," I whimpered. I hung up but was already running in circles again.

What am I supposed to wear? My husband just died. What does a widow wear? I have to get out of my robe.

I paced back-and-forth from the bedroom to the living room. I picked up one piece of clothing at a time and set it on the couch. Then I'd sit down for a moment before returning to my room to choose something more appropriate. I couldn't figure out what to wear. I grabbed a pair of socks and walked to the living room with them, set them down, and then stared at the socks. I picked up those socks and took them back to get some panties. Then I walked back to the couch with the socks in one hand and my panties in the other, and set down my underwear. I carried pants and t-shirts back-and-forth from the living room to the bedroom, changing my mind after every trip, taking one garment and then bringing it back to where I had started.

I was no longer in charge of my body or my mind.

People are coming over. I haven't even gone pee yet. Or had coffee. Don't need coffee today. Gotta brush my teeth. Gotta put on clothes before Cal gets here. We're broke. Jesus, Bart. Why did you fight me on life insurance? I'm gonna lose everything. But I just want you! Fuck, oh God. I'm a widow. Oh, baby. I'm sorry for everything. I'm sorry I made you cut your hair. I'm sorry I ever disappointed you. I'm sorry I'm not out there with you. Maybe I could have saved you. I hope it didn't hurt. Please tell me it didn't hurt. What do I put on my body?

Okay, okay, okay. Think.

Sweat pants and a t-shirt will be good. Yes. Wear your blue sweats. Put on a bra. That's right. Brush your teeth.

The Coast Guard called to tell me they were in contact with the boat. The man offered his condolences. "Since Bart has passed, we won't be sending a helicopter. The crew and men from the other boats are taking good care of your husband. Is there anything you want me to tell them? Anything you want them to do?"

"Make sure he's wearing underwear. He likes to be naked, but not when he's dead. I don't think he would like that. And he has to have socks on. His feet get so cold when he's not in the tropics. Make sure he's wearing socks."

"I'm so sorry ma'am. We'll take good care of him."

The phone rang as soon as we hung up. First, my dad called. I could hear him trying to be strong but it sounded as if he was attempting not to cry. "I know your Mom's on the way, Honey. I'll come with her."

"No, Dad. I think I need you there. I'll need to you to come here when we get back. I don't know what I need, but maybe you should stay there for now." Then I broke down. "Daddy? What am I going to do?"

"Oh, babe. I'm so sorry. We're all here for you. Just say *when* and I'll be there. I'll call Mike and Paulette. They need to help you with the boat."

The phone beeped, showing my brother Bryan was calling, so Dad and I hung up.

"Sister. Oh, Sister, I'm so sorry. I know it hurts. I'm so sad for you. I'll be there as soon as you want me to come. Mom's on her way and Dad and I will come too. Just say when."

The landline rang repeatedly with calls from family and friends beeping through call waiting. The cell phone rang at the same pace. Word spread rampantly through our small community on San Juan Island.

Two of my closest friends, Kami and Susan, were on their way. I needed help packing, getting dressed, and assigning duties. Some things I couldn't deal with—like who would feed my cat and water the plants. Who would check my voice mail and get messages to me? Who would help me plan the memorial? My friends and neighbors rallied in a way that warms my heart—to this day.

* * *

Cal arrived at the door in tears. I lost it. I described what happened and he held me while we both cried.

"Have you told Gavin yet? His brother needs to know right away," Cal said.

"No, not yet. Will you tell him? I can't do it. He'll have to call Bart's family. I can't do it."

"I need to go tell him now, sweetheart. He needs to hear this in person. Why don't you take a shower? It will make you feel better. Just do that and I'll be right back."

"Thank you for going to him. Hurry back—please don't leave me alone too long."

"Will you be okay?"

"Yes. No. I don't know."

"You'll feel better if you take a shower," he assured again. "Get in the shower, T."

"What am I going to do, Cal?" I squeaked as he closed the door behind him. Cal's face showed pain and confusion. He may have wanted to offer his support to me but he looked as if he wanted to run away instead. His friend had just died and he had to go tell Bart's brother the dreadful news.

I collapsed on the floor again and found myself crawling to the nearest corner. Then the keening took over. The intensity of my sobs forced my mouth open, allowing the loud cries to pour out— the cries that identify a dying soul mourning deeply. You know it when you hear it. It's the sound of a broken heart. One that might die from the pain. My whole world had just exploded and I had no idea how many more explosions would soon follow. No idea.

Love

To give and not receive
The ultimate in love
It feels so good
But at times it hurts so bad
Good-bye
Just what
Kind of word is it anyway?

~ Bart Mathews

Chapter 2:
Bart

B ART GREW UP IN ST. CHARLES, ILLINOIS. He was the youngest member in a family of five. He had one older brother, a sister in the middle, and loving parents named Craig and Betty Mathews.

Bart was the most free-spirited of the three kids and in early 1974, when he was seventeen, he just couldn't wait any longer to take off on an adventure. Against his mother's wishes, he left high school early to hitchhike across the country where he landed in Corvallis, Oregon. There he finished his high school courses, sent his diploma home to Betty, and resumed his path in search of his calling.

Still in Oregon, he found himself on the docks of Newport where he met Woody, a valuable member of the tight community in that small coastal town. Woody introduced Bart to Wes, a local fisherman who became instant friends with Bart. Soon after their introduction, Wes hired Bart to crew his commercial vessel. The salt poured into Bart's veins immediately. But he also loved forests full of trees and the comfort of a good woman. The pull of both options tormented him.

One day between fishing trips, he spotted his friend Lynn. She was walking down the sidewalk with her two kids in tow. Faye was seven and Skyler was four. Lynn had finally had enough of her abusive husband and left. Bart took them in immediately and became the kids' father from that day forward. Bart and Lynn married a couple years later and settled in the backwoods of Toledo, Oregon, where they lived off the grid.

Bart logged off and on, and ran a local tavern for a while. But Mother Ocean kept calling his name. He ignored her magnetism as long as possible, but he needed to provide better for his family and his desire to be near boats won out. He stumbled upon a deal he couldn't pass up when he heard about a marina that was for sale. The marina was just out of Toledo and allowed him to have the best of both worlds.

Living in a houseboat was a lot fun for the kids, but unfortunately, Bart ended up being taken for a ride by a couple of shysters over the deal. Bart lost his shirt in the transaction.

In 1988, he applied for a harbormaster position in Friday Harbor, Washington, on San Juan Island and got the job. Bart brought his family north in a moving van. Once on the ferry to the island, they were transported through the Straits of Juan de Fuca to their new home in the quaint town where they settled in. But Bart and Lynn had been struggling with marital issues and a short time after their relocation they divorced.

Bart married again and was lured back to commercial fishing at the encouragement of his wife, who agreed to go with him. But only a few weeks before it was time for them to leave, she backed out. Shortly after, Bart's second marriage ended. After a few seasons at sea, Bart decided to live the best of both worlds. So he took another harbormaster position in Roche Harbor at the northern tip of the island where he could be surrounded by trees, saltwater, and boats.

As the new harbormaster at Roche, Bart oversaw the expansion of the resort's marina. He also purchased a little cabin right up the hill from the resort.

Meanwhile, the elite fishing group that he was part of—The Hyenas—kept him in the loop of what was occurring at sea and they continued urging him to return. Mother Ocean's influence was strong, so back to sea he went. And once again, all was right with the world.

When Bart came back from a three-month trip, he learned his teenage son had gotten into trouble. Like many kids that age, Skyler was restless and made some poor choices. If he didn't get his act together, it would be difficult for him to turn things around. Bart gave Skyler two options: Go to jail or go fishing. Removing the derailed teenager from a suspect environment seemed the only way to get the boy back on track. The decision was easy for Skyler, but he was in for a surprise—commercial fishing is no vacation!

Bart was not about to cut his son any slack however, and was determined to teach the boy a few lessons. Bart had always tried to instill good work ethics, proper manners, and "doing the right thing" in the kids, but sometimes that was not always enough.

Out fishing, Bart taught Skyler everything he knew about the trade—the rules at sea, the electronics of the vessel, the hydraulics, the mechanics, patience... everything. The anger and disappointment Bart felt when the trip started faded when he witnessed Skyler's efforts. Bart also saw what a wonderful young man Skyler became when out on the water.

The fishing was good and they both worked hard to keep up with the demands of running a boat—a difficult task for only two people. While one stood watch, the other slept, making "their turn" at the helm a long run. When they landed on a school of fish that bit their lines as fast as they could clear them, Bart would have to help Skyler pull fish. Bart would alert the other captains that he'd be on deck for a while, and then he would set the controls for the vessel to troll in a circular motion. Everyone else would simply stay out of their way.

There's something to be said about hard work. To see what

happens to people who are in sync with each other working a laborious project is truly amazing, and that experience was not lost on Bart and Skyler. Father and son were bonding. An unexpected gift for both.

Another month or so remained before they would see land again and both men were exhilarated by their adventure. Just when they thought life couldn't get much better, their freezer died—the freezer containing their provisions. Fortunately, they caught it before the food thawed and spoiled. Plus, JB on *The Waluda* was fishing nearby. Like a true Hyena, JB offered to have them store their food in his freezer.

JB's crew would have to move things around and get creative to make room, but the arrangement worked. Everyone acted quickly because a storm was moving in and the weather had already started to pick up. If the transfer wasn't complete within a couple hours, it would be too dangerous to complete the mission and their provisions would have to be tossed overboard. Not a minute was wasted. Everyone rallied as if they had done the transfer a hundred times. The last hour was hairy when the seas grew to about four feet. Four-foot waves are not a big deal when you're in a seventy-foot or one-hundred-foot steel vessel. But when you are in a rubber raft, they can be deadly.

Bart and Skyler stayed extremely focused. They continued operating as if their bodies were on autopilot, allowing both youth and intuition to work in their favor. Once all the food had been transferred to the *Waluda* and the skiff had been secured, Bart returned to the wheelhouse to get them back on course. By then, the seas had grown, but they were safe.

Bart and Skyler completed their trip, staying close to the *Waluda* in order to access their food as weather and fishing conditions would allow. Despite their challenges, they filled up the boat with albacore and returned to the island with a new respect for each other... and a new perspective.

They completed their tasks and returned the vessel to its owners, Scott and Kathleen, two of the nicest people on earth. Scott resembled a surfer, from his wind-blown trusses and a wide smile that lit up a room, to his easy-going energy that was rarely rattled. Kathleen emitted a gentle energy and kind spirit as her lean body moved with the grace of her soul.

Bart provided Scott and Kathleen with a list of necessary boat repairs and a recap of their trip. The owners were relieved to learn captain and crew were safe after enduring their unfortunate mishap with the freezer. The vessel was otherwise in excellent condition.

With the boat transition complete, Bart and Skyler returned to life on San Juan Island. They opened all the windows of their home that had been closed tight while they were fishing, and immediately unpacked their sea bags. Father and son adjusted to life on land and settled into their routines.

While Skyler was finishing high school, Bart met a woman. A woman who came from a fishing family and was willing to go to sea with him. Later that year, when the fishing season started, Bart, his new girlfriend, and Skyler embarked on a fishing adventure together. The woman's ex-husband enjoyed having their daughter full time, but she missed the girl far too much and she chose to go back home to raise her daughter. With the challenges that come from being separated for months at a time, their relationship ended after a couple of years.

Again, as a single man, Bart figured his odds of meeting someone to grow old with while living on the ocean were not great. But at least he was doing what he loved. Fishing was what he knew, and he did it well.

When the Cadillac of albacore fishing vessels—the *Maverick*—

was in need of a captain, Bart threw his hat in the ring and was hired to run the vessel. Skyler joined him for one of his trips on the *Maverick,* along with Bart's niece, Ainsley, and a Kiwi (a loving label for someone from New Zealand) named Brandon who had previously fished on the *Waluda.*

Bart was like a kid in a candy store. He loved his beautiful, burgundy steel schooner. She was a safe, well-maintained boat that had a reputation for catching a lot of fish. And the *Maverick* had some high-end features you don't always find on a fishing vessel—such as rolling chocks, a bow thruster, and a galley that was more like a yacht salon than anything normally found on a tuna boat.

Bart was at a high point in his career. His son was doing well, and his daughter was not only married to a good man, but they had given Bart a healthy baby grandson. Life was good and it seemed that just when he thought life couldn't get any better, he met the love of his life. Me.

Bart circa 1975

The Mystery of Love

For all that is given
For all that is received
For all that is taken
For all that is taken for granted
Why can't it be understood?

~ Bart Mathews

Chapter 3: Falling

BART AND I MET ON SATURDAY, OCTOBER 24, 1998. We had been invited to a party in Bellevue, Washington, by a mutual friend who instructed us to meet at her house for the pre-function activities. Because I arrived twenty minutes early, I had the chance to visit with Jeannie before everyone else got there. While she was still getting ready, a knock sounded on the back door.

"Oh, that must be Bart," she said. "I'll be about ten more minutes. Will you let him in and get him a drink?"

"Sure," I replied.

I was looking forward to meeting some new friends and she had told me Bart was single.

I hope he's cute! I thought as I walked through the kitchen of Jeannie's old house. I opened the door and to my surprise and delight, a tall handsome man stood before me.

"Hi!" I said with a little too much enthusiasm. "I'm Theresa. Are you Bart?"

"Hi, there," he answered with a little chuckle. "Yes, I'm Bart."

We shook hands and I lingered like that a bit too long. I tried to cover up my awkwardness for acting like a teenager who'd never seen a boy before by making a joke of it.

"Oh, would you like to come in?" I said, stepping out of the way so he could enter. "Good grief, where are my manners?! Please bear with me. I'm a little wound up tonight."

"You're cute!" He laughed again.

"What can I get you to drink?"

Looking at the glass in my hand, he said, "A glass of wine would be just fine. Thank you."

His eyes were locked on mine and I didn't move. But then I said, "You got it," and forced myself away from him. *Oh my God!* I almost said out loud as I turned away from him to get his drink.

I could feel him watching me. I moved smoothly, careful not to do anything klutzy. I grabbed both glasses and turned back to face him. His eyes twinkled with lust and adventure while they burned through me like lasers.

The teenager in me was gone and the woman had returned. Just in time.

"Here you are," I said without taking my eyes off his. "Cheers!"

"Cheers," he purred, clicking our glasses together, "It's nice to meet you, Theresa."

Oh, I like the way he said my name. "Nice to meet YOU, Bart. Shall we adjourn to the living room and wait for Jeannie?"

"That sounds nice."

He followed me around the corner. I felt his eyes on my ass. *Oh, my. This is fun!*

"Bart, is that you?" Jeannie hollered from the back room. "I'll be right out, you guys!"

"Take your time," he smiled as he made himself comfortable in a chair across from mine.

We made small talk for a couple minutes and then more people started showing up. All the conversations stayed fluid and lively.

Bart was a wonderful blend of sophistication and blue collar. A man's man. He wore a pair of Levi's 501 jeans, an oatmeal-colored fisherman's sweater with one dark brown leather button near Bart's right collarbone, and he wore brown leather loafers. His hair was mostly gray, but I could tell he used to be a blond. He had a neatly trimmed beard and mustache that had turned a medium-gray. All in all, his hair was a nice compliment to his gorgeous blue eyes.

"Can I get you another glass of wine?" he asked.

Oh! This gentleman wants to wait on me. How nice! "Oh, yes, please. Thank you." *I like him.*

More guests arrived and the seven of us visited for another thirty minutes, then headed out in our cars for Bellevue, which was just a short drive from where we were in Kirkland. It took us about fifteen minutes to get there. Jeannie rode with Bart in his Corvette, and I hopped into one of the trucks with Jeannie's friend Lisa.

"Oh, I like that Bart!" I told Lisa. "Do you know him?"

"First time I've ever met him," she said, tucking in behind Bart's Vette at the stop sign. "Jeannie never mentioned him before so, unless they're on a first date, I think they're just friends."

"She told me they're just friends and he's not married. So I think he's available. I think he's cute and he sure is nice."

We parked under a big oak tree behind the old farmhouse. The white building and covered wrap-around porch was illuminated by candles and lanterns. Laughter and chatter echoed across the lawn as we approached the house. Sounds of upbeat 1930s jazz poured out the windows, setting the pace for swing dancers to occupy the large hardwood floor inside.

Smiles spread across our faces as we entered the small kitchen and made our way through the crowded room to the front porch where the hostess, Kate, was recovering from a round on the dance floor with Gene, a guest who danced every song.

Our group scattered, enjoying all the interesting people who gathered at Kate's house. I lost sight of Bart and was fine mingling with everyone else when I saw him spot me. He was heading in my direction when Kate's boyfriend, Scott, asked me to dance. I'd never danced to swing music and had always wanted to, so, I gave it my best shot. After finishing the song, we made a beeline to the porch to cool off and approached Bart and Kate who were standing together. I wiped the sweat off my upper lip and Scott said, "Do you always lead or are you just a shitty dancer?"

    I didn't know whether to slap him or bust out laughing but my mouth dropped open. "Really? Um. Actually, I've always been told I'm a good dancer but I do tend to lead when I'm with someone who can't."

    "Good one!" Kate chimed in. "Don't be a dick, Scott. Jeez. What makes you think you're so hot? Don't listen to him, Theresa."

    "Sorry, but you kind of suck," he defended, looking toward me.

    "Wow," I said, rolling my eyes.

    "I thought you looked great out there," Bart said. He shot Scott a look of disgust and then said, "I'd love to dance with you and I don't care if you lead."

    "Perfect!" I said and accepted Bart's hand. We left and walked back inside. Bart wasn't a good dancer and since I didn't know what I was doing either, we made a great pair. We laughed, danced, and had a wonderful time until it was time to leave.

    I packed myself in between Jeannie and Bart in his Root Beer-colored Corvette for the ride back to my car. I thanked Bart and gave him a hug, and just as he drove away, I told Jeannie, "If he asks for my number, you'd better give it to him."

    Bart called the next day. I had some vacation time saved up so I was available to spend a good chunk of the next two-and-a-half weeks glued to his side before he had to go fishing again.

    Although it was a little chilly that time of year, Bart took me for a ride on his Harley. That was hot! And we stopped for lunch at a Chinese restaurant. A couple of days later, he surprised me by booking first-class tickets for us to San Francisco for the weekend in search of Thai food restaurants and adventures.

I didn't want the minor detail that I'd never flown first-class before to be obvious so I choked down my, "Oh my God, really?!"

We had a blast in the city. When I visited San Francisco many years earlier, I remembered visiting a rockin' bar on the pier that attracted people of all types: chichi, sophisticated, punk, biker, preppie—you name it. The bar played wonderful blues and I'd always hoped to go back there again one day.

After we indulged in some fantastic Thai food, Bart and I headed toward the water in search of that very bar and spotted a sign that read, THE BLUES AT LUE'S. We ventured inside, grabbed the only table left, and the music started a few minutes later. The place was packed-out with people who came to listen to E.C. Scott & Smoke perform. They were amazing! I bought the two CDs they were selling, and now, every time I listen to either soundtrack it takes me back to that glorious weekend with Bart.

When we returned to Washington, Bart took me over to Port Townsend where the *Maverick* was moored. This was another first for me—seeing a fishing vessel like that. It was lush on the inside, unlike the other working boats I'd been on, and it was huge. We spent a few more days enjoying the charming town of Port Townsend, playing pool, eating at wonderful restaurants, and exploring the seaside community.

For our next voyage, we drove onto the ferry that transported us from Anacortes on the mainland, to Friday Harbor on San Juan Island. The boat ride took an hour since that particular sailing didn't include stops to other islands along the way. We drove to Roche Harbor, where he rented out his little cabin to his brother, Gavin.

After a weekend "on the rock," as locals liked to call the island, we went to town to catch a returning ferry to take us back to Anacortes.

While we waited for the boat, we strolled into the local

bookstore and purchased a memoir entitled *Red Sky in Mourning*, which his friend, Tami Oldham-Ashcraft, had recently published. After returning to the car and waiting to board the vessel, he flipped open the book and was about to begin reading to himself. But we had bought the only copy the store had left in stock so I asked him, "Will you read it out loud?"

"Really?" As quickly as he seemed to reject the idea, he reconsidered and decided it might be fun. "Sure," he said, and Bart began reading.

Tami's book is about love, loss, adventure, and survival at sea. We lived Tami's journey vicariously through each page Bart read to me. He knew about her life through their friendship, but still Bart was moved to tears as he read the details about her experiences. We were falling in love, and reading the book together—a story that is so tragic and tender—was part of what deepened our feelings for one another.

Then, Bart left for three months.

First, he flew to Tahiti to meet Miguel, the owner of Bart's boat *Maverick*, and to get everything ready for the South Pacific season. He surprised me by sending a gorgeous black pearl necklace before they left for the fishing grounds. It was the nicest thing anyone had ever given to me and was another example of his excellent taste. But more importantly, it symbolized the deep feelings he had for me.

We hated the separation, so we wrote to each other as often as possible, trying to survive our broken hearts. While he was at sea, he started a diary for me where he wrote his thoughts, dreams, and his expressions of endless love.

Back in those days, the only means of communications from sea to land were through Inmarsat, a global satellite system that allowed us to receive and send email, but was extremely expensive to use. He sent notes to me via his friend Paul, who had a computer.

I would pick them up from Paul once or twice a week when Paul called to tell me he had received notes from Bart that were for me. Paul said he didn't read them and I prayed he was telling the truth!

Bart and I also communicated via two-way radio but it took some planning to ensure I wouldn't miss his call. A week in advance, he'd email a note suggesting a phone date. I would respond with my schedule and keep my calendar open until we had a date and time nailed down.

When our date would arrive, a radio operator would call me. There was always this strange delay hearing the operator's voice come through, but the static on the other end meant it was him calling me! The problem with the two-way radio was that whenever Bart and I talked, anyone on the ocean could listen in. It felt like a scene straight out of World War II, which made it cool but also sort of weird.

After living our intense, action-packed love affair for two and a half weeks and then being separated for three months, well, it was tough on me. Until then I had never considered what fishermen's wives go through.

Bart was due home from his fishing trip in February—the day before my birthday—a day I'd been looking forward to for three months. That was the day we would be in each other's arms again... something I had dreamed about for ninety days. As his return approached, I felt as if I were being courted by a ghost, a fantasy, a man who didn't really exist. It was as if I was in love with being in love. I mean, I was happy to see him, but I was also confused.

The emotional adjustment I underwent was at a completely unexpected level. I told him so and he told me he would wait for me to figure it out. I couldn't bear the thought that I might lose him if I took too long. Thinking about it nearly killed me! Which is when I knew Bart was "the one." Our love continued to grow stronger and deeper. We made every minute count during those few months we spent together—before he had to leave and go fishing again.

He spoiled me and I loved it. Often, when I came home from work, he would have washed, folded, and stacked my laundry. He'd have cleaned the apartment. He'd have lit candles, prepared a tray of *hors d'oeuvres*, had wine chilling, and had dinner prepped and ready to cook whenever we were ready. We were in heaven.

With nearly three months before he had to leave again, I decided to send him off with a notebook of special messages—one for each day he would be gone. He needed to know that I was in the relationship to stay and that I loved him dearly. I had only prepared ninety pages, hoping he would come home to me sooner. But if he needed to be gone longer than ninety days, he could simply start from the beginning and re-read each message.

Some pages said, "I Love You." Some were merely jokes; some were long messages that contained dreams of our future together. I drew little diagrams on some pages. Others were X-rated. Bart told me he loved them all. He said he enjoyed the surprise of what he'd read the next day, so he tried not to jump ahead.

The day before he left again, I needed to paint my toenails. "Will you do them for me?" I asked.

He looked both scared and honored.

"Don't worry," I added, "you can clean up the cuticles afterward."

He did an excellent job as he concentrated on covering the whole nail while not making too big of a mess.

"They look beautiful, Babe. Thank you!" I said, admiring my pretty feet. "Now let's do yours!"

"What? Are you kidding?" he said laughing. But after giving the idea a quick ponder, he said, "Sure. Why not!"

He accepted the project as another adventure.

First, I washed his feet and gave him a mini pedicure, which he thoroughly enjoyed. Then I painted each of his toenails a different color. With a contrasting color, I made designs on his toenails. I painted stripes on one, polka dots on another, zigzags on one, a smiley face on one big toe and an M (for Mathews) on the other.

He loved it! He told me he received a lot of strange looks when he picked up the boat in Hawaii sporting fancy *Teva* sandals, but he didn't care. He told me how happy it made him every time he looked at his toes during those three months we were apart. Looking at his feet, he said, made him think of me and he'd smile.

From then on, I sent him off on each fishing trip with freshly decorated toenails and a notebook with a page for each day he'd be gone. That became our ritual.

Our love was deep, we had magic, and we wanted to be together. So when Bart talked about how great it was to go fishing—making it sound like a cruise and telling me, 'The most stressful part of any day is deciding what to have for dinner,'—well, he had me—hook, line, and sinker!

That's when I decided to join him on the *Maverick*.

Bart and Jack at sea discussing a game plan

Chapter 4:
The Reunion

THE SUN WAS WARM AND THE AIR COOL on that summer day back in 1999. Paul offered to give me a ride to meet Bart when he brought the boat in, which I gladly accepted. We arrived at the West Mooring Basin Marina in Astoria, Oregon, where the *Maverick* was securely tied to the dock. The seagulls squawked, announcing their presence as they scavenged for bugs and scraps. The pungent smell of seaweed, tiny crab, and other sea remnants scattered across the rocky beach brought a welcoming scent I'd missed.

I had butterflies in my stomach so bad I thought I might puke. It had been three months since I'd seen my Bart. I quit my job in Seattle to go offshore fishing with him. I never liked sport fishing, but Bart had a way of making the commercial stuff sound romantic, adventurous, and downright fun.

We'd been dating for only nine months but we both knew early on that we were in love. I had to be in love to leave a good-paying job in the city where I was encouraged to wear nice clothes, makeup, and jewelry, and take a three-month job as a deckhand on a fishing boat thousands of miles from anywhere, wearing sweats, rain gear, and rubber boots.

Proudly displaying the shape my legs had taken from months of aerobics, I stepped out of Paul's white Lincoln Continental wearing a pair of black Laura Petry-style capris, a periwinkle blue blouse with three-quarter length sleeves, and a pair of simple black sandals with a wide two-inch heel. I had applied makeup to my fair skin extra carefully that day and had gotten my straight blonde hair cut short for the long trip. Somehow, I knew the gun-powder-bronze nail polish would be gone within two days, right along with my long fingernails.

"Hi, Honey!" I shouted as I approached the steel vessel.

Bart came around the port side of the *Maverick*. His six-foot-one-inch frame climbed off the stern to the dock where I stood with his buddy Paul. Bart's sparkling blue eyes led him toward me. His neatly trimmed gray beard and mustache framed his round face, and his straight teeth beamed through his wide, joyous smile. We ran the few remaining feet that separated us, not wanting to spend one more second out of each other's arms.

Like the scene in *Gone with the Wind* when Melanie and Ashley reunite, the whole world disappeared around us when we embraced. The magic between us was electric. Paul patiently leaned against the car in the background while Bart and I did our dance.

"How are you?" I asked, my arms tightly secured around his broad shoulders.

"Better now," his deep voice purred. "You feel good."

"Mmmmm, thanks, baby. So do YOU."

He gave me another kiss and released his grip around me. Taking my hand, he led me over to the car.

"Hey, man," he greeted Paul with a strong handshake.

"I got her here safely, buddy," Paul replied as the men exchanged a one-arm hug complete with a double pat on the back to let each other know they meant it but that was enough.

I mused at their contrasting physiques. *Mutt and Jeff*.

Bart's thick middle showed how much he appreciated good food, and yet his long legs gave the overall appearance of a tall, lean man. The three-month growth of his baby-fine locks added a couple years to his handsome face. His thinning gray hair blew freely in the wind.

Paul's five-foot-seven-inch stocky build and full head of thick reddish-brown hair made him resemble Oompa-Loompa, a quirky elf from the movie *Charlie And The Chocolate Factory*. His ruddy complexion, dense red beard, and a mustache that surrounded his bulbous nose completed the look. At forty-eight, and with very little gray in his hair, he looked younger than he was.

"Let's get your things on the boat, Hon. I can't wait to see how much you brought," Bart teased.

"The bag is full, Bart, but she didn't do too bad for her first time," Paul chimed in, opening the trunk.

"Wow, it IS full isn't it? But ya did good, Hon. I expected a lot more than this."

I had stuffed my borrowed orange four-foot-five-inch canvas bag to the brim with clothes, shoes, books, and toiletries. Bart pulled the bag out of the trunk. "Jeez, this thing is heavy," he grunted, tossing it over his shoulder.

I just stood there and smiled, resisting my natural urge to jump in and defend myself. Both men applauded my ability to pack for a three month fishing trip.

Good Lord. Me on a three-month fishing trip! Please tell me I'm not insane!

Bart's free hand held mine as we walked toward the schooner—my new home. The *Maverick* was the nicest tuna boat I'd ever seen. Her fresh coat of paint made all ninety-two feet of her look like royalty. She proudly sat there all-knowing in her power, grace, strength, and ability. She welcomed us with open arms.

I should have been intimidated by her, but I was excited and comforted at first. I was entering unknown territory—this *man's* world. Then, with each step I took, I felt more like an insecure kid. I felt the self-confident, grown-up woman slip away little by little. *Oh my God, I'm going to play with the big boys now. I hope they keep me on their team. I hope I don't disappoint them. I hope I don't lose ME in the process. Oops. Too late! There I go! Relax, dummy, relax. YOU are the one who wanted this!*

Bart took my hand and helped me onto the bow. We walked across the spotless deck to the starboard side and headed toward the stern where we could enter the main cabin—referred to as "the house." Mario and Brandon stood at the landing tables where they were preparing the gear for the next trip.

"Hey, guys, this is Theresa," Bart introduced. "Mario and Brandon," he continued.

We greeted one another and shook hands.

Mario had been a young man in his twenties when he and Miguel, the owner of the boat, met while in the South Pacific twenty years before. They became friends immediately and Miguel offered Mario a job aboard his boat. Mario had been on the *Maverick* ever since. Like most crew on commercial vessels in the tuna fleet, Mario was Filipino. At forty-two, he stood five-foot-three, had medium-brown skin, deep brown eyes, and jet-black hair.

Brandon was twenty-seven and gorgeous. He was at least six-feet tall and kept his dark blond, wavy tresses cut short. His blue eyes twinkled in a mildly flirtatious manner atop his lightly freckled face. He spoke using that delicious Kiwi accent.

This is either going to be a lot of fun or pure torture.

Miguel sat at the galley table sipping his Jack Daniels with a splash of water. "Hi, Theresa," he said deliberately. "Glad you decided to come." He wore a grin that told me he was genuinely pleased.

Miguel was traditional when it came to relationships. He believed a woman should be with her man, no matter what the man chose to do for a living. His wife, Aleelat, had fished with him for many years, even though she was seasick for the first five of them.

"Thanks," I replied, kicking off my shoes. I walked into the master stateroom on the starboard side of the vessel and set my purse down on the bed. I went back outside and met Paul at the bow, where he handed over a plastic grocery bag that contained my tennis shoes and a couple of pairs of sweats. I had hold of only one side of the bag when Paul let go, dropping one shoe into the drink. With no fish in the hold to weigh us down, the boat sat high in the air, so there was a noisy splash when the shoe hit the water.

"Oh, shoot!" we both yelled in unison.

"Quick! Get a net!" Paul shouted to the stern.

Immediately, we heard a few loud thuds as Bart came to the rescue. With his face full of drama and purpose, he quickly retrieved my drowning shoe.

My hero!

Miguel appeared a moment later to see what all the yelling was about.

"The way Bart ran, I thought YOU fell in," Miguel taunted. "I didn't know he could move that fast."

Everyone laughed and with a red face and a few chuckles, Bart led us back down the starboard side of *Maverick* to the house where we would drink together. Bart poured me a glass of chardonnay, and fixed Paul and himself a Canadian Club on the rocks. Bart sat next to me at the galley table, resting his hand on my leg while we talked.

An hour or so later Gail showed up. Gail had been in this business her whole life. Her father was a fisherman and she had been a fish buyer in Ilwaco, Washington, for over twenty years. She wore her thick reddish-brown hair about three inches above her shoulders. She had a voluptuous figure that made her five-foot-five-inch frame seem taller than she really was. Years of smoking gave Gail a raspy voice, and her charismatic personality had an energy everyone in the fleet appreciated.

"Hi, Theresa!" she said enthusiastically, "I've heard so much about you. It's great to finally meet you."

"Same here!" I jumped up to shake her hand.

"Bart, you were right. She's gorgeous!"

Gail approved.

Bart beamed and patted my butt. I felt my face flush so I quickly turned away to fetch Gail a drink.

"Wine or whiskey? I'm having chardonnay," I said.

"Chardonnay sounds good, thank you."

The conversation livened with Gail in the house. Listening to tales of life at sea and the wacky things their fellow ocean dwellers would do is the kind of entertainment I can handle for hours. But before long, the discussion turned to business. The price the fish buyers were paying for albacore was not as exciting as the stories, but it was the topic on everyone's mind. By then, the day was disappearing and the alcohol was taking affect.

"Let's get some dinner," Gail commanded. "I'm taking you all to Clemente's."

"That's a fine idea," Miguel chimed in.

"Sounds good to me," everyone agreed.

"C'mon, guys, you wanna get ready? We're going to dinner," Bart informed Brandon and Mario who were just coming inside.

I grabbed a denim jacket from my bag. The air was still—no wind—but it was damp and cool from the overcast skies that hovered above the Columbia River. The weather wasn't what I expected for the first part of August, but it was a common forecast for southern Washington and the northern Oregon coast.

That night, there were only seven eating dinner. Typically,

when fishermen gather for a meal on the beach, it isn't unusual for fifteen or more to show up. Every fisherman I've ever met loves to pick up the tab. I mean, no one worries about how the bill will be distributed, or if they will end up paying for more than they consume. These people either announce early on that they are "getting it" and then order everything from appetizers to plenty of expensive wine, to lobster, to one of everything on the dessert menu. Or they will just throw in a handful of $100 bills at the end of the meal and simply feel good about generously contributing. Everyone gets their turn to pay. And to them, it's an honor, not a burden, to pick up the tab.

As expected, the meal was delicious. The energy around the table was like that comfort level you get when you're with family or close friends at Thanksgiving. When you are with people who really *get* you—and you *get* them. When you know it's safe to be yourself. When you share something special. As if you stand out in a crowd but you're not alone because you have your kin.

We ate until our bellies were full. We laughed until it hurt. And we drank until the buzz was deep.

Miguel was staying on the boat with the crew until the next day when we were scheduled to head out. So, Bart and I got a room at a hotel within walking distance of the dock.

Finally, we had our chance to be alone.

Chapter 5: Getting Ready

THE NEXT MORNING, BART AND MIGUEL WENT OVER the boat list, which included repairs that had required immediate attention. Every necessary project that needed completion before embarking on our trip was done. We ate breakfast at the Pig N' Pancake and then bid farewell to Miguel.

The four of us spent the rest of the morning at Costco, choosing food we liked. I picked instant oatmeal, Lean Cuisines, and Healthy Choice Asian Bowls. All three men reached for mixed nuts and various candies and cookies, explaining how the salt air created a craving for sweets. Brandon tossed frozen bean and cheese burritos, cold cereal, and Oreos into the cart. Mario found his favorite Top Ramen, Asian instant soups, and spicy sausages. Bart loaded up on V-8, bread, peanut butter, lunchmeat, and a couple of apple pies.

"We're gonna be out there for three months, so make sure you get enough of what you like," he ordered. Bart placed enough fresh meats, coffee, various frozen cuisine, and other food staples into the carts to fill both chest freezers and the two empty bunks. The bill was just over $3,000 and the attention we got from fellow shoppers was fun. The shopping project was perfectly orchestrated by these men who had the system down.

After unloading the groceries onto the boat, we went back to town to shop at Fred Meyer for toiletries and enough fresh produce to last two weeks.

The key was to buy only enough ripe fruits and vegetables for one week and the rest of the produce should be as green as you can find. Preparing produce for storage on board a fishing vessel was a new experience for me. Cabbage keeps up to a month, much longer than lettuce. So we bought a dozen heads of cabbage, a couple of heads of iceberg lettuce, and three bunches of green leaf lettuce.

We wrapped each head of lettuce and cabbage in newspaper and placed them in the fo'c'sle (pronounced fokes-ul)—a storage area located at the bow of the vessel where tools, canned goods, large plastic containers of flour, sugar, rice, a chest freezer, and a stack washer-and-dryer were kept. The word originated from the word forecastle, or "forward castle," which refers to the upper deck of a sailing ship and forward of the mast. "Fore" on a boat means the forward part of a ship, and on some boats that is where the sailors' quarters are located.

We placed the lettuce on top of the cabbage because it would perish first. The trick was to unwrap each head once a week and peel off the outer layers, revealing the fresh leaves, then replace the heads back in their newspaper cocoons. If the task was not done religiously, the rotting outer layer would permeate the remaining leaves and speed up the rest of the vegetable's demise.

With nowhere to buy fresh food at sea, the produce was a welcomed treat that needed to be cared for. We also stored boxes of oranges and apples in the fo'c'sle where we could keep the food safe from overexposure to light or heat, and where it was relatively dark and cool, away from heat generated by the main engine.

The guys opened each family-pack of meat, and divided them into four servings before re-wrapping them and placing the portions in the freezer. They put away the dry goods while I went through the canned goods. I threw out all expired rations or cans with rusty lids in order to make room for the new fare.

I finished my chore and when I came up out of the fo'c'sle, I noticed a young couple in their thirties sitting on the boat tied up next to us. The man sat on a white plastic bucket turned upside-down reading what looked like an instruction manual. Fixing broken parts, electronics, motors, and anything mechanical is a constant activity with boat owners, especially commercial vessels in continuous use. With her long bony fingers and perfectly manicured nails, the woman very methodically fed him red grapes. He reminded me of a helpless, nestling robin waiting for worms from its mother.

She seemed to be trying to project the image of a loving, dutiful wife, but her far-off expression told me she was anywhere but with this man. Plus, the grapes weren't always fed one at a time! After carefully placing a couple of single grapes onto his tongue, it seemed her far-away fantasy sped up, which affected the pace she grabbed those grapes.

She shoved three, four, or five into his mouth at once. She must have anticipated his struggle with the grape overload because, without missing a beat, she cupped her hand under his mouth to allow him to eat from her palm. Then she shoved her palm into his face, which forced his head back. At that point, she poked the last grape into his mouth so it wouldn't fall to the ground. All the while, he just looked at her with adoring eyes and chewed. It was as if her devoted attention was all he wanted and her chilly disconnect went unnoticed.

What a couple of fucking weirdos!

I quickly looked away so they wouldn't catch me staring. I was disgusted by the scene and my expression would have given me away. Then those wing nuts boarded our boat!

The man, Dave, was a long-line fisherman whose primary target was swordfish. His wife, Melanie, stayed home and spent most of her time shopping and going to baseball games. She was neatly put together: tall and thin, with shoulder-length dark brown hair, and good looks. I sensed that she was pretty impressed with herself—a trait that always annoyed me no matter who it was.

Dave was a handsome man of average height. He had dark hair, lightly tanned skin, and a five-o'clock shadow. He was sweet and polite and seemed slightly envious, and maybe even a little sad that I was going to sea with my boyfriend when his wife refused to go out on his "stinky boat" with him.

Melanie and I visited for a while onboard Dave's significantly smaller boat while Bart showed Dave around the impressive engine room of the *Maverick*. She was actually fairly nice, but definitely had her priorities mixed up, if you ask me. "Spoiled brat" was the term that entered my mind as she cackled on and on about what was wrong with her husband and how she didn't sign up for this.

In time, I would come to understand her frustration with a fisherman's lifestyle, but for the time being, I was excited to try something new and attempt to understand the power this life had on my man. I honestly thought I was tough enough to embark on such an adventure.

* * *

The sun came out and warmed the crisp sea air, beckoning us to sip our iced tea in its soothing blanket of summer's embrace. Melanie and I responded to the shift in the weather and I developed a better appreciation of her. The sunshine helped me see more clearly who she was. A nice woman struggling with the life she was living.

We grabbed our beverages and departed Dave's boat, making the few steps across the dock to board our boat. Melanie and I reclined in deck chairs on the Maverick's bow. With sunglasses that made us look like Hollywood insiders, we pointed our faces to the bright rays like spring flowers thirsting for solar nourishment. That afternoon felt more like I was going on a cruise than the eve before a fishing trip.

I heard Bart's voice first. "Look at those beauties, Dave," he said as they walked toward us. "We definitely hit the jackpot!"

"I was just thinking the same thing," Dave agreed.

I never felt half as beautiful as Bart claimed I was, but being adored was a feeling I was getting used to and I really liked it!

The time eventually came for us to go. Brandon and Mario untied the lines that allowed us to drift slowly from the dock. We bid farewell to Dave and Melanie, and then cruised up the channel a short distance. We needed to top off the fuel tanks and pick up a set of Grunden raingear and Extra Tuff boots for me. We also needed a couple more packages of extra-large blue Atlas gloves for the guys.

Steering from the bridge deck where he could get a better view, Bart approached the pilings that framed a concrete wall in front of Englund Marine. Being careful to properly align the door on the bulwarks with the steel steps bolted to the thirty-foot pilings, Bart slowly slid the *Maverick* into place while the guys positioned themselves to tie up the boat.

I anxiously awaited my orders. But Bart just glanced down at me and said nothing. Brandon and Mario scurried around the deck making knots in the tie lines, securing them to cleats, and slipped them under scuppers to toss over pilings on the dock.

Boys on the dock stood waiting. They had no expression on their faces. I ran around in a panic wishing I was a cool-chick-crewman but instead, I was a fish out of water. I didn't even know where to put my body.

God!

I wanted to help but didn't have a clue about what I was

supposed to do. So I stood there looking like the greenhorn I was. I no longer felt like a cherished girlfriend, just foolish and in way over my head. The expressions on the faces of the men at the dock confirmed my insecurity.

"What do I do, Brandon?" I asked.

"We're just going to tie up," he said.

"How do we do that? How can I help? I don't even know what to do with the ropes," I said.

"Lines," he patiently corrected me, "Just watch me, you can help next time."

"Lines—right." *I should know that.* I felt stupid.

Brandon moved so quickly that I couldn't see what he was doing with the lines. I asked him to slow down and explain it, which he did but still I didn't quite get it. I had never been good at knot tying anyway, and I figured this was in the same category. I also knew I over-think things when I'm out of my comfort zone.

"Don't worry, Hon," Bart called from above. "You'll pick it up."

His smiling eyes gave me some relief, but I still felt stupid.

The other men's five sober faces staring down at me from the dock made me feel as though they were all thinking the same thing: *What the Hell is she doing on that boat? Little princess here has no business going to sea—she can't even tie up a boat. Dumb girl doesn't know what she's doing or what she's getting herself into.*

At least it looked to me as if that's what they were thinking. I have to believe that Bart spoke to his crew before I arrived because they were polite and seemed to put some effort into making me feel better about my shortcomings.

We all climbed the ladder from the boat and went inside the marina's store for our last few purchases before taking off. The guys walked around the store while Bart and I made a beeline for the raingear and selected mine.

We ran into a few fishermen Bart knew, and he introduced me as "his new partner," which made me feel less like his "new love" and more like I'd been tricked into doing a boy's dirty job. I was hurt and a little angry by the reference of "partner," but realized later that he'd probably been trying to make me feel better by referring to me as someone with status—a real member of his team. I wanted to please him and be good at everything, but at that time, I felt clueless, as if I was in everyone's way, and I was embarrassed about that.

We were all back on board within a half-hour and I waited inside the wheelhouse with Bart while the guys untied the lines. Within seconds, we were underway.

The water was flat calm, which made the transition from the river to the ocean undetectable except for the change in the water's color. We had barely pulled away from the dock when the guys began climbing the mast to lower the poles. Once we were a couple of miles out, it was safe to get the gear ready.

"Let's drop a line to see what we get," Bart suggested.

The giddy look on their faces was priceless, but I watched the land behind us get smaller and smaller.

I climbed up to the most forward position on the bow and securely placed my feet on two steel plates bolted to each side of the vessel's anchor hole. Resting my body against the bulwarks, I gazed out at the aquatic abyss ahead, occasionally glancing down to see the boat cutting through the deep blue ocean. It felt more like I was in a scene from *The Titanic*, or on a super cool carnival ride than beginning a journey into the unknown.

No room for second thoughts. Enjoy the moment. I am committed now.

* * *

I reflected back on my life. Working as a recruiter had been fulfilling to me even with the job's stresses and having to cope with city traffic. The money was good, I liked the work, and I was good at my career. All those facets gave me an enormous sense of self-worth.

The separation between Bart and me shortly after we first met had been tough on both of us. That separation made me wonder if having a career was worth not having Bart. When he came back in the spring, he talked about fishing as if it were a spiritual experience filled with fun and relaxation. I think maybe that was just part of his plan to get me out there with him—and obviously it worked.

But the morning after I'd arrived in Astoria, he began to reclaim his status as captain. Not that he had ever lost it… it's just that I had never seen him acting the part before. Clearly, he was going to treat me as a member of the crew. I didn't think I would like the dynamics, but hoped I would adjust.

Captain and crew during the day and lovers at night. Ick. I like my boyfriend a lot better than this guy in charge. How do couples do it out here? My ego might be too big for this, but I am doing it now and there is absolutely no turning back. Thank God I trust Bart's seaman abilities, the boat, and the skills of the crew. At least I am in good hands. I guess I can do anything for three months. Shoot. That thought process is the very thing that got me out here in the first place!

The sound of the bell at the stern told us we had a fish on. I snapped out of my doubt-filled wandering mind and, with one hand on the edge of the bulwarks, steadied my gait as I headed back to where the action was. Bart ran down the steep steps on the back deck to see what we'd caught.

"It's a salmon!" he shouted, "Quick! Get this thing on board before anyone sees us. We don't have a license to catch this and I'll have to pay a hefty fine if we get caught."

Brandon tossed the fish on the landing table and unhooked him while Bart stood by with a fillet knife, ready to take charge. Like a Benihana chef, Bart's skilled hands flew high in the air tossing fish parts into the ocean after each cut.

"Run in and grab me some mayonnaise and lemon, will yah, Hon?"

I quickly obeyed without uttering a word. Within two minutes, that seventeen-pound fish—still quivering—was ready for the grill. Someone had hosed off the deck, and not one spot of blood sullied Bart's white cotton shirt during the gutting.

"Whoa!" was the only word that fell out of my gaping mouth after the impressive show.

Brandon made a green salad and barbequed the salmon. Mario made Thai Jasmine rice in the large rice cooker and set the table. Meanwhile Bart and I enjoyed a beverage together in the wheelhouse and listened to the soundtrack from *City of Angels* until dinner was ready.

I found a glass jar containing a scented candle and lit it before placing it in the center of the table. Brandon and Mario looked at the candle, looked at each other, and then looked at me. Before I could speak, Bart said, "Classy isn't she?"

"We like to eat by candlelight and since the weather is calm I thought it would be a nice touch tonight," I explained.

"It's perfect," Brandon said.

"I think it's going to be good having you on board," Mario agreed.

Dinner and dishes were done by seven that evening and everyone settled into their routine. After a couple hours, however, the continuous movement of the boat across the water made my head feel funny. And even though we had the luck of a smooth ride, I drank a 7-Up and nibbled on Saltines. I still couldn't quite shake the nausea, but fortunately I kept my delicious dinner down. Bart allowed me one day to adjust to the sea before my first turn at standing watch.

Watch? Shit! He never told me I'd have to take watch! But then, why wouldn't I?

I knew this wasn't a cruise, for cryin' out loud. Yikes! What had I been thinking?

***Maverick* at sea**

Chapter 6:
The Slaters

JACK AND SUE SLATER WERE TEENAGERS WHEN THEY MET. Both worked on sport fishing boats out of San Diego, California. It didn't take long for them to know they had found their callings and to decide to pursue their captain's licenses. Jack embarked on a couple of ventures out of state, but within a few years, he was back in his homeport where he ended up running a long-range sport fishing boat.

The couple's romance blossomed from that point. They married in 1988 and started a family shortly thereafter. First came their daughter, Jaime. Megan joined the clan a year later.

The Slater family settled in Three Rivers, California, so the girls could be raised in a small town while Jack worked on long-line fishing vessels, which is where his journey had taken him by that point. In between trips, he always made sure he and his girls went on a variety of fun adventures.

On one of his months off, Jack happened to be available when someone asked if he would deliver a newly built commercial fishing vessel through the Panama Canal. It was a trip he'd dreamed of for years. And since Jack was a man always willing to take on a new venture, he eagerly accepted. John, the owner of the boat, quickly learned what an exceptional captain he had with Jack, and since the owner hadn't hired a captain, he encouraged Jack to stay aboard the vessel. However, the boat was built for a fishery that wouldn't make as much money as albacore fishing. Since Jack had friends in the albacore fleet, he encouraged John to switch industries. With a blast refrigeration system on board already, it was easy to convert the vessel. So, Jack started jigging.

At that time, the Hyenas hadn't established their group name yet, but they were a closed group—a group that brought in only the best members. At the encouragement of Stephano (aka Pops, the father figure in the group) and Steamer (whose name was often sung to the jingle for Stanley Steamer), Jack was invited into the group and was unanimously accepted.

Jack was given the alias Ultimate, which he acknowledged without hesitation. The name was initially assigned as a joke but he pulled it off beautifully and it just seemed to suit him. He was clearly "the Ultimate fisherman on the ultimate fishing boat."

The albacore fishery has been family-friendly for many years, which allowed Sue and the girls to join Jack at sea on several trips. They ended up logging more than two years of sea time as a family while living aboard a few different vessels. Jack fished the entire Pacific Ocean and was able to visit some exotic ports ranging from the Aleutian Islands to New Zealand, frequently landing in Hawaii.

One of my favorite stories about Jack and Sue—one of the first stories Bart told me about them—took place back in the late 1990s when their two daughters were seven and eight. The fleet was congregating in Hawaii like they always did in the spring. Some of the boats were coming up from the South Pacific after finishing off the season, and some were stopping on their way through before beginning the North Pacific season.

As boats pulled in, the captains and crew from other boats wandered over to the new arrivals for a meet and greet. Jack and Sue were running the *Lady Smith* and had already settled at the dock when Mikey (aka Guitar-man), captain of the *Mercator*, and his reliable crewman, Steve, came in on the boat. Steve's long blond hair was an identifiable feature for many years and his heart of gold could be felt whenever he was around. Jack and Sue gathered their girls and walked over to greet the new arrival. When they got on board, they noticed cat stuff everywhere. Mikey's cat was pregnant and about to have her kittens. The girls turned to their dad, looked up at him with their pleading puppy-dog eyes, and before they had a chance to say a word, he just replied, "Yes!"

The whole family was excited to know they'd have a kitten on board to love and play with as they embarked on their next fishing trip. As the girls expressed their excitement, Mikey assured them, "You'll get first pick of the litter since you were the first ones here."

"Oh, goodie!" they squealed. "I wonder when she'll have the babies."

"Any day now," he said. "Start thinking of a name for your kitten and I'll let you know when they arrive."

The cat delivered three kittens that night.

The next day, the girls walked down the dock to the *Mercator* as early as Jack and Sue allowed. They couldn't wait to see the kittens!

Naturally, they chose the fluffiest kitten. She was gorgeous, with long black hair and perfect white markings. Her face, feet, and the tip of her tail were white, and she had a really cool white stripe up the back of one leg and down the other. The stripe looked like an upside-down smile. She had an exotic look, like her mother, and resembled a female version of Sylvester the Cat. The girls oohed and aahed at the kitten's beauty and how precious she was. They loved the name Rosie, so that became their kitty's name.

Two captains in the group, Slider and Eastwood, each claimed a kitten that day, and the next morning Mikey left for the fishing grounds, taking all the newborn kittens with him.

Jack and Sue still had two weeks' worth of boat work to

complete, as well as the standard last minute shopping for provisions before they'd be ready to head out. Mikey continued to provide daily updates on the stages the kittens were going through. In fact, he got on the radio every time he noticed something new. He watched them open their eyes, stagger around their mom looking for milk, and play with each other. He described in detail all the cute things kittens do and took extra care to watch Rosie so he could give the girls a play-by-play account of her progress.

Eventually it was time for Ultimate, Mrs. Ultimate, and the Little Ultimatums to go fishing. The weather was calm, with a slight breeze as the crew untied the lines. Jack set the waypoint to the fishing grounds. Sue and the crew prepared the gear, and the girls completed their chores as the boat sailed away in a northwesterly direction.

Sue wore many hats when she fished with Jack. She was the engineer, first mate, deck hand, cook, relief captain (she was excellent at finding and staying on fish), and she home-schooled the girls. Jaime and Megan (the Little Ultimatums) had assigned chores as well. The first job their daughters held was to bleed the fish. The girls would wait on the bow at the end of the chute with paring knives in hand. One would grab the fish by the tail and the other girl quickly slit its throat and reached for another fish while her sister moved the fish out of the way and prepared to bleed the next fish in line. They worked like a smoothly oiled machine—a solid team that enjoyed contributing to the day's production.

Since the family and crew were just starting out and hadn't landed on a spot yet, the girls completed the light chores they had been assigned and enjoyed busying themselves with fun activities until the real work began. By the time the kittens were seven weeks old, someone in the group had found the fish and the boats were all fishing close to each other. The only breeze that day came from the movement of the boats trolling at three or four knots.

The water was glassy slick, making the ocean feel more like a giant swimming pool than open sea. All the fishermen had been watching the weather more closely than normal those past few days, keeping track of the hurricane moving in. Enjoying the calm before the storm, Mikey decided it was a great time to pass out the kittens before the hurricane blew the group into a scattered mess. Naturally, he sent Rosie to her new family before the others.

When you pass a package at sea, normally you put the item in a heavy black plastic bag. But Mikey didn't want to put the kitten in a bag. Instead, he took his life ring and put the kitten carrier on top of the ring, secured it with a bungee cord, and tied one end of tuna cord to an empty bleach bottle saved from his last trip. He filled the bleach bottle one-third full with water, for buoyancy.

To prevent the cat carrier from taking on water, Mikey used Duct Tape to secure a piece of cardboard to the front of the crate, which unfortunately prevented the Slaters and their crew from seeing inside to look at Rosie. He then gently placed the container on the water.

Wanting to surprise the kids, Jack and Sue hadn't yet called them out of their stateroom. They anxiously watched the crated kitten float on top of the life ring across the flat, calm, open ocean. Sue later told me it was the cutest thing they'd ever seen. Jack wanted to get nice and close to the life ring so he could snag the package on his first attempt. Well, the *Lady Smith* was a beast to turn. He hadn't considered the enormity of the wake the bow would make, so, as he pulled up on the kitten, the wake overtook the crate and the life ring and the whole assemblage separated!

The cat carrier rose to the top of the wake and when it slid down the backside, it was no longer stacked on top of the life ring. Everything was still attached by tuna cord, but now the cat carrier was sitting in the water without a float device. The bleach bottle had floated furthest away and pushed everything out of reach so the crew wasn't able to grab it with the gaff. Keep in mind that all the gear was still in the water.

The Hyenas close enough to see what was going on all sat idle, watching. Jack had to pull that big boat back around and try again. Being careful not to overtake the kitten with another wake, he stayed back—just a little too far back—and slid past the precious cargo. By then the cat carrier was sinking! Jack had to make yet another attempt and by this time, Sue was freaking out.

"The kitty is sinking!" she cried out as she kept her eyes on Rosie's carrier.

Mikey was watching the fiasco from afar, staying in contact with Jack on the radio. The next time Jack came around he got it right! Sue snagged the carrier with a gaff and pulled the bleach bottle up within reach. The *Lady Smith* sat a good fifteen feet above the water, so it was a long way to haul the kitty. A deck hand grabbed the string on the tuna cord, but by then the carrier was full of water and when he lifted her up, the weight was too much and the tuna cord broke.

The carrier fell back into the water and the boat slid right past it on the wake. Sue knew there was no way they could go back around to try again. She also knew the cat was going under!

So she threw off her jacket, kicked off her boots, and jumped in to save the cat. Meanwhile, Jack was on the radio giving Mikey the blow-by-blow.

"Got the cat," he said first.

Then, "Cat's in the water."

And then, "My wife's in the water."

And finally, "This is not good!"

Fortunately, Sue was able to land clear of the jigs and not get hooked. She swam over and grabbed the cat out of the carrier, which sank immediately after retrieving Rosie's little body out of it. But she was too late. The cat was wasn't moving.

Sue felt very sad as she put the cat on her shoulder. She was thinking the kids were going to want to have a funeral for Rosie. She figured that while she was in the water, she might as well help Mikey, so she swam over and grabbed Mikey's life ring and waited there while the crew pulled the gear out of the water.

Jack came to get Sue, and carefully drifted next to her so she could grab hold of the boat and get back on board. Sue climbed up the pigeonholes on the starboard side and handed Jack the cat.

"Well?" Jack asked.

Sue shook her head no. "Honey, the cat is dead," she said.

Jack had brought a towel for Sue, but instead of giving it to his wife, he wrapped the cat and gently rubbed her itty-bitty body. When Sue finished boarding the vessel, she noticed bubbles coming out of Rosie's tiny nose.

Sue looked up and said, "Jack, give her a couple blows."

The crew chimed in, "You can do it, Jack!"

Without hesitation, Jack put his mouth over the kitty's nose and performed CPR. Her little sides expanded, so he gave her a bit more air. The kitten started to breathe on her own!

Jack handed the kitten back to Sue and went upstairs to update the group. Instantly, Jack became everyone's hero, and Sue was deemed "Susie the Rescue Swimmer." It didn't take long for Rosie to gain back her strength and everyone enjoyed watching her grow into a healthy, playful kitten. Jack even gave Rosie her own stateroom. She'd wake in the morning and go charging up the steps to see Jack. Everyone on board could hear Jack say, "There's my sweet kitty!" She'd play all day with her little toys and scatter them everywhere. Luckily, everyone thought it was really cute, and it was obvious to all that Jack and Rosie loved each other. She was a funny little thing, and although the family and crew loved *her* and she liked everyone—she loved only Jack.

Slater family

The Slaters' vacation, 2006

Bart and Jack

Chapter 7:
Death's Journey

A FEW HOURS AFTER LEARNING OF BART'S DEATH, Bart's brother, Gavin, drove me to the small airport in the town of Friday Harbor for my 1 p.m. flight to Seattle. Mom would pick me up there and we'd drive to Astoria, where I would meet the boat that held my husband's body.

Gavin and I didn't always get along. But that day, the day Bart died, Gavin and I came together. Our grief and trauma consumed us. We were family and we needed to pull together to get through what was in front of us.

My friends Kami and Susan took care of my cat, processed their own grief without me present, discussed what was next, and locked up my house. Another dear friend who ran to my side when she heard the news was Brenda. She met me at the airport. She expressed her condolences to Gavin and assured him she could "take it from here." We checked my bags and sat on one of the benches waiting for the plane to arrive.

"This wasn't supposed to happen," I said in disbelief, staring at the floor. "It's not part of the deal."

"I know, Honey," Brenda consoled. "You love him so much. Every time he comes home, you're like a kid in a candy store. Skipping around, making sure your hair is freshly highlighted, your toenails painted, the house clean, and the fridge stocked with his favorite foods. It's so cute to see you that happy. It's as if the honeymoon is about to start all over again. I'm so sorry, Sweetie. No, this wasn't part of the deal."

She held my hand and I rested my head on her shoulder as we sat waiting. Waves of tears washed over me and then subsided. I walked through the next phase of horror like a zombie in shock.

My plane arrived and Brenda hugged me goodbye. She placed a small item into my hand—it was a bright red shiny heart made out of hard plastic. "Keep this in your pocket and think of Bart's love every time you get sad," she told me. "And know that we're here, holding your heart in ours, sending you strength. I love you. Call me if I can do *anything* for you and I'll see you when you get home."

"Okay," I said. "Thank you."

There was a young girl, about eight years old, traveling alone on the plane sitting in the seat in front of me. She noticed me crying. I noticed her courage. I told her how brave she was to travel all by herself and pointed to the beautiful islands below. She smiled and I apologized for being so sad that day. I knew by the way she held my eyes in hers, as if she were hugging me, that this little girl was a wise old soul.

When I arrived at Boeing Field in Seattle, Mom wasn't there yet. Her 300-mile drive from Spokane took longer than expected. Recurring sobbing attacks forced her to make frequent stops.

I called my friend Barbara who is like a sister to me. She lives in Kirkland, a town northeast of Seattle. Susan had tried to contact Barbara, but was unable to reach her that morning. So I had to tell her the dreadful news myself. Barbara couldn't believe what she was hearing. I wish I could remember the name of the kind woman who was sitting nearby and heard me weeping as I spoke with Barbara. When I ended the phone call, the woman asked if I was okay.

"No," I said, "My husband died this morning."

I told her I was waiting for my mom to pick me up and drive us to Astoria where we would meet the boat and get Bart. She held me as if I were family and I cried some more. She handed me a little stuffed animal—a mini St. Bernard—the breed she raised.

"These dogs bring good luck," she said. "Good luck, my dear. I wish you a safe journey and a heart that heals quickly."

Mom arrived twenty minutes later. Our embrace weakened our knees but gave us strength at the same time. I introduced my new friend, who cried with Mom as if she'd been waiting for her all day. Mom forgot to pack her earrings and, bless her heart, she was a little concerned about that. The gentle stranger came to the rescue again. She had just bought several pairs of earrings during her visit to the city and generously offered Mom a lovely pair of blue earrings that made my mom's eyes shine.

It's funny how, when we are in the midst of such tragedy, we can focus on things that really aren't important. Maybe that's a gift in a way—a survival instinct that kicks in just when we need it. If we allow ourselves to focus only on what is so devastating, we may not be capable of living another minute.

Mom and I bid farewell to our new friend who we knew we would never see again. We left the airport and made it back to Interstate 5 (the main interstate highway on the West Coast running from Canada to Mexico), and promptly got into a traffic jam. We listened to Neil Diamond sing, hoping to take a break from reality. I interrupted the distraction to share what hit me like a ton of bricks.

"Mom, he's gone," I said. "Really gone. I can feel him leave the earth. Right now, this very minute. I can see him in the back of my mind's eye. He has overgrown fisherman's hair trailing behind him like light beams. His cheeks are moving in the wind from the G-force. He's happy. It's like he's saying, Whoa! He's having the ride of his life and he's going so fast he can't help it. He's not going to linger, Mom. He can't. His spirit is in a big hurry. I can see him, Mom! He's not in pain and he's going to be okay. That makes me feel better. I just wish he could have said goodbye first."

"Oh, my darling," Mom said as she reached out and took my hand.

We rode in silence for a while. Tears came and went throughout the drive. A stretch of silence was interrupted when Bart's daughter Faye called. "Oh, Theresa! Is it real? Tell me it isn't real," she begged.

"It's real, Faye. God, I'm sorry."

"I'm so sad for you, Theresa. Bart loved you more than anything in the world. I'd never seen him so happy. We were so glad he finally found someone who gave him so much joy. This is so terrible. I'm worried about you. We are family and we'll get through this together," she cried.

"I know, Hon. Thank you. I'll call you later. Love you."

When I wasn't consumed with my broken heart, I tried to figure out what I was going to do with the boat, the crew, the debt—oh, the enormous debt. Thank God I had three of the best Hyena men and their wives available to help me with the immediate issues like the boat, the foreign crew, the boat's owner, and the fish on board.

Mike and Paulette (Senior and The Admiral) reserved a room for Mom and me at a Best Western near the marina. It was the same hotel where Bart and I stayed the last time we were in Astoria together. He was still running the Maverick at that time.

Mom stayed strong, like she has always done for someone in crisis—even when she is in crisis too. We tossed our bags on the beds in our room and immediately went over to the suite next door to be with Mike and Paulette. They had dropped everything to help me in a way that only family could.

When they met us at the door, we all embraced and cried. It seemed as though there was an emotional reserve set aside for that very moment. As if each of us was in shock and experiencing our own grief, but a new and different depth of pain took over once we were together.

Paulette poured us each a glass of wine and we sat down and tried to make sense of everything. I sat on the bed, and Mike—who has always been very appropriate, by which I mean cautiously distant with women and clearly uncomfortable with expressing emotion—held my hand. I leaned into his shoulder and we cried together.

Gail, who bought fish from the Hyenas for decades and was truly a member of our fishing family, showed up moments later. After we numbed our pain with wine and memories of the good old times, we made a plan for the next day.

* * *

My body ached from head to toe. My ribs felt as if I'd broken every one of them. The hours spent sobbing had poured lactic acid into my stomach and back muscles. Mom said I cried in my sleep. In the shower, I sang a few words of "Amazing Grace" before I started crying again.

One day I won't cry. I don't even think I want that day to come. Will it mean I don't miss him anymore? Will it mean I'm "healed" from this trauma and sadness? I feel as if I'm dying and that feeling keeps me closer to him, maybe. Oh, Bart. I want you to come home now.

Sue Slater drove all night from California to be there for me. Her husband Jack would be arriving later that morning on the *Delena*. The knock on the door of the motel room at seven o'clock signaled one more sign that Bart's death was real.

"Oh, Theresa," Sue cried, hugging me while Mom stood by

waiting for her turn to hug Sue and holding back her own tears so she could be strong for me.

"I can't wear mascara," I told Sue as if she would care. "I like this green blouse. Bart likes me in green," I said.

"You are beautiful, Theresa," Sue replied. "You don't need make-up at all. Bart will like that blouse. It's a good choice."

"Yes, Honey. That's a very good choice," Mom chimed in.

Both women looked a little concerned. I was talking as if I'd lost my mind and I knew Bart couldn't see my blouse—or would give a shit even if he could. But for some reason, the detail mattered to me. My attire had always mattered to me—especially when I was going to see my Bart. Why would that day be any different? Just because his eyes didn't work anymore?

Mom made me eat some of the food she'd brought up from the lobby. Nothing tasted good to me. In my new autopilot, robotic state, I called a friend and co-worker, Jeanine, to discuss a deal we were working on. She said she had everything under control, which forced me to pull back in and deal with what I was about to endure.

It was time to go to Bart.

Nick was a U.S. crewman who had been working aboard the *Alaska* and was the man who tried to save Bart. He was the person who brought the boat within view. The U.S. Coast Guard took Mike out to the boat. Then Mike brought our boat, the *Lady Barbara*, into the dock.

When our boat came into view, I felt the punch in my gut and my knees buckled at the sight of her. One of the crew had set her flag to fly at half-mast. Her captain had died. My Bart.

Soon I would see my love again, but he wouldn't hug me with those big, strong arms this time. I wouldn't see the twinkle in his eyes or hear the sweet sound of his deep voice.

The Federal Bureau of Investigation had boarded the boat.

Following a death at sea, it's standard practice for the FBI to run a full investigation even when there is no suspicion of any wrongdoing.

"The crew is like family to us and they are devastated beyond belief," I warned them. "Do your job as you must, but if you disrespect those men in anyway, I will prosecute you to the full extent of the law."

Not that I would have been able to do anything, but in my whacked-out state of mind, I don't think anyone wanted to chance it.

Jack tied up his boat, the *Dalena*, across from *Lady Barbara* where Mike had secured our vessel. They would not let me, Mom, Sue, or Paulette walk down the dock to the boats. Sue needed to go to her husband. Paulette needed to go to hers. I needed to go to mine. Mom needed to hold me up. Paulette got tired of waiting and we all felt as if we were being punished, so Paulette walked past the authorities and said she was going to the boat for a cup of coffee.

We all followed and Sue barked, "What are you going to do to us?"

No one had an answer.

"Just don't talk to your crew yet, Mrs. Mathews. Please wait until we advise you that it is okay."

"Sure," I replied.

I walked past *Lady Barbara*, where the crew stood at the edge of her bow, waiting for me. The crew had also been ordered not to speak to any of us yet so no one said a word. We looked at each other through our wet eyes and sad faces. I placed my right hand over my heart in a fist, signaling the pain we shared. I touched my fingers over my lips and then to the air in the direction of the men as they watched us board the *Dalena*.

When we could finally gather again, we comforted each other

as we waited for the crew to join us. We were safe and "okay" with Jack in charge.

The authorities finally let the crew come over to us while our boat was being "cleaned up." The crew was traumatized and kept apologizing to me as they relived every single minute. They talked as though it was their job to save him. They tried so hard. They had worked on him for half an hour before Nick got there to take his turn and to document the series of events.

Shortly after the crew and I were allowed to talk to each other, Bart's son Skyler, and his fiancée Melissa arrived. Skyler ran to my arms and we hugged tightly as if to make it stop hurting. But the pain didn't stop. I tried to comfort Skyler and he tried to be strong for me.

We all agreed I should wait to see my husband until he was ready—ready for me to see him—after they got him to the mortuary where they would prep his body and I could be alone with Bart. Someone alerted me when they were going to remove Bart's body from the vessel. That was a scene I did not want etched into my mind, so I looked away.

The crew and Jack helped me on board. My chest was tight as I slowly guided myself along the starboard side of the vessel. My left hand slid across the bulwarks, steadying me as if we were out to sea and combating the constant movement of the ocean. As we neared the house, I could smell bleach and cleaners, yet an unfamiliar scent lingered in the background. Something foul. It was the smell of death.

My knees began to shake as I steered my trembling body towards Bart's stateroom. I carefully crawled inside his stripped bunk. The fetal position controlled the shaking of my body while I sunk under my blanket of pain.

Will this weight ever get off my chest? Will I ever be able to breathe again? Bart, please come get me now. I'm ready. I don't want to do this without you. Baby, please come get me.

They told me that Bart's body would be ready for us to say our final goodbyes by late afternoon. Mike and Paulette hung back to handle a few details, stating they'd catch up with us shortly. Jack, Sue, and Mom coaxed me out of Bart's bunk from a dead slumber to take me to lunch.

Everyone was hungry and we needed to eat. Food had never been such struggle to eat as it was then. I forced down half a turkey sandwich, but that felt as if I had completed a dreadful duty.

We had at least an hour remaining before the mortuary would call and we all needed a drink. Without discussing what was next, Jack, Sue, and I looked at each other and in unison said, "The Chinese place for drinks?" We nodded in agreement and walked across the street to the restaurant where the Hyenas went to do their serious drinking. It was dark inside, and off the main drag.

We filtered in and I spotted Wes. We hugged each other tightly. Wes had lost his wife, Pam, four months earlier to brain cancer and there he was to comfort me in my loss—the loss of his best friend.

I joined his club and I don't like it. I thought the membership was closed. I don't want in this club!

Just as we ordered a round of stiff drinks, my phone rang. I stepped outside to take the call.

"Theresa, this is Keegan. I'm sorry about your loss. This may not be a good time, but we need to discuss the money. You know I loaned Bart a lot of money."

"Yes, I'm aware of that."

"I also screwed up last time Bart unloaded fish to us and I didn't honor the price. I assured him I would give him two thousand dollars a ton the next trip, so I will honor that for you. Are you going to unload this week or send the boat back out first?"

"I don't know yet, Keegan. I have to deal with my dead husband first," I snapped.

"Of course, I understand. And you don't have to give me an answer right away on the loan either, but we'll need to draw up a document soon. Bart and I never got around to that."

"That's too bad. I'll get back to you." I hung up the phone.

Are you fucking kidding me? The fish buyer loans Bart money without documentation or any insurance to protect it and I'm supposed to pay it all back? And he calls me the day after my husband dies to tell me the debt needs to be paid? He screwed Bart in the last trip, but he'd like to get his money back on THIS deal? Wow! I can't handle this right now.

Back inside the Golden Luck, we reminisced about fishing stories and cried in between, when the flash of reality—the tragic reason we were there in Astoria at that moment—brought us back to why we had gathered together again. Jack was our leader that day. "Ultimate" was like "Midnite"—they both had a way of guiding the group through everything we were up against.

Even though the authorities said the crew (Filipino foreigners) were not allowed to disembark the vessel, we decided that they were family and should—and must—be at the funeral home for the final viewing. I had my Hyena family taking care of the boat details, but I was in charge. And being a grieving widow—we all believed the authorities would cut me some slack if they found out that the crew had left the boat. I was not going to ask permission. I asked Mike to bring them along and he agreed. We took them with us.

No one said a word as we walked from the funeral parlor's parking lot into the building. The manager inside told us Bart was ready and for us to take our time. I went into the small room where he lay on a table, closing the door behind me. I'll never forget what it was like to see my husband's dead body. He looked so purple. He was hard as a rock and very cold. I tried to warm him up—*how silly*, I thought later. I stroked his beard and straightened his mustache—it must have gotten crinkled when he fell to his death the previous morning. I gently kissed his soft lips for the last time and noticed a single dried tear that trailed from his left eye and stopped near his nose. I wondered if that was for me.

Then I carefully took his lifeless hand in mine and wiggled his gold wedding band over his knuckle until it came loose. I will miss holding those hands until I take my last breath.

Skyler and Melissa entered the viewing room so that Skyler could say goodbye to his dad. Then Mom went in, then the crew, and everyone had their moment with Bart for the last time. Jack even put a special message in the pocket of Bart's shirt—a private message between the two men. The man at the mortuary collected Mom and me and guided us to a room in the back, where I chose a hand-carved wooden urn for Bart's remains.

* * *

Mike and Paulette took the crew back to the boat. Jack escorted me, Mom, and Sue to the Fred Meyer in Warrenton, Oregon, so I could buy a gold chain to hang Bart's wedding ring around my neck. Mom helped me choose the perfect weight and length of chain. Sue picked out a necklace for herself in memory of her dear friend. The lady who waited on us wasn't very friendly, but softened when she realized what the chain was for. She was a widow also. She was part of the club. I didn't want to be in the club.

We needed to pick up groceries for the boat, so Jack took us to Safeway. The rest of us quietly waited in the Suburban while Jack and Sue went into the store and evidently caused quite the ruckus. That was not an uncommon occurrence for those two! We drove through the parking lot laughing as they told their story—

something about a conversation they'd had with the checker about Pog and Rum, when Jack suddenly stopped the car.

"Honey?" Jack shouted. "Did you forget to close the hatch?"

"Oh shit! I think I *did*!" Sue giggled.

We all turned and looked toward the hatch to see a trail of plastic bags with groceries spilling out of them. Fortunately, nothing broke. Hysterical laughter broke out in our car full of middle-aged adults. We were amused by the Laurel and Hardy-like scene we created.

Man, we needed that! Bart would have enjoyed that little diversion. Thoughts of him brought me back. *Oh God, what am I going to do?!*

Lady Barbara and *Maverick*, **Honolulu, Hawaii**

Awareness

To become aware, the ultimate
To be in tune with what
Is going on around you
And at the same time,
Be in tune with what
Is going on inside you.

~ Bart Mathews

Chapter 8:
The Board Meeting

BY MID-AUGUST OF 1999, we had been underway for two weeks. It was the second half of the trip for Bart and the crew, and my first time out. The weather was calm, with a light chop in the water, a low breeze on the bow, and partly sunny skies. We'd caught a few fish here and there, but had not come across any big schools. I used the slow time to try to perfect the art of pulling fish, but I couldn't seem to get the "wrap" down.

I grabbed hold of the monofilament fishing line (mono) and wrapped it around my hand a few times but it kept slipping down the length of my glove. That prevented me from getting a tight enough grip to give me control of the line so I could pull the fish out of the water. I had given up for the time being, but knew I would have to keep trying.

This isn't rocket science, but why can't I do it?

Time ate up the days with each of us occupying ourselves with activities and distractions. Bart kept a movie playing in the VCR of the wheelhouse while he checked water temperatures, talked with other captains on the radio, and looked through the binoculars in search of birds that might be feeding on bait. Every couple hours he went down to the engine room to monitor the gauges, the bilge, refrigeration conditions, and check a number of alarms, batteries, and other devices that kept all our equipment and back-up sources running.

When the guys weren't rigging gear, tying knots in tuna cord, or building some groovy device to keep their stations organized, I'd find them relaxing in white plastic lawn chairs behind the landing tables, reading magazines as they waited for fish to bite. I cleaned, wrote in my journal, read books, watched movies, scanned cookbooks for recipe ideas, and planned meals for two weeks to keep myself busy. The latter was my preference and often inspired me to get up and cook something right then. I enjoyed cooking and it made everyone else happy, but it also made me fat because I liked to eat what I cooked.

It was a slow start to the season as we tried to get located on fish. We hit another slow spot but were still scratching along and caught an average of 150 to 200 fish each day. One morning, during a lull around 10:30, I went upstairs to check in with Bart.

"Hey, Hon," I said, reaching the top of the wheelhouse steps.

"Hi, there! I was just thinking about you."

"Oh, yah?"

"Yah. We're just running right now so if you want to talk to Paulette, you can."

"Really? Cool! I don't want to take up radio time if you guys need to talk about fishing strategies or whatever."

"Thanks, but nothing is going on. I'll let you know if I need to get on there." He handed me the mic and kissed the air in my direction. I returned the gesture.

"Hey, Paulette! Are you on here?"

"Hi, Theresa!" she came right back. "How are you doing over there?"

"I'm good, thanks. How are you today?"

"Oh, fiiiine," she continued. "I don't know what to make for dinner. I run out of ideas and I'm so sick of the same old stuff I always make. Do you have that trouble too?"

"Really? It's not like that for me. When it's slow, I sit at the galley table and go through piles of cookbooks. It gives me ideas and I write down recipes. That way I can see the variety and try not to repeat anything for a while. I come up with new dishes all the time. I love it! I am going to make a chicken curry tonight, though. Nothing too difficult."

"Oh, I wish I was like that," Paulette said. "I'm just not that creative, I guess. Maybe I'll make enchiladas. Either that or meatloaf," she giggled.

"That sounds good actually. I haven't made meatloaf in ages. Maybe we'll have that next week. Mexican food sounds yummy too—I think I'm planning to make chimichangas on Wednesday—I have to look."

"Okay, well we should let the guys have their radios back. Nice talking to you, Theresa. Call me anytime!"

"Will do, Paulette. Have a good day. Over."

"You, too. Over."

I hung up the mic and thanked Bart for letting me have some girl time. I really needed that.

"Maybe we should have a board meeting," Bart suggested.

"Really? That would be *awesome*!" I told him.

A "board meeting" at sea is like a board meeting on the beach. Captains are like the CEOs of companies. They also "board the vessel," which gives the practice another meaning. The entire crew of the ships (like the employees of companies) get together for what on land would be a company picnic. Team morale is important for smooth sailing—just like corporations host employee functions to establish synergy. When the captains/CEOs get together to discuss industry strategies, challenges, and so on, the crew/staff discuss their challenges and ideas of life in the trenches.

Bart and Mike talked about the fishing conditions, weather forecast, and the plan for the next day. The weather doesn't usually turn nasty until the middle of October, which would likely give us plenty of good days for a board meeting, but with the calmness of *that* day, it seemed appropriate to hold a get-together right then. It was decided. We were going to have company!

Paulette and I discussed the menu. The water had been calm with only a gradual roll all day so, we could make anything we wanted and not have to worry about creating a dangerous or messy cooking scene. When the seas come up, the galley can be a treacherous place to be. We agreed on a simple meal of BBQ chicken, potato salad, and a "green" salad made from iceberg lettuce, cabbage, carrots, and one of the last good tomatoes Paulette had in their fo'c'sle.

The guys were managing the deck just fine without me, so I started making the potato salad. I placed bacon in a frying pan and gathered the rest of the ingredients. As I waited for the potatoes to boil, I fixed tomato soup and grilled cheese sandwiches for lunch, and resumed my project after everyone was fed. Once the potato salad was complete and I had created a spot in the fridge large enough for the bowl, I cleaned up the galley and went back outside to see if there was anything I could help with. I was surprised and thrilled to see about thirty fish on the bow deck.

"Wow!" I said to Mario. "I had no idea we had this many on."

"Yah, we been pickin' away at 'em. Brandon is stacking more down below. I'm going down to help. Will you listen for the bells on the stern? We'll be right back."

"Sure! I'll get these rinsed and take care of new ones."

We counted twenty-eight in that batch and ended the day with seventy-six. Not great, but not too bad for a dry spot. As long as we caught an average 200 or so per day, we could fill the boat within a total of ninety days out. We had seventy-six days to go—if we found a good spot to work and kept catching.

At 5 p.m., we hadn't caught a fish in more than two hours. It was time to pull the gear and lower the skiff from the upper deck to the waters below so Brandon could go pick up our guests from the *Wendy Seaa*. Mario brought the Hibachi and briquettes from the fo'c'sle to the landing table where we would cook. He made a fresh batch of rice in our large rice cooker since there would be three Filipinos on board for dinner. I went to our stateroom to get ready.

Wow. I get to wear makeup, jeans, and a top that I don't have to worry about ruining—this is great!

The skiff returned twenty minutes later with Mike, Paulette, and a cooler that held their contributions for dinner. Mario and Bart met them at the door to the starboard deck. Brandon tied the skiff to the boat while Mario secured the ladder to the side of the vessel with lines that tied to nearby cleats. He reached down to help Paulette steady herself as she climbed out of the skiff and up the side of the *Maverick*. Mike grabbed the lower ladder rungs with one hand and placed the other on the back of his wife's legs to ensure she was covered in case Paulette lost her balance. Mike hung onto the ladder while Brandon handed up the cooler, and then Mike went up the ladder. Brandon untied the lines and went back to the *Wendy Seaa* to gather the crew.

Bart was right. Paulette and I liked each other from the moment we met. She was shorter than I was, standing about 5-foot-1-inch, with an average frame, and shoulder-length dark brown hair. Her skin was olive-toned, making her painted red rosebud lips stand out when she smiled. For a woman who worked so hard, knew how to pull fish, and understood every engineering and mechanical piece of that boat, I was surprised to see such beautiful hands and perfectly shaped long fingernails.

What a cutie! And she's nice and fun—YAY—a buddy for me at sea!

Everyone was excited to take a break and be physically near

other people—our friends. I handed Bart a glass of Canadian Club on the rocks, then poured a glass of Chardonnay for Paulette and me. Mike even joined us with a glass of Boone's Farm blackberry wine—his favorite. We clicked our glasses and said in unison, "Cheers!"

While many boats at sea are "dry boats"—boats where alcohol is not permitted (sometimes this applies only for the crew)—there are a handful of captains who enjoy their evening cocktails and believe their crew should be allowed the occasional beer, especially at a board meeting.

Before everyone arrived, Brandon and I decided on the music for the evening and loaded the CD player with a mix of sixties, seventies, eighties, and nineties music across several genres. The five crewmen hung out on the back deck, enjoyed their beer, and nibbled on the tuna rolls Paulette brought for an appetizer. Mike and Bart grabbed a couple of tuna rolls and made a beeline for the wheelhouse to talk business. Paulette and I put the rest of the food out and sat at the galley table to visit while we waited for the briquettes to heat through. We were done with dinner by 7 p.m. and feeling no pain when Paulette and I got up to dance. Within fifteen minutes, three of the crewmen (Brandon, Matt—a Kiwi, and Elmer—Filipino) had joined us. Bart and Mike waited for the right moment to cut in, while Mario and Oscar were more reserved and chose to stay outside to observe the action from the sidelines.

"Rockin' Robin," by Bobby Day, was blasting from the speakers when Mike couldn't hold back any longer. He took Paulette's hand and twirled her under his arm, sent her backward, and pulled her to him again, then the two of them sidestepped to the beat as if they were professional dancers. We laughed and sang all the words and verses we thought we knew, while trying to keep our moves fluid as the boat rolled from side to side. We had a blast!

Before we knew it, it was 8 p.m. It would take at least an hour to get everyone back to the *Wendy Seaa* and secure the skiff on our upper deck. With the clear skies overhead, we had enough daylight left. Mario delivered the crew to their vessel while we finished gathering food and beverages that belonged to our friends. Just before Mario returned with the skiff, Paulette suggested I come over to see their boat.

"Sure—that sounds like fun. I'm up for a little adventure," I said to Bart, looking for approval to leave our boat in the middle of the ocean.

"Go for it, Hon. Be careful and don't take too long. We still need to put the skiff away and we'll be getting up at four-thirty, like normal," he reminded me.

"Cool. Be right back," I said and gave him a kiss.

"I'll take her over, Bart," Brandon said.

"Thanks, man," Bart said, placing my safety in the hands of his crewman.

The guys helped me into the rubber boat and we were off. I didn't let fear get in the way.

Several years later, I realized that although no one would do anything stupid—especially Mike, who was very cautious—to leave a boat and get into a tiny raft thousands of miles from anywhere is dangerous. If we had fog roll in at the last moment, it wouldn't take anything at all to be lost at sea forever. Thank God, that possibility *never* entered my mind while I was "out there."

We reached the *Wendy Seaa* within a few minutes. Their boat seemed huge compared to the *Maverick*. It was 120 feet long, stood thirty feet up from the water line to the top of the wheelhouse, and drew thirteen feet from the water line down. With only fifteen tons of fish onboard, the water line was far from touching the water, which made the vessel look gigantic from where we sat in the skiff.

Matt lowered the ladder and stood at the gate. Elmer helped us board safely. Paulette went first to show me how she maneuvered their ladder. Unlike the *Maverick's* steel ladder, the *Wendy Seaa's* ladder was made of wooden rungs and rope that allowed it to move easily back and forth. I was a bit nervous using the flimsy support, which was the only thing keeping me out of the open ocean, but I followed their instructions and moved slowly. Mike stayed in the skiff to steady me from below while Elmer held the ladder from above and Matt leaned down to pull me up once he was within reach. I moved slowly and succinctly and only looked up, never down, so I would not fall in the drink.

"Holy crap!" I said with relief once I made it on deck. "That was kinda scary."

"Yah, it can be intimidating the first few times," Paulette said. "But as long as you go slow and steady and don't look down, it's not too bad. I still get nervous and I've been on that ladder a hundred times."

"Good thing I didn't have another glass of wine," I said.

"No kidding," she said with a chuckle.

Mike climbed the ladder next, followed by Brandon. Mike and Paulette led me through the massive boat, giving me a quick tour. It felt more utilitarian than the *Maverick* because of its individual rooms and long hallways (the *Maverick* had an open floor plan with large windows in the galley and salon). *Wendy Seaa's* foredeck had two large booms, which stood nearly thirty feet up. Walking around on the boat felt more like being on board a large ship rather than on a fishing vessel, but it more closely resembled what I had always thought a boat like that would be like. The *Maverick*, on the other hand, was more like a yacht than the other boats in the fleet, so I was a little spoiled—or at least exposed to a different perspective.

With the sun out of sight, we needed to get back to the

Maverick. Brandon climbed into the skiff and steadied the ladder for me. I hugged Mike and Paulette, then turned to say goodbye to Matt, but he grabbed me and planted a kiss smack on my lips. We all gasped and Mike nearly punched him.

"What are you doing?" I snapped, pulling back, my eyes wide.

"Matt!" Paulette barked. "Leave her alone! She's Bart's woman!"

"I know. I'm sorry," he replied. "You are just so beautiful I couldn't help myself. It will never happen again."

"It better not," Mike said firmly.

"Thank you for the compliment," I said to Matt, "but don't ever try that again. Next time I'll slap you."

"Okay, I promise. I'm sorry," he said and then looked away as if he knew he'd been out of line and felt bad for it.

I took a deep breath and carefully climbed down the wimpy-ass ladder and sat in the skiff. We waved goodbye and thanked our friends for coming over, and then headed toward home.

"Hang on," Brandon said.

"Okay," I said, grabbing onto the handles inside the skiff.

When he gave it some gas, my body slid tight into my seat as we sped toward the *Maverick*. We were back safe and sound in no time. When I climbed up our steel steps, I appreciated the secure feeling of that ladder. Back in the comfort of my home at sea, the satisfaction of the exciting escapade lingered for days.

I crawled into bed and tucked myself under Bart's arm to snuggle.

"Thanks, Honey," I said. "That was awesome."

"Yah, it was fun, wasn't it? Glad you had a good time, cause it's probably the last board meeting we'll have this season. We try to have at least one per trip, but it doesn't always work out that way—especially as we approach fall. The weather is going to turn soon."

"Well, I'm glad I got to experience one. Love you."

"Love you, too. I'm really glad you're here," Bart said before he kissed me goodnight.

"Me, too," I lied. Sort of.

Bart getting ready for a "board meeting"

Paulette, me, and Matt at our "board meeting"

Chapter 9:
The Browns

FOR MORE THAN THIRTY YEARS, Mike and Paulette Brown have represented what it means to be a solid team. From rags to riches and back several times, they stayed together through thick and thin, always staying the course.

Mike had been around boats his entire life. When Mike was just five years old, he helped his father, Chet, build boats in San Pedro, California. He didn't just hand his dad tools and sit around. He worked grinders, handled every tool in the shop, and learned how to arc weld by the time he was eight. He continued perfecting his boat-building skills throughout his childhood—until he joined the Navy at the age of eighteen during the Vietnam War. After six years in the military, Mike returned to civilian life in Santa Barbara, California, where he and Chet built a fifty-four-foot steel jig boat, called the *Dawn Star*. Once the boat was complete, they fished the boat together.

During a turn-around, Mike's sister brought a couple of her friends to the boat for a visit. Her youngest friend, Paulette, was only sixteen at the time, but the mutual attraction between her and Mike was instant. They eventually went on a date and married a year later.

They bought a beat-up wooden boat, fixed it up, and took it dragging for rock cod, halibut, and other bottom fish, as well as jig fishing for albacore out of Santa Barbara. They continued to fish and to make improvements on the boat as they had money, and eventually sold it when someone offered them an amount they couldn't pass up. Mike and Paulette had returned to boat building and were not fishing anyway, so the timing was perfect. They were working hard to finish building the steel vessel, *The Wendy*, when Paulette became pregnant. They named their first daughter Wendy Seaa, and later named a boat after her.

They continued to fish on *The Wendy* and to build boats between trips. Then they decided they needed a bigger boat. As luck would have it, they were tied up at the dock when Greg Noll—a famous surfer—walked up and offered them $350,000 for their vessel. They accepted the generous offer and moved to Oxnard, California, where they spent the next two years building two other boats. One of the boats was a sizeable schooner designed for albacore jig fishing. They named the boat *The Mikette*.

Then Paulette delivered a second daughter, Kami Michelle. That child was the inspiration for naming two boats—both named *Kami M*. The first was a 130-foot vessel that they built then sold. Later, they purchased a smaller boat to run and renamed that one the *Kami M*.

The family lived in and around boats as they toggled between land and sea. The girls quickly grew from babies to toddlers to young girls ready to attend school. When the kids were not in school, they were at sea with their parents. As soon as they were able to see over the stern, they learned how to pull fish and were put to work. The girls picked up the trade naturally and before long, they were home-schooled on the vessel with the help of a courageous tutor Mike and Paulette hired.

Paulette was strict about ensuring that the kids studied, completed their assignments, and were tested—to be certain they wouldn't fall behind their landlocked schoolmates. Learning was the priority over work, but those little girls would rather pull fish with the crew than be stuck in the galley, so they obeyed their mother and plowed through their homework.

Wendy and Kami learned about discipline, resilience, and how to respond to dangerous and frightening situations. Despite the perils at sea—such as a fire in the engine room, rough weather that bucked everyone out of their bunks and practically swallowed the boat, getting cut by fish teeth or jigs that popped off a gill, and spending a lot of time away from their friends, the ocean was where they both wanted to be, especially Kami.

Kami was only fourteen when she met Pacific who had been hired to run her parents' boat, the *Kami M*. She convinced her parents to allow her to fish with Pacific two years later. Just like her mother, she was still a teenager when she married, committing herself to life at sea as the wife of a strong captain.

* * *

The most frightening event Kami experienced could have been pulled right out of a scene from *The Perfect Storm*.

The year was 1995. Kami was sixteen. She and her sister Wendy were on the *Kami M* and they were 500 miles off the coast of Oregon heading toward Honolulu when a series of low pressures moved in. They had heard the weather was going to get real bad, so most of the boats scrambled for shore. Since they were ultimately headed south to New Zealand for a haul-out, they stayed the course instead of heading in, and they became caught in the storm.

The waves were huge and towered over the top of the boat. The seas were so rough, they couldn't move around without falling or getting thrown across the room. The staterooms of the *Kami M* were tucked up in the bow due to its forward-cabin design. The bow was the bumpiest place on the boat, which made it difficult for them to sleep in many normal conditions, and impossible in rough weather, so the kids kept a mattress under the galley table—the most stable place on the boat. The girls had never been more scared! They tucked themselves under the table and hung on tight to each other. One minute they were clinging to the legs of the table and the next minute they were thrown into the hallway. Books, movies, everything that normally stayed on the shelves during bad weather, flew off the shelves and through the air.

The bungee cord that kept the refrigerator door shut blew open for the first time. A mayonnaise jar dropped off a shelf and became wedged in the door, which caused food to fall out with every roll of the boat. A head of cabbage tumbled out and rolled across the floor, but there was nothing they could do. Kami said it was pure chaos!

Pacific never left the wheelhouse. Not even to pee or get something to eat. Everyone on board was terrified. The girls knew it was bad when Pacific yelled down from the bridge, "Get your survival suits out!"

Even with the violent movement of the boat and flying debris, Kami somehow managed to get herself up the steps to the bridge. By that time, night had fallen and it was pitch black inside and out. The only light she saw came from the white water outside the windows. The overwhelming power of the storm blew all the color out of the water.

They heard May Day stress calls continuously from voices of men going down. As awful and eerie as that was, they also felt an odd sense of relief because none of those voices belonged to anyone they knew. And yet people were dying out there.

Kami said the only thing they could see when they looked out a window was water. She said it looked like the inside of a washing machine. The little boat would fall off a big wave and crash to its bottom. But *she* kept trying as *she* climbed up the wave in front, as other waves thrust themselves upon *her*. Antennas broke in the mayhem, but not a single window busted out or even cracked. Kami told me the only thing that separated them from all that madness and certain death was God.

Then something went wrong with the boat. The pump that kept the fish frozen lost its suction and they had to add salt in order to re-prime the pump. The only way they could re-prime the pump was to go downwind, and they were going upwind. Turning a vessel in those conditions is dangerous and could be the end if you get hit broadside with a wave or two.

With only twenty-six tons of fish on board, the fish might have shifted during the turn, which would have added more weight to the downside of the vessel. Talk about stress. Pacific was only twenty-one years old at the time and he had the owners' daughters on board! But he figured that was exactly what he had to do. He decided that as soon as he got the boat turned around, the girls would have to go to the lazarette, located at the very edge of the stern, to retrieve the salt. They had to act quickly and they had to do it twice in order to get enough salt for the mission.

The back deck did not have any shelter. Nothing acted as a barrier between those young girls and the enormous waves above them. Being the oldest, Wendy crawled down the steps into the deep hole of the lazarette and hurried to the forward sides where the salt was stored. Kami stayed on deck to catch the salt bags as Wendy tossed them up to her, when all of a sudden she saw a massive wave coming. She screamed at Wendy to find cover and then ran toward the cabin to secure her body. But Wendy didn't hear her.

Wendy heard a loud thunderous sound and turned to see a tunnel of water rushing toward her. She was certain she would drown in that hole, but figured at least she wouldn't be sucked overboard.

The next thing she remembers was that Kami appeared at the opening to the lazarette yelling, "Hurry! Get those salt bags up here. We have to hurry!"

Those young women, who couldn't have weighed ninety pounds soaking wet, hauled enough twenty-five-pound bags of salt up the manhole to get the pump re-primed. How they managed that risky maneuver in the wild ocean was a miracle. No one slept during the entire ordeal. Pacific still wouldn't leave the bridge, and those kids were tossed around for nearly two days. Finally, the storm passed. The *Kami M* was a sturdy vessel and the people on board matched her strength and endurance. That may have been the thing that kept Mike and Paulette sane as they helplessly listened to the weather reports from the beach.

* * *

Another major event in Kami's life was when the *Defiance* went down. The weather was nasty. Everyone in the group had shut down and was drifting. For some odd reason, Kami was on the bridge reading. She remembers hearing the "May Day" come over the radio and said that sent chills down her spine. It was Popeye (Barry), and she heard the clear ringing sound of terror in his voice.

Pacific was at the top of the steps in seconds, having heard the "May Day" from down below. They were the second closest boat to their friend and unable to reach Conway, who was running the *Maverick*—the closest to Popeye.

Pacific ran below to crank the engine into high gear. Even though they had no business going anywhere in those conditions, let alone at that speed and with that force, they were not going to let their friend go down with the boat. They were charging ahead when Conway answered on the radio and said he was able to reach Popeye and his crew.

The *Defiance* was a bait boat, which means part of the hull was filled with water that contained live bait. One of the lines that filled the well broke, and by the time Popeye realized what had happened, the boat was listing. The boat was not able to recover and stabilize by the time the next wave hit, which kept them tipped over. The boat went down so fast it's a miracle no one was trapped inside.

When Kami and Pacific learned everyone was safe, they gathered everything they could to help out—clothes, food, anything. When they became close enough to pass a package of supplies, Kami saw Popeye standing near the edge of the stern. He was wearing a hot-pink shirt.

As soon as the guys came out of the water, the *Maverick's* crew handed them whatever clothing they had available. Everyone on board wore an expression that signified a range of emotions: relief, terror, and pure shock.

* * *

Kami's parents have always been her greatest heroes. Even after she left the family boat to fish with Pacific, Mike and Paulette were almost always out there with them. Although it was through the radio, they were never more than an hour or two drive across the water, which made Kami feel connected, safe, and never alone.

One year, after Kami and Pacific had married and purchased the boat from Mike and Paulette, they took the boat to the southern hemisphere and the weather was flat and calm. They didn't see another boat in any direction for days. She said they were just driving the boat around looking for fish when all of a sudden there was a horrendous noise. The boat lurched and made a huge banging sound. Pacific jumped in the water and swam under the vessel to investigate. He emerged from the waters and announced that the shaft had broken.

"We are screwed," he said. "That noise was the propeller grinding on the rudder."

Luckily, the boat was twin screw, but it really needed both engines to operate properly. To be in the South Pacific when you are dead in the water is a recipe for feeling desperate and consumed with total devastation. No one can come that far to tow you in, no helicopters will come, the Coast Guard will not arrive. All you have is each other.

They called Kami's parents. As they sat in the middle of the ocean feeling the panic mount, Kami looked up and there they were. She saw the unmistakable bright light and the huge boom on the bow of the *Wendy Seaa* as it came up over the horizon.

"Mom and Dad came to the rescue," she said. "Again. They came every time."

Mike worked with Pacific to secure the shaft and propeller, and to ensure the remaining engine was in good working condition.

Although it was hard to steer the boat, their speed was cut in half with only one working prop, and the air conditioning had gone out, they managed to fill the boat and make it back safely without further incident.

After many more years at sea, Mike, Paulette, Kami, and Wendy now operate their family tuna fishing business from the beach—*High Seas Tuna*.

The Browns—Wendy Seaa, Paulette, Mike, and Kami, 2008

Wendy Seaa **in the North Pacific**

Chapter 10:
The Detour

THREE WEEKS INTO MY FIRST FISHING TRIP I felt as though we had settled into our routines. Well, the guys were settled in pretty much from the start, and although I tried to keep busy every day, I continued to adjust to that new world. My restless spirit tormented me in the love/hate struggle with life at sea.

The weather was fairly consistent. The five-to-ten knot winds on our stern gave us a little push across the steady rolling seas as they lifted up our rear and shoved us forward and over the short swells. We had caught few fish that day but I asked Mario to save a peanut for me for dinner. "Peanuts" are small fish weighing less than nine pounds.

I cooked fresh albacore medallions, onion, celery, mushrooms, and garlic in a white cream sauce I made from a roux. I served it over rice, accompanied by crunchy bread and a salad. After we ate and I cleaned up the galley, I decided to visit with Bart and start my shift early in case he was ready to turn in.

"Hi, Honey," I said as I reached the top of the wheelhouse steps.

"Hey, there," Bart replied. "Ready for your watch?"

"Yep—all set."

"We're heading into Newport to get the bellows fixed," he said.

"What's that?"

"I won't bore you with the technical details, but basically it's a metal device used to close the inside of a pump from the outside world. It prevents leakage."

"Oh, that's serious," I said.

"Yes, it's critical, but we'll be fine till we get it fixed. We are not going to sink, but I'm glad we found it now while we're not that far out—it won't set us back too far."

"No kidding!" I agreed. "Would hate to have this happen at a thousand miles out."

"Mike and Paulette have a couple hiccups they'd like to get fixed before we get too far into this trip, so they're going with us."

"I know we're out here to catch fish, and I'm looking forward to learning how, but I have to admit I'm excited that we get to go in. I can't wait to see Paulette again," I said.

"Yah, I knew you two would like each other. She's a real sweetie. But don't get used to going in after being out for only a few weeks—this isn't normal and most likely will never happen again."

"I know."

"You remember what to do, right?" Bart asked me.

"Yep—I got it."

"Since we are going in, there will be more traffic the closer we get to the beach. The *Wendy Seaa* is following us in, but if you see boats and don't know what to do, get me up."

"Deal."

When Bart kissed me, he made that little purring sound of his. It made me smile.

He disappeared down the steps as I put a tape in the VCR from season two of *Sex and the City*. I situated myself in a comfortable position on the couch and called out the *Wendy Seaa* on the radio.

"Ya pick me up, Matt?"

"Aye, Theresa. How are you tonight?" the Kiwi crewman on the *Wendy Seaa* replied.

"Doing great. I'll be on watch for the next two and a half hours so call if you get bored and want to chat."

"Sounds good. Call me if you need anything—I'm right behind you."

"Thanks. Over."

"You bet. Over."

An hour and a half of uneventful time went by. The winds were light, practically undetectable, which made the water calm— aside from a six-inch ripple. The episode of the TV show ended and the credits were rolling on the screen. I looked out the windows and on the radar to see if anything had changed from the last time I'd checked ten minutes earlier.

I saw bright lights on the horizon at about two o'clock. The big green blob on the radar screen confirmed my sighting of a vessel headed toward us. I pressed the left arrows a couple times and that took us slightly off course, which would provide a little more room for the boat when it got closer.

I was fixated on our unexpected company and kept turning us further to the left because it didn't seem as if they were moving away from us. Instead, they were getting closer. Sometimes I found it difficult to determine the direction another boat was headed when they were still several miles away. Distant vessels showed up as a blob on the radar that moved back and forth rather than continuously in one direction, until we were closer to them.

"Yah... Aye, Theresa... ye pick me up, okay?" I heard Matt call me out on the radio.

"Hi, there."

"Do ye see that ship out there?"

"Of course," I replied. *Duh!* "I'm trying to get out of his way but it seems like he's getting closer instead."

"Yah. Um. According to my calculations it looks like yer

heeded straight fer a collision."

"What?"

Just then, Brandon appeared from his stateroom in the wheelhouse. I was totally embarrassed.

"Aye, Theresa, how's it going? Do you mind if I take over fer a sec?" he asked, immediately holding down the right arrow on the dashboard as he forced the boat to make a hard right turn—not waiting for my reply.

"Of course—thank you. I don't understand. I thought I was steering us out of his way."

"It's okay, I got this. If things don't look right, you can always get me up. I was only half asleep anyway but when I heard the word *collision* I was wide awake."

"Shit, Brandon, I'm sorry. I feel so stupid. I really thought I knew what I was doing or I would have asked. Good thing we're being followed, but I suppose at some point I would have realized my strategy wasn't working and I would have gotten you or Bart up. It just never occurred to me to steer toward on-coming traffic."

"I understand, but you see here?" he said, pointing to the plotter." You were steering right into his path. If you would have turned right like we're doing now we would have tucked in behind him."

"I see that now. Thank you."

"Yee. Ya bet," he said with his strong kiwi accent.

"Nice to see ya turn out of the way, Theresa," Matt called me out on the radio.

"Yee there!" Brandon answered his buddy. "I heard you on here and thought I'd give 'er a hand, man."

"Nice job, man. Looks like we'll make it in just fine." I could hear him grinning.

"See ya tomorrow."

"Night."

"I'm sorry, Matt," I called out. "Like I told Brandon, I never thought of turning toward the boat and thought I was doing it right or I would have asked for help."

"Ye did fine, Theresa. No worries. I wouldn't have let you crash! It's all good. Will be nice to see you tomorrow."

"Thanks. See you tomorrow."

I was not only embarrassed, but felt a sense of fear because I had almost driven us straight into an oncoming vessel. When the boat passed us, we were less than a quarter mile away from them so I could see the enormity of that ship. It was huge, which means it would have taken two miles for them to turn a few degrees. *Fuck! That was close.*

When I got up in the morning and grabbed a cup of coffee, I went upstairs to see Bart.

"Good morning, Hon," he greeted me.

"Hi," I said.

"Looks like you took a pretty big detour last night," he said pointing to the tack on the radar.

"Um, yah. Well, there was a ship out here with us and I tried to get out of his way, but evidently, I was steering us straight toward him. Matt noticed I wasn't doing a very good job and said something on the radio just before I was going to ask for advice. So Brandon got up and took over. I'm sorry."

"It's okay, Hon. It looks like it all worked out fine. You need to remember if you don't know what to do you can always get one of us up. Don't wait till the last minute. That's how accidents happen."

"I know. I'm really sorry."

Bart kissed the air in my direction as he looked into my eyes with softness and compassion. He knew I felt terrible.

I could have killed us! GOD, what is wrong with me?

I did my best to shake off the feeling of what could have happened, and that it would have been my fault. *Wow.*

Once both boats were tied up in Newport, Mike and Paulette came to the *Maverick*.

I said hello to the crew and thanked Matt for helping me on the way in. He was gracious and made light of it, then the crew went off and left the four of us to get reacquainted.

"We heard about the ride in," Mike said to me.

"Yah, Theresa. Sounds like you had some excitement!" Paulette chimed in. "What happened?"

I told them my version of what I saw and why I made the decision I did—including not asking for help—since I thought I was doing exactly what Bart had taught me to do.

"I've decided I DO NOT like seeing another boat on my radar!" I told them, trying to keep things light. Everyone laughed and nodded.

"Don't feel bad, Theresa," Mike said. "Our youngest daughter spent most of her life out here and responds the exact same way. And this is your first time at sea. She never did get over that."

"Yah, Theresa. You did good," Paulette interjected.

"I'm proud of you, Hon," Bart said. "I'm glad you're here with me and you're doing fine. You'll get this stuff. Just remember that if you aren't a hundred percent sure, just get me or Brandon up."

"Thanks, you guys. I still feel bad but I'll learn. Shoot—I haven't even pulled a fish in yet."

"You've gotta learn how to pull fish! It's easy—and it's fun. But you haven't pulled fish yet and you're gonna have to learn do it right away," Paulette added.

"I know. I will."

Miguel, Aleelat, and their five-year-old daughter JD arrived. The men discussed the mechanical mishap and how best to fix the bellows to get us back out there the next day. After several phone calls and trips to the hardware store, the captains and crew worked quickly repairing the *Maverick*. Mike and his team made the minor repair needed on the *Wendy Seaa*, and both boats were back on course in less than thirty hours. Thank goodness we were close enough to the beach to come in and not lose a lot of time getting there. I would have preferred just going home, but we hadn't even started.

Wow. Okay. So the three-month voyage basically begins now. The last few weeks were a snapshot of what it's like out here, what I don't like about it, and that I have a lot to learn. Oh, boy, here we go!

Chapter 11: Nippers

THE BELLOWS WERE FIXED AND WE WERE ON OUR WAY. Again. It was still August and the sun was shining when we left Newport. The breeze on our bow and the two-foot chop wasn't bad as we ran in a northwesterly direction.

Bart's job was to stay focused on keeping us safe—and to find fish. He was a great captain. Mario and Brandon kept themselves busy by rigging gear, checking the engine room, organizing their workstations, and reading magazines or watching an occasional movie. I kept up with housework, meal planning, cooking, and trying to get those damn fish on board when they bit one of the bowlines.

We were approximately 400 miles out by the third day back on the water. We caught a few fish, but the numbers weren't significant enough to stop and work an area. The guys who had a better sign were nearly 100 miles away, so Bart set the waypoint to their latitude and longitude.

Since I watched the guys pull fish during the past three weeks, I was anxious to start pulling fish too.

"Can I get the next one?" I asked Mario and Brandon.

"Sure," Brandon said. "I'll stand back here to assist if you need me."

"Perfect," I replied. "It looks easy and I need to learn."

A few minutes later, we had fish on both sides of the vessel.

Mario stayed on the port side and brought his fish in. I reached for the tag line and secured it to the gripper so I could grab the mono, just as I'd seen Brandon do. I pulled the mono to the hydraulic pinch puller and looked at Brandon for affirmation.

"Yep, that's right," he said. "Now turn the lever on and keep your hand over the mono to make sure it stays in there. You got it."

"Cool," I said, pleased with myself.

When the fish reached the stern, I turned off the hydraulics and leaned over the rail, grabbing hold of the mono. I wrapped my hand around it several times until I thought I had a solid grip and then lifted the fish out of the water. The mono slipped and the fish went back in the water, so I reached down and made a couple more wraps. I successfully landed the fish but I had created a little ball of mono in the process. The guys smiled patiently.

"It's okay. You'll get it with a little practice," Mario said watching from his station.

"Yah, don't worry about getting it right the first time," Brandon agreed.

"Thanks, guys. I didn't expect the mono to slip like that but maybe after I pull a few it will become second-nature."

"No worries, it's all good," Brandon said.

The bowlines gave me the same trouble. The guys made pulling fish look easy, but I struggled. And labored. No matter how small the fish.

The mono slipped whenever I grabbed hold of it when I wore small or medium-sized blue Atlas gloves. The small-size ones were snug and caused blisters after heavy use. The medium-size were big enough to leave excess material hanging off each fingertip. So Bart taught me how to make nippers.

I took old wetsuit material and cut strips to fit around the palm of my hand, making sure my hands were covered from just under my fingertips down to my wrists. I created a slit for my thumb. I triple-threaded a needle thick enough to get through the rubber, then sewed the ends together so I could slip them on like gloves.

I attached another piece of wetsuit material from the back of my hand at mid-knuckle and wrapped that around the palm for added density where I would be gripping the mono, and then secured it to the other side just past my pinky knuckle. Sewing was never my thing, but I was quite pleased with myself for being able to create those cool gadgets.

The bowlines were not attached to tuna cord that tripped a bell when fish bite, although that's the way the stern lines were rigged. Instead, the tuna cord was attached to the bow poles that were tethered to the vessel, which kept the lines in place with weights to prevent them from blowing in the wind or flying up over the boat. The mono was connected to the tuna cord, and a two-pronged metal jig (hook) was attached at the end of the mono. The mono was then covered by a bright rubber skirt that (hopefully) resembled a squid in the eyes of an albacore. The jig trolled behind the boat a few inches under the water's surface.

Basically, the rigging was the same as the lines that ran off the stern poles, but they did not drag as far back in the water and they didn't have the bell to alert us when a fish was on the line. That meant the person most responsible for the bowlines needed to keep an eye out for fish dragging alongside the boat. The captain had a good view from the wheelhouse and could yell to us, "Bowline!" Or, if one of the other crewmen was walking by and noticed, they could simply pull the fish in.

Since I was the bow-girl, I did my best to get those fish onboard but I still struggled with a proper wrap of the mono around my hand. The nippers helped by reducing the slippage, but sometimes the mono around my hand would slide toward my fingertips before I had enough of a grip to get the fish out of the water. I'm lucky I didn't lose a finger, for Christ's sake! I knew I shouldn't still be struggling with the procedure by that time, but I just couldn't seem to get it down.

But think about it. We were in a ninety-two-foot steel vessel, cruising at four or five knots, and those ten-to-fifteen-pound fish were pulling in the opposite direction. That was a lot of force! And it didn't take into account the weather. So, getting the flow just right took time.

Did I mention how strong albacore can be? When traveling in search of food, they are known to make quick spurts that reach sixty miles per hour as they lunge for their prey. That was a great feature when they bit a jig since it tripped the bell. We could hear that bell outside no matter what noise surrounded us—music, a movie soundtrack from the VCR, engine noise, wind, waves, thunder. In fact, we would even hear the bell during a big boom when the boat slammed down on the other side of a large swell as we steamed across the ocean.

The strength of albacore is especially noticeable once they are out of the water. They flap and pound their bodies in a fast, powerful frenzy as they gasp for air and try to free themselves from the steel hook. The trick is to grab hold of the mono close to the fish's head and tighten any slack in hope that it will steady the fish enough to reach inside its mouth and un-hook the jig. It is common for those fish to shoot themselves toward the fake squid so fast that they actually swallow the jig, which makes the task of releasing the jigs a nightmare. It was, for me, anyway.

I loved my nippers, but they had a downside too. With my fingertips exposed, and each fish squirming with all its might, I was repeatedly poked by tiny fish teeth and the intermittent stabbing of sharp metal prongs when the fish went from lying still for a moment to flipping over their entire body—just as I had a good hold of the hook.

By the second day in action, my fingers were swollen, cut, and sore. Most evenings after fishing was done, I sat at the galley table and carefully and generously applied Bag Balm to my fingers, then wrapped each one with a thick Band-Aid. I placed my nippers in a bucket of bleach to soak overnight. When I pulled them out of bleach and slid them over my wounds each morning, I cringed with pain. By the time I pulled a couple fish, the cuts were re-awakened and I did my best to ignore the discomfort until the end of the day when I could tend to my injuries.

After the first month of those shenanigans, I realized my fingers might never heal and would keep getting worse if I continued to expose them to more trauma. We had enough wetsuit material onboard to make a third set of nippers and I decided to use a different strategy on that go-round.

I wrapped the rubber strips around each hand while I wore a pair of medium-sized gloves. I ensured the new nippers were tight enough to keep the gloves on my hand while still allowing sufficient give to pull the gloves on and off without too much effort.

Oh, my brilliance is endless!

My routine soon changed from Bag Balm and Band-Aids at night, to Neosporin and Band-Aids in the morning. My skin eventually healed but the constant tight gripping of mono caused "claw-hand" at night. I would have to peel my hands open in the morning and stretch them back into place by pressing them backward against the counter top. My tendons were so sore I was unable to grip my toothbrush without wincing. Of course, continued use of a paring knife to slit the throats of hundreds of fish per day could have contributed significantly.

I was thankful for all the medicine and remedies we had

onboard to help with pain management. Eventually, soreness became just part of the deal and it lessened each time I worked those muscles and tendons again.

Me pulling first fish, 1999

Chapter 12:
Highs and Lows

WE CAUGHT 75 FISH THAT DAY, SO BART DECIDED we would run to a new location through the night. Since I took first watch, I had slept in. Bart came to wake me and got undressed, sliding his naked body under the covers next to mine.

"Who's driving?" I asked in a sleepy voice, happy to get some lovin'.

"Brandon's got it for a while," he said, reaching around to touch me gently. "I told him I needed a nap."

"Nice," I purred. I was delighted we could take as much time as we wanted and even have a little pillow talk afterward. It was also a turn-on knowing the guys probably knew what we were doing, but it was less risky than when we did it upstairs in the wheelhouse.

I hoped the wonderful feeling I had from our connection would keep me in a good frame of mind all day. Bart had to get back to work and I needed to pull the chicken out of the freezer so it would be thawed in time to make dinner. I couldn't decide whether to make a green curry or enchiladas, but I definitely wanted spicy.

There was a light breeze at our stern and a little chop in the water, which made great weather for running. We saw an occasional albatross cruise above us as it swooped down from time to time to grab a bite to eat. They are cool birds to watch.

With their wings motionless and outstretched up to seven—or twelve feet for some species— albatross are one of the largest of all flying birds and are able to soar for hours. They can remain at sea for five to ten years and cover thousands of miles. I read that they live long and mate for life, producing only one egg every one or two years. Due to their hollow bones, they weigh only a few pounds and fly fast. They eat small fish, squid, fish eggs, and crustaceans. Some cultures believe albatross are the souls of dead sailors and that killing them will bring bad luck.

* * *

The air temperature was in the mid-sixties, and humid. With the sun peeking through the clouds only occasionally, the skies cast a dreary spell on me. Fortunately, when the sun squeezed its way through and pushed those clouds out of the way, everything lit up like a Christmas tree—including my mood. That was, until the clouds moved back in and shut off the lights again.

The fog in my mind and spirit made me feel as if I had entered the twilight zone. My emotions flipped back and forth like a ping-pong ball. It seemed as if the weather controlled my emotions. And time. I had too much time to be in my head.

I went upstairs to see Bart. "Hey, Babe. How's it goin'?"

"Hi, there," he said flatly. Our morning sex seemed to have worn off. He was captain and I was crew again.

I couldn't think of anything to say. What do you say when you are stuck on a boat and running to where you hope the fish are? I learned early on that if I spoke about life on the beach, it was not fun for Bart. He got mad when I focused on where I would rather be as opposed to being present wherever we were. Didn't he tell me that when you're on the ocean you want to be anywhere but out there? And when you get home, you can't wait to go back? Well, I was in the "I want to be somewhere else" part and wanted to talk about what we would do when we got home.

Since he didn't like that kind of discussion, I stopped trying to talk about it. But that was not fair. I have never been mechanical, so I did not want to discuss the engine or hydraulics or those types of things. The thing was, and I've said it before, the ocean changes people. I got quiet. My natural energy has always been upbeat, conversational, enthusiastic. When that part of me was silenced, my mind turned dark and run amuck.

I am alone on this boat. Alone with three men. The man I love is now my boss. This great guy I admire—damn but he's really let himself go out here. My God, can't you trim your beard, your hair, your fingernails! And use some fricking deodorant?! What the hell? Your GIRLFRIEND is on this boat with you for crying out loud! And SHE cleans up! Better watch it, mister. There's a hottie on the back deck who talks to her.

I removed myself from Bart's deafening silence. Mostly to keep from blurting out thoughts I would surely regret if I gave voice to any of them. Those thoughts seemed to come from someone—something—else. Not me. I loved and adored my man. Mother Ocean was messing with my head.

I did need some conversation though. And since Bart wasn't interested in talking to me, I went outside to chat with Brandon-- that hot young man from New Zealand.

Oh, my! Stop it! Don't you dare do anything to jeopardize your relationship. Slut. Wait! What am I thinking? Flirting is healthy and Bart is a huge flirt. Right. We are both harmless flirts, because it's in our DNA. We love each other, so neither of us would flirt too much or be misunderstood, or put ourselves in a compromising situation. I'm good. Yah. Don't be so hard on yourself, Theresa. God, help me!

"Howdy!" I said, stepping out onto the back deck as I latched the door to the house behind me.

"Howdy," Brandon replied in that fabulous accent of his. "What er ye up to?"

"Nothing actually. I just went upstairs to talk to Bart but he never talks to me. I don't know why he wanted me to come out here if he's just going to ignore me. I'm going stir-crazy and I feel like I don't even know my own boyfriend anymore."

I probably made that poor guy feel really uncomfortable. I wanted to turn up the flirt-meter but I pulled it back. I needed a friend. That was all.

"Ah. Yeah. Well, that's pretty normal. He probably wants to talk with you but he's focused on finding fish. I know he's really glad you're here, even if he doesn't say it, or act like it."

"I don't know about that. At home, we talk easily. Out here, I can't even think of anything to say. It's weird."

"You can always talk to me, you know. I get bored, too. The ocean can make a person restless, so you've got to use whatever you can to keep your mind busy or you'll go nuts."

"I think that's what's happening. I'm not stimulating my brain enough and I keep thinking of what I wish I was doing instead and that just makes it worse. But I want to talk about things that are part of me because that also makes it better. For me, anyway. I want Bart to engage in conversation with me, but he just isn't interested. Then I get mad at him and the frustration takes over. I had no idea this would happen out here."

"The ocean changes everyone," Brandon responded. "You just have to manage it, cause we've got a long way to go before we're done with this trip."

"God help me!" I said. "I'll take you up on the conversations, but you may regret that offer."

"Naaa. No worries at all. Really."

My heart went thump. Not because I had feelings for Brandon. I planned to ignore them. Or at least keep them to myself. *Maybe I will let Bart be the beneficiary of my silly crush, and having a secret could be my own little thrill. Oooh, that's fun.*

Anyway, I felt enormous relief just knowing I would get through it. I was elated that I could survive the loneliness I felt out there because now I had a buddy. Brandon helped me to not be mad at Bart. There was hope I would get through such an overwhelmingly confusing time. I knew I would have to rely on my new friend to pull me off the ledge—until we were on solid ground and everything fell into place again. But at least there was hope.

Mario was at his station on the port side of the stern and chimed in.

"The ocean definitely changes people. There are guys a lot tougher than you who come out here thinking they're going on a great adventure. But once they can't see land anymore, their minds get the best of them and some have gone crazy. They may have been 'off' a little to start with, but adding all this time to be alone with your thoughts? Well, it can mess with a person's head."

"He's right," Brandon added. "Lots of fellas have cracked out here."

"This one guy was hanging out at his station when they were running to a better spot," Mario said. "They were still running when it was dinnertime. But no one had seen that guy for a while, so everyone searched the boat. They never found him."

"Oh my God," I said, trying to imagine the scene.

"Some say he fell asleep and fell in, but no one heard him scream and the boat was moving too fast to find him. They looked, but never saw a trace."

"That's terrible," I said, imagining the terror of being in his shoes.

"Some think he was a little goofy to start with and he just snapped. There have been suicides out here when guys couldn't take it, so he could have been one of them."

"I heard about that guy," Brandon said. "And there was a guy who tried to kill the captain. Crazy bastard. They had to lock him up till they were done with the trip."

"Wow." I just shook my head.

Deep in our individual thoughts, the three of us leaned against the landing tables and stared off the stern at the light chop in the waves. With nothing on the horizon to separate water from sky, the earth's curvature was visible in all directions. The clouds brightened with sun breaks that ripped through the clouds as if there were holes in a thin piece of fabric. I was mesmerized by the ease at which the albatross flew above the ocean. The movement, the sounds, the changes in weather—and the lack of change. It can all be hypnotic.

"Well, no one on this boat is gonna go swimming!" I said, breaking the spell. "In fact, let's make a pact right now. I don't mean to be a freak about it, but we need to be aware of where each of us is at—at least most of the time. In case someone is in the hold and falls, we will know they've been gone too long. Or, if one of us hasn't been seen for a long time, we should ask each other. What if we get into bad weather and I'm alone back here and fall overboard? You guys would be racing around doing your jobs, picking up the slack, thinking I went inside or something. If you keep going and it's dinnertime, Bart would come looking for me but it would be too late."

"That would never happen!" they said in unison.

"But you're right," Brandon added. "We do need to keep an eye out for each other."

"Yep, I agree," Mario said.

"Good," I said, satisfied. We had bonded and I was happy we made a pact to take care of each other.

"Shall we call you Mom?" Mario asked chuckling.

"No!" I said. We all laughed. "I'm going in to get some water. You guys need anything?"

"No thanks—I'm good," they both replied.

I went into the galley to fill up my water bottle just as Bart was backing down the steps. He had a routine when he reached the bottom step of the wheelhouse. With his right hand, he'd reach for a pair of earmuffs that had been placed on the back of the couch in the salon across from the door to the engine room. He would put them securely on his head to cover both ears.

With his left hand resting on the back of the couch to steady himself, he would turn to face the galley and open the engine room door with his right hand. The noise from the engine was really loud. But as he did this, if I was in the galley, he would blow me a kiss and I might say something to him. That really seemed to annoy him because he would roll his eyes, close the engine room door, take off his earmuffs, and say, 'What's that, Hon? You know I can't hear you with these things on.'

Well, this time I was feeling a little frisky, so just as he turned and opened the engine room door, I moved my lips as if to say something—like watermelon watermelon watermelon—just to look like I was starting a conversation. Dramatically, he shut the engine room door with a little more force than normal, yanked his earmuffs off, and slammed them on the back of the couch, while shaking his head and rolling his eyes.

Before he could say a word, I busted out laughing and stuck my arm out as I pointed my finger right at him.

"Gotcha!" I shouted. I grabbed my stomach and laughed even harder. "I didn't say anything! Ha ha ha ha ha!"

He chuckled at himself, blew me a kiss, covered his ears with the earmuffs, and headed back down the steps to the engine room. The look on his face before he realized what happened was hysterical. He was like, 'What's so funny? Oh. Oh my God. You got me.' I was still giggling when he came back up. I had to rub it in.

"I got you good! You should have seen the look on your face."

"Yah, you did," he said smiling. He came up and grabbed my waist, pulling me close to his body with gusto. We kissed and he went back upstairs.

I love that man!

It was definitely going to be curry for dinner.

Bart taught me how to make green curry with chicken and red onion. Sometimes I added mushrooms and chopped potatoes to make it a little more hearty. I looked out the window above the sink in the galley. The view was similar to the one off the stern, but the waves came from the left instead of toward us. I had a moment of happiness. I felt satisfaction, a sense of belonging, completely tethered to the world and to the universe.

An albatross came into view. Freedom. Peace. I felt safe. We were out in the middle of the ocean. Literally. And I was safe. For the moment.

Hope

Touch upon happiness
And sorrow
More good times
Are always brought
With tomorrow
With the sunshine
Of your smiles.

~ *Bart Mathews*

Chapter 13:
Walking Through Molasses

BACK AT THE MARINA, AFTER "THE VIEWING" of Bart's body and our ruckus at Safeway, we each grabbed a bag of groceries from the car and walked down the dock toward the boat. Once on board the *Dalena*, Jack and Sue put food away, made sure we each had a beverage, and tried to make the dreadful situation seem as normal as possible. We had a few hours before Bart's ashes would be ready for me to pick up.

The conversation turned to—What should Theresa do with this boat?

Mike, Paulette, Jack, Sue, and Wes shared their opinions. The discussion went from—You've gotta keep it going. The fish are still out there and you have a chance to make more money. This was Bart's dream. Don't let Art take the boat back!

To—Just walk away. This is too much for you, and without Bart to run the boat you'll just have another headache and won't make any money because you'll have to pay a captain.

We went round and round on what was the best thing to do. Longline (aka Dirty Don) and his wife Vicky lived just up the road. Vicky fished with her husband for many years as the only deckhand. Longline came down to offer condolences and propose the idea of running the boat for me. But the percentage he said he required wouldn't leave me a penny. That wasn't going to work. Jack and I talked about another alternative.

"What about Skyler?" Jack asked. "He knows this business and yah, he'd need some help from the rest of us, but any captain you choose will need the group to get them located. Bart would be proud, and I bet Skyler would be honored. I think he can handle it and would do well. The rate you'd have to pay him to make it worth his while isn't as high as Longline's, so you'd get a cut too."

"You think he's ready? That's a pretty good idea," I said.

Skyler was honored and excited about the offer. So I needed to order his passport and have it delivered overnight in order to send him out there on time.

My uncle, Harold, called. He was known as Uncle Halibut because he had spent most of his career as a halibut fisherman. Uncle Harold was married to Aunt Jan, my mother's sister. Both of them were sad to hear the news, and he, too, offered to run the boat. They were in the middle of building a home in Montana. Harold had been retired for a number of years, but they knew running the boat would be something they could do to help me, and they wanted desperately to lend a hand wherever they could.

"Oh wow," I said in disbelief and gratitude. "That's so generous. But I think Skyler might run the boat. We are talking about the logistics and I need to get him added to the insurance. The board members of the pool have to approve him before I can do anything, but I should know by next Wednesday—the day of Bart's memorial. Can you guys come to Bart's memorial? It will be in Friday Harbor and I'd love for you to be there."

"We'll be there," Harold said, with Jan chiming in. "And I'll be prepared to take the boat if Skyler can't do it. I used to be on the board myself so I know it wouldn't take but a phone call to get me approved and added to the insurance."

* * *

In order for a U.S. fishing vessel (F/V) to be insured, the underwriter must approve the captain who will be running the boat. If that person is not approved, they will not be insured and the owner needs to find a different captain.

Harold and I discussed terms of payment, and how long Uncle Halibut would be able to fish. The generosity was mind-blowing! Although there were eight to ten weeks left in the season, he could commit to running *Lady Barbara* for three weeks, which gave me a little time to figure things out and transition the boat back to its owner.

"Thank you. I don't know what to say."

"No need to say anything. We're family and we love you. This is what we can do for you."

Jack needed to be back out on the water. He had broken his trip to help me, and by not catching fish for those five days, he had already lost thousands of dollars. Mike and Paulette were retired—but only from fishing. They had captains running their boats, so they had time to run the boat to Roche Harbor. We decided not to unload since the boat had caught only fifteen tons and needed to get back out before the season ended. No telling if we could fill the boat for the season, and the boat wouldn't be ready to go for another eight days anyway, so time was of the essence.

The FBI completed their investigation and cleared my crew to leave port with the boat. I went in to let the guys know and to talk with Mike before we parted. Mike told me the guys were pretty freaked out about finishing the season. He said the crew wanted to go home immediately because the boat was cursed.

"Oh, no!" I said. "I NEED them! They were ready to stay on and fish with my uncle yesterday!"

"I know, Theresa, but they won't go now. Let's talk to them. Maybe there's a way we can get them what they need," Mike said.

We gathered on the dock next to *Lady Barbara*. I was compassionate and respectful of their concerns, but I got right to the point. "Hey, guys, I understand you want to go home now. I can only imagine what you must be going through, but I need a few weeks of fishing this boat or I could lose everything. Is there anything I can do to make things better? Is there something we can do to the boat to make it feel safe and whole again?"

"There is one thing that might help," Jaime said, looking at Arvn and Flavio for support. The two men nodded as he continued. "This boat is cursed by death but if it can be blessed by a Catholic priest, it would be cleansed and only good spirits would remain. We cannot go out in the condition it's in now," he said. "I'm very sorry, Theresa."

"Okay, I'll find a priest. Will you be able to ride up to Anacortes with Mike, and we can bless the boat there?" I asked.

"Yes, that would be okay," Jaime said, looking at the two other men.

"Yes, we can do that," they both agreed.

"Thank you, Theresa. We really appreciate it," Jaime said.

"I'm grateful for all of you. I know Bart is, too. I'll take care of you. Let me get a priest lined up before we head out, then you'll know we are all set."

"Thank you," they kept saying to me.

I made a few phone calls and finally reached a woman at St. Mary's Catholic Church in Anacortes. I gave her our ETA and she proceeded to tell me the priest would not be available at that time because it was after his working hours. I explained our situation in detail and uttered my final plea. "With all due respect," I said as panic set into my voice. "We NEED this priest and I'm sure God would want him to be there for us. PLEASE help."

She almost cried right along with me. "I'm so sorry for your loss, ma'am," she said with true sadness in her tone. "I can't imagine what you must be going through. I will make sure he is there to bless your boat."

A sigh of relief came over all of us and the guys were grateful. We waved goodbye to the boats, hugged Sue, and then Mom and I followed Paulette out of town. I had to refocus into my business head and make some calls to the accountant and the attorney. I'd set an appointment to stop in Ballard to meet my probate attorney on the way north.

You know how some doctors don't have good bedside manner? Well evidently, they teach "disconnectedness" in law school too. My husband had just dropped dead and I had no safety net to help me with the enormous debt that accompanied that loss.

Bart had hired an attorney to write up the charter agreement for the boat. That allowed Bart to take over managing the boat. The agreement covered all the legal details that Bart and the owner of the vessel agreed to, including (our) option to buy. Bart's sister and her husband also agreed to lend us money so Bart could upgrade the refrigeration system in the boat, which would—in theory—help us make more money from the fish due to a better market price for higher quality fish.

The same attorney wrote up the promissory note to my in-laws. When Bart died, our attorney's partner was defaulted to be my probate attorney. Both men seemed annoyed I was taking up their time by crying.

They stuck to the facts. I don't even know if they bothered saying the customary polite thing: "I'm very sorry for your loss." People are funny. They are funny because they don't know what to say or do, so they say the wrong things. Or they just say nothing and avoid *your* reality, because they have no clue what it's like and it scares the shit out of them. Or they see emotion as a weakness and they just don't get it. Lucky for them that they don't.

My friend Susan and the neighbors were at home planning the memorial. I wanted it to be a celebration of life—the only way Bart would want it. I wanted the men to wear aloha shirts, which were Bart's favorite. He had more of those shirts than anyone I'd ever known. I wanted the women to wear something colorful—no black. Bart wouldn't want mourning clothes. Those were my only requests. My friends took care of everything else.

* * *

We arrived at Lovric's Shipyard in Anacortes, which is located just a few minutes away from the ferry landing where we embark the vessels that carry us to the San Juan Islands. The detour to the attorney's office took longer than we expected because we ran into thick traffic on the way up Interstate 5. As a result, we arrived only an hour before Mike and the crew showed up with the *Lady Barbara*. That gave us just enough time to purchase a St. Christopher medallion for each crewmember, and meet the priest at the dock.

Mom and I made a beeline to Burton Jewelers on Commercial Avenue to look for the perfect medallion for the men. They had four in stock. Three were made of sterling silver, and one was made of gold. I bought them all, with chains to match. The gold pendant would hang in the wheelhouse to bless the captain, and the crew would receive the silver pendants. I would keep the gold necklace when the season was complete. That felt good.

Kami's husband, Pacific, was at the dock when we arrived. He was between fishing trips on the *Kami M*, and had been enjoying his sport boat for a few days. We hugged and acknowledged (again) the shock and grief we felt. Moments later, the *Lady Barbara* appeared and Pacific caught the lines.

I gave the guys their pendants.

The priest arrived fifteen minutes later, ready to perform the blessing. He blessed each room of the vessel—galley to the head, to the staterooms. He took special care in Bart's room, and proceeded to the engine room, the wheelhouse, the fo'c'sle, and even the landing tables and the bow of the vessel. He didn't miss an inch.

The heaviness that consumed the boat was suddenly lifted, as if a thick blanket had been removed. The air seemed fresher, thinner, easier to breathe. We thanked the priest and I immediately felt like we (all) could take the next steps.

Mike and the crew would bring the boat to Roche Harbor the next morning. Pacific offered to give Mom and me a ride home in his sport boat as soon as we were ready, which would be much faster than taking the ferry to the island. I introduced Mom to Joyce Lovric and explained to her what had happened. Joyce expressed her condolences and said the boat could stay tied up to the dock that night without charge. She also allowed Mom to park her car by their house above the shipyard and pick it up a week later, after the memorial service.

Mom remained strong for me and pushed her own grief deep down where no one could see it. Pacific was sad, but stayed on autopilot. Everyone around me kept their grief hidden from me. They acted as if I was made of glass or eggshells and might shatter into a million pieces.

I sat quietly in a trance as if, once again, I was not in control of my body. The moment to just "be" was both a welcomed distraction from my state of frantically trying to figure out what I would do, how I would survive my new reality, and to adjust to the torment. Grief—an inevitable process—was something so powerful it nearly killed me.

* * *

The following Wednesday was the service. Our next-door neighbor, Dave (Bart's best friend on the island), and his girlfriend, Dom, offered their guest cabin to my dad and stepmom, Carol. My mother and brother stayed in our house with me. One of my best friends, Denise, came from the other side of the state, bringing things I just might need like laundry detergent, cat food, muffins... just stuff. Barbara, one of my other best friends (I am lucky to have three) came up from Kirkland. My cousins from the Seattle area arrived while I was getting ready.

"I can't believe you look so beautiful," my cousin Gail said to me. It's funny what people say when they don't know what to say.

People spilled out the doorway of the pavilion at Roche Harbor Resort. At least 300 people attended the memorial. I cried during the video of Bart's life, mostly when "Pirate Looks at 40" by Jimmy Buffet played in the background. That song truly represented Bart's soul.

Dave spoke about his treasured friend. Cal had a good story to share, and Bart's brother Gavin shared stories and feelings that were perfectly delivered. Jaime, Bart's first mate, spoke of how Bart was like a brother to him and a second father to his son Arvn, as well as to Flavio, the other crewman.

Kami told us how special it was to meet Bart when she was fourteen and he had been hired to fish the family boat. She told how excited she was when Bart fell in love with me. He had shown up in Honolulu to start the North Pacific season with brightly colored toenails, each a different color with a separate design on each toe. 'My girlfriend did that,' he had proudly told her. "We knew Bart had found true love when he let her do that to him. We were so happy for him!" Kami said.

I had a hard time putting anything together for the memorial. Where to start? Where to focus? How to summarize who Bart was. My speech wasn't crafted as well as the others' were, but I spoke. I felt my body slouch and my words get softer as I continued, but I wrapped it up by straightening my body, standing tall, and saying in a strong voice, "Now let's party!"

Skyler arrived with his arm in a sling.

"Hi, Honey," I hugged him tight. Stepping back, I asked, "What happened to you?"

"I was blowing off some steam and I wiped out on my motorcycle. I broke my arm."

"Shit. You realize you won't be able to run the boat now? What the fuck, Skyler?"

"I know. I was wondering about that. I'm really sorry, Theresa. I want to take the boat out, I do! It would make Bart proud. It was an accident. I'm pissed too."

"Right," I said. "I understand. I'll find someone else. Good thing I put a rush on your passport. God."

Just what I needed... another wrinkle.

I was swarmed by well-wishers, all of whom were grieving. Bart's daughter, Faye, was strong for me even as she tried to deal with the death of her dad. Bart's ex-girlfriend, who never stopped loving him, was there. Our dear friends, Scott and Kathleen from Port Townsend (who had leased their boat, the *Middlepoint*, to Bart many years earlier, and we had planned to buy the boat from them in 2000 but the deal fell through) had offered up their next-door neighbor's guesthouse in Mexico to us as a honeymoon gift. We'd had a ball! Seeing them made me think of our honeymoon.

So many other friends, family members, and islanders expressed their condolences and personal sadness. Everyone was in shock at the loss of Bart. So sudden. So sad. A huge hole had been created in our community.

An hour later, it was time for the *Roche Harbor Colors Flag Ceremony*, commonly known as "Colors." This is a nightly event during the summer months that the resort has been putting on for many years. It honors the United States and Canada.

Scott, a long-time employee of Roche Harbor, turns on the loud speaker and asks everyone to be quiet for the ceremony. The servers in the restaurant stop whatever they are doing and face the marina. The dock crew—usually teenagers dressed in white pants and dark green sweatshirts with the Roche Harbor logo—march in unison toward the flag poles. "O Canada" plays through the loudspeakers overhead as they lower the Canadian flag, "God Save The Queen" is played as they lower the British flag, and the "Star Spangled Banner" is played while they lower the United States, Washington State, and Roche Harbor flags. Immediately afterward, they shoot off the cannon, which generally startles people due to its noisy blast.

The marina then fills with the sound of boat horns honking and patrons celebrating on and off the docks. "Colonel Bogey's March" plays as the crew marches out of sight. Scott might announce the weather, welcome new and/or returning guests, or recognize special occasions being celebrated around the resort. Then people resume conversations and the staffs at the restaurant and bar once again bustle around as if there had just been a freeze frame in a movie.

But that day, "Colors" was a bit different. My mom, dad, stepmom, brother, aunt, Uncle Halibut, friends, and I poured onto our boat, *Lady Barbara*, which was moored close to the resort. After they lowered the flags, Scott gave a special tribute to Bart, asked for a moment of silence, and then played taps. He saved the sounding of the cannon for his conclusion, which seemed like a perfect closing of Bart's memorial service. There wasn't a dry eye on the boat, but we were ready to enjoy each other and what was left of the sunset. "My people" settled in various places around the vessel—some inside the salon, and some remained on the deck until the sun had completely disappeared.

Once the crowd on the boat cleared out, my immediate family

and a few of our closest friends gathered around me in the wheelhouse. People tried to help by telling me what I should do with the boat.

"She needs to get it back out and finish the season," someone said.

"She doesn't have to do anything else tonight," Dad responded.

"Yes, you're right. I'm sorry."

The people around me were tired. We were all spent. I was a zombie again. I leaned my head into Dad's chest. He held my hand and stroked my hair. "It's been a long day, Honey," he said. "I think we should gather our things and go get some sleep."

"Good idea," echoed everyone on board.

Dad and Carol settled across the street in Jerry and Margi Rehn's guesthouse. Jerry and Margi had become my "island family" when Bart was fishing and I stayed home to manage things from the beach. Our friendship grew organically and remains rich to this day. They rallied the way family does in a crisis. And speaking of a family that rallies… Kevin and Ann live next door to the Rehns and they offered their guesthouse to my Aunt Jan and Uncle Halibut. Small towns work that way. Neighbors become family.

Mom, my brother Bryan, and I went home. I got into my jammies and went into the bathroom to wash my face while Mom and Bryan rearranged the living room to accommodate their sleeping quarters.

I looked at my reflection in the mirror and saw pain. I kept the water running in an attempt to drown out the roaring sound of my cries. I ended up on the floor, sobbing so hard my ribs hurt. Again. The day had taken its toll. I pulled myself together and entered the living room. Mom and Bryan sat on the settee and hung onto each other for comfort. Neither of them said a word. They stared at the bathroom door and watched me emerge. They could not fix me. They could not make the pain stop. They could not bring Bart back.

They looked scared. And sad.

"I'll be okay," I told them. "I'm just really broken right now." They hugged me tight and we called it a day. After a while, I finally slept.

In the morning, Mom said she was certain she saw Bart, as if he were struggling to see through the living room and around the doorway to the bed where I lay.

When Bart was home we left the curtains open over the French doors in the bedroom so the morning light would wake us and we could start our day with a view of the backyard. But I had closed those curtains that night in hopes of sleeping past sunrise, and that must have been what blocked Bart's view of me. I left the curtains open every night for the next year—just in case he tried again.

Me, Bart, Flavio, Arvn, and Jaime on *Lady Barbara* **in port**

The Drifter

Meeting people
Traveling day by day
Life-long friends
Along the way.

~ Bart Mathews

Chapter 14:
79th Day at Sea

SUMMER WAS GONE AND FALL WAS UPON US but it was hard to tell the difference. The temperature was getting cooler, but otherwise it wasn't much different from any other day at sea. No bright colored leaves fell from the trees and landed in the yard like a new carpet. No frost to cover the grass and windshields of our cars. No soft scarves and trendy boots. No crackling fire burned in the woodstove. Just the calendar I looked at every day told me how long I'd been stuck on that boat.

I miss my life, and yet... this IS my life.

The air had a chill and the wind, rain, and rough seas came more often. Other than that, day 79 was just another day.

We had been picking away at fish and since no one else had found a better spot, we shut down and stayed put for the night. When Bart left the stateroom, I let one of the rolls of the boat from the portside give me a boost out of bed. I steadied myself as I walked to the head, keeping one hand firmly planted on the windowsill, then on the built-in cabinet in the corner, then on the doorframe so I wouldn't get flung across the room.

I dressed in a pair of jeans, tank top, and a sweatshirt, then headed for the galley, applying the same strategy I had used to move through our stateroom. I poured myself a cup of coffee, added hazelnut creamer, and hung onto the railing of the steps with one hand to get up to the wheelhouse without falling.

"Good morning," I said to Bart.

"Mornin', Hon," he replied.

"What's new?" I asked as I set my coffee on the non-skid that covered the desk. I draped both hands across the back of the bench to steady my body and hoped to start a conversation.

"Just trying to find our school so we can get to work," he said very matter-of-fact.

"I see. I'll go cook then."

Bart kissed the air in my direction to suggest that was a good idea, but as usual he didn't have much to say.

It's funny… when we were home, I couldn't care less about a little quiet time in the morning since I've never been chatty that early. But at sea, I needed dialogue to feel connected. I felt ignored if we didn't engage in some conversation—to just reassure myself of something. Anything. Perhaps that the romance hadn't died, or that WE were still good in every other way, or that there was some "normal" in my life out there.

I grabbed my cup, took my annoyed self to the galley, and let my negative thoughts run rampant.

I fucking hate it out here! I want to go home! I want my boyfriend back. Maybe I need a new boyfriend! I am always out of my skin, doing stuff I don't like, on a boat that is thousands of miles from anywhere. What the Hell was I thinking?!

Chop chop chop. I cut up an onion.

Ooh, bell peppers would be good. Oh, I think I'll throw in that leftover taco meat.

Cooking calmed me right down and gave me something to do that I enjoyed. I decided on breakfast burritos that morning and added plenty of spice. Enough to match the mood I was trying to snap out of. Brandon walked in and smiled at me.

"Smells good in here," he said. "Ya making Mexican?"

"Yah, I thought we'd have something different today," I said smiling back. "I'm trying to shake off a crabby mood and cooking is helping."

"You're feeling a little salty, are ya?" he asked in that flirtatious Kiwi tone. "Wake up on the wrong side of the bed?" Snicker snicker.

Ha ha ha ha ha! We both laughed. There's only one side of the bed to get out from on a boat—the other side is against the wall.

"Thanks, Brandon," I said. "I needed a good chuckle."

"No worries. Anything I can do to help?" he asked, looking toward the stove.

"I've got it, thanks," I told him. "Breakfast is just about ready."

"I'll let Mario know," he said grabbing the handle to open the door.

Just as he called to Mario, a few bells went off. We had fish on. I wondered how those fish always seemed to know when it was time for us to eat.

I put Bart's burrito together, added salsa and sour cream, grabbed a can of V-8 (his morning choice), and headed upstairs. I pushed my butt against the wall as a way to steady my body since both hands were full.

"Looks good, Hon. Thanks," he said. "Nice little school of fish we're on. Love you," he added with a twinkle in his eye.

"Love you, too," I said and went back downstairs. I wasn't mad anymore and I needed to eat quickly and get outside to relieve one of the guys so he could take his turn for food.

The weather picked up, which made it difficult to hang on. The wind blew about fifteen-twenty knots so the lines tangled easily—something I had very little patience for. The guys were good at managing the lines when Bart turned the boat around for another tack.

If we turned in a leftward direction, for example, Brandon would grab the mono of all the lines that had crossed into Mario's lines and secure them on a gripper by wrapping them around it a few times. Once the turn had been completed, he'd release the mono from the gripper and the lines would usually fall back into place.

During one of the turns, a fish bit a jig and took off with a powerful force as it tried to get free. The fish swam back and forth across the other lines and managed to create a massive tangle. Brandon got the fish onboard, cut his throat so he would bleed out (a technique we were trying that trip, thinking it would eliminate bruising of the meat), pushed him down the chute, rinsed his station, and got straight to work on the tangle.

I just pulled the few fish that were on the bowlines and returned to the back deck to watch Brandon carefully free each line and toss it back into the water. Amazing. Those guys made everything look easy.

We scratched along the rest of the day as we tacked back and forth and moved further to the northwest. We got into a spot where fish bit off and on, but it wasn't wide open when Brandon noticed that the tuna cord on one of his longer lines had tightened so much it looked like the whole rigging was caught on the bottom of the ocean.

"I either have a big fish on or we're dragging something huge here!" he said.

"Wow look at that line," Mario said. "I'll get the gaff."

Brandon worked hard and steady to get that line in. Mario assisted. They both knew we had something significant hooked. The end of line moved closer to the boat and finally they saw it.

"Holy crap! That thing is huge!" Brandon said.

I ran up to let Bart know we had a big one on and he slowed the boat way down to make it easier for the guys to get it on board. Bart stood at the steps, calling out words of encouragement as they worked. I stood in awe.

Brandon and Mario were a professional team, perfectly in sync with each other as they double-gaffed that fish and pulled him out of the water. The fish was so big, it was longer than the landing table! They brought the massive tuna to the bow of the vessel and we all admired the enormity.

Mario retrieved the scale from the fo'c'sle and hung it from the mast so we could weigh that thing. Fifty-six pounds—a rarity for jig fishing. Of course, we had our pictures taken with the spectacular specimen.

The next hour or so was uneventful. We caught a few normal-sized fish but the weather started to come up and grew more aggressive by the minute. Waves collided into the boat and violently crashed over the sides. It became harder to hang on, but we kept moving and did our best to let the roll of the boat help us pull the fish out of the water. Since they were still biting, we weren't about to stop fishing. We ate our simple meal of Costco lasagna and a piece of garlic bread in shifts that night. Then we washed our dishes, suited up, and went back out into the wind and wet.

The rain started late that afternoon, which increased our discomfort in the miserable conditions. The guys and I wore our rain gear, but I couldn't decide which was worse... getting soaked to the bone or sweating to death under the rubber to stay dry.

The rain collected on the bridge deck and sloshed back and forth as the boat plowed through the rough seas. I was at Brandon's station while he stacked fish in the hold. As I pulled a fish and spun around to heft him onto the landing table, the boat rolled starboard and released a bucket of rain from the upper deck onto my head.

"Fuck!" I yelled. "I'm gonna drown out here!"

No one heard me. No one would have cared anyway. The music was playing loudly, the wind was howling through the stern, the rain was pouring, and the boat's engine was working hard. It was noisy out there and my damn hood was too big so it was hard to see.

I had to breathe with my mouth open to keep from drowning. Rain poured down my face from the top of my hood whenever I pushed the hood back far enough to see out from underneath it. When I turned back to the stern and tossed a jig back into the water, a wave that came from the other direction slammed into the portside of the vessel and nailed me in the face with enormous force.

"Goddamn it! I fucking hate this mother-fucking shit!"

I was not happy and my temper tantrum was on. Again. No one heard me. No one cared. I was on a workboat and everyone was enduring the same—or maybe even worse. I was not special.

Eventually the fish stopped biting and Bart came outside.

"Wow, what a tack, huh? I'll have Brandon pull 'em when he gets back here. I didn't think they'd ever quit biting. How many do we have, Hon?"

"About 450, but Mario has the final count. He should be back from the hold in a few. Seems like we got more than that, but maybe that's cause we had to fight with each one," I said.

"Well, that's a pretty good day. I know it's wet out here, but you should be happy about all those fish," he said with a disappointed tone.

"I am happy we caught fish but this weather sucks!" I snapped.

He shot me a look and went inside.

Fuck. Why can't I whine a little? This is not the romantic adventure he promised and I'm pissed. I want to unleash a major temper tantrum, but I have to stuff it and be a tough guy. This is the day I might just lose my mind!

So here's the deal... there were moments in those miserable conditions—on that day and many others like it—when I got caught up in the physical exertion, the adrenaline of catching fish, knew we were making money, and it felt good to be just plain working hard. The excitement of catching a fish that was almost as tall as me was incredible!

But then I would feel my aching bones and over-heated body, slip on the deck, get blasted in the face by a massive wave—one too many times—or flinch from the water that fell from the aft deck above when it dumped down my back inside my rain coat.

That's when my mood would switch gears and I'd wish I was anywhere in the world than on that damn boat. The worst part was when Bart ignored me or judged me for not being happy. He chided me for being miserable and lonely. I hated him sometimes. The ocean can do weird things to a person. It changes everyone.

To not be able to go home at the end of the day, change your surroundings, or be in control of your situation is difficult. With an average of ninety days per trip—that's a lot of time to be with your thoughts. And boy, can those thoughts mess you up.

When Bart turned his back and went inside the wheelhouse, I stuck my tongue out at him and flipped him off. That made me feel better. Thirty-five going on seventeen. That was me, and I didn't care. I braved the short walk to the bow deck to help the guys finish up for the day.

Just then, Bart appeared at the bridge and hollered down to me.

"The guys can get this, Hon. Why don't you go ahead and take your shower," he said sweetly.

"Okay," I said looking up at him. He blew me a kiss. I returned the gesture. I loved him again. I loved him still. I will love him always.

Me with a 56-pounder

Brandon with big fish on *Maverick*. Mario on the right

Chapter 15: The Visitor

WE HAD BEEN ON A GOOD SCHOOL OF FISH for a few days and the boat was filling up. A couple more days and we would head south to American Samoa to unload. The trip to the island would take up to two weeks, depending on the latitude/longitude we ended up on when we filled up, and what kind of weather we ran into on the way south.

I got out of bed as soon as Bart was dressed and out of our stateroom. My hands were sore from squeezing mono since we'd caught more than 400 fish per day during the previous two weeks, and one day the count was 1,289!

My thumb and fingers had a hard time gripping my toothbrush. I had to place the handle between the palms of my hands and work it back and forth across my teeth to keep it from falling to the sink.

I washed my face and stretched my hands to get them working, then grabbed a clean pair of jeans and a sweatshirt from the cupboard above the bed. With a squirt of Wings by Giorgio Beverly Hills (my favorite perfume), and a swipe of lipstick, I was ready to enter the galley. I wanted to start the day looking and smelling like a girl.

As soon as I pulled back the curtain from the stateroom and secured it to a hook on the inside wall, Mario met me with a greeting and his index finger to his mouth. He whispered, "Shhhhh. Walk gently. Look there... under the table." Brandon stood by the galley table and pointed underneath toward a little black and white bird.

"We've been keeping him warm for you so you could see him before we let him go. Mario got up early and found him on the back deck. He was cold and wet and seemed disoriented, so we wanted to make sure he wasn't injured. He should be ready to go in a few minutes if we can keep him calm that long."

"Oh my God, he's so cute! What a precious little guy. Wish we could keep him."

"We thought you'd like him," Mario said, beaming for his thoughtful decision to rescue the bird and share him with us.

The little bird sat there quietly and looked around. He didn't even try to fly around the house, which surprised me.

"Is he hurt?" I asked.

"No, he's just warming up I think," Mario said.

"Do you know what kind of bird he is?"

"I'm not sure. He looks like he could be a tern, a petrel, or perhaps a shearwater."

"He's so cute!" I was thrilled to be that close to a sea bird.

"He won't hurt you," Brandon assured me. "Let me get a picture with you holding him."

"Oh, cool!" I said.

Brandon grabbed his camera from the couch while Mario bent down and carefully scooped up our little friend.

"Here you go," Mario said as he placed him into my hands.

"Hi, little fella! Where did you come from?" I asked, gently holding the bird as I posed for a photo shot.

"I think he's ready. What do you think, Mario?" Brandon asked.

"Yes, I think so. He seems fine, so we shouldn't keep him any longer," Mario replied.

Both guys looked at me.

"Do I get to do it?" I asked.

"We think you should," they both agreed.

The rain had stopped, but it was gray and breezy and the spray coming off the tops of the short waves made us wet.

"Thank you!" I said. "Let me put on my rain pants before you hand him to me, okay?"

"Of course," Brandon said. "Mario will take him outside and I'll get the camera ready to capture the image when you let him go."

Bart watched from the wheelhouse window. I released the bird and hoped he'd fly away and not drop into the drink. He flapped his wings immediately and off he went.

What a thrill. I still find it hard to wrap my brain around how anything smaller than an albatross can get so far off shore.

We were cruising southbound and still had approximately one week of running before we'd find land.

My research revealed the following: white-faced storm petrels are very small seabirds that migrate to the tropical eastern Pacific for the offseason (May through July) and are found in the seas around New Zealand during breeding season (August through April). Some fishermen and boaters claim the birds "walk on water" due to their little bounding hops and minimal wing movement when they feed. Terns go to land only to breed and will spend anywhere from three to ten years at sea, soaring above the waves or resting on its surface.

Like most birds with several species in each family, the shearwater can be found around the globe. Many breed on southern islands and in tropical climates across the Central Pacific Ocean and can be long-distance migrants that travel in a circular route across the ocean.

The freedom a bird must experience is something most humans dream of. I felt joy and envy as I watched our little friend return to flight. I wondered if he would reunite with his flock, or if he'd be a solo-flyer. As the word maverick is synonymous with individualist, nonconformist, and lone wolf, I thought it was appropriate that he landed on the *Maverick*.

Me holding a small bird, 1999

Me setting the bird free

Mother Ocean

I dream of being on the ocean
It is so nice and quiet
To talk to the waves
Listen to them
Waves will talk to you
Out there
They'll keep you company
When no one else will
Sunshine on the water.

~ Bart Mathews

Chapter 16:
The Dream

SEPTEMBER 15, 2006 WAS EXACTLY ONE MONTH from the day Bart died. My alarm went off at 5:30 a.m. Bart went into the shower at 5:30 a.m. a month ago—just like every other day of his life. I hadn't slept well, which was a common theme in my life those days, so I turned off the alarm and lay back down. I woke again at 6:55, cleared the cobwebs from my head, went to the bathroom, and looked again at the clock.

It was 7:06. That was the exact time Jack had called one month earlier to tell me Bart was dead. Interesting. All those time stamps. The dream I'd had during that hour-and-a-half replayed in my mind.

Dreams are very real when we are dreaming them. They may remain fluid and clear as one scene (or person) quickly morphs into another. When we are awake and recall what occurred in our dream-state, we may find the message is poignant or confusing and difficult to explain. I hope I can articulate just how powerful each dream scene was for me because it continues to remain a permanent picture in my memory today.

* * *

DREAM: I entered a tall glass building. I'm not sure where I was or how many stories the building contained, but I knew I was a long way off the ground. All that surrounded me was sky. Bart was standing there waiting for me. He was wearing his Levi 501s and a cobalt blue button-up heavy cotton shirt, the one he wore during winter months. His eyes were blue and shiny, his beard gray, his body large. I ran to him.

We hugged tight and I could feel *it was him. Really him*! We both cried. I comforted his tears.

"I'm sorry," he said. "I miss you so much and I love you. I don't think I have the patience for this."

"Oh my God," I said. "It really is you. I've been waiting for this moment to hold you."

Next scene ~

We were in his room, which was decorated in contemporary Ikea wood furnishings. Not his style or mine. The floor of his room was hardwood—pine I think—and shiny.

"There are stages to go through," he said. "And lots of tests. The men and women are separated for the process. Each stage and test determines if we are ready—or worthy—to be men and women."

I didn't comment. What do you say to that?

Bart and I just hung out there and chatted about nothing really. We checked out his new digs and life—or way of being—now that he was no longer alive on earth.

Next scene ~

Bart went to lie down and crawled inside a small black body bag. It looked like it would hold a guitar, or maybe a large cue-stick. He didn't zip it up all the way, but he did cover his face.

I told him, "Honey, don't go yet… I'll leave soon."

I lay down next to him and peeked inside the bag so I could see his face and kiss him gently and touch his beard. I asked, "What if I die of old age? That's such a long time to be without you."

He reached out and put his arm around me, looked into my eyes and said, "You'll find someone and love again. I know you will."

"Not now! Not yet," I told him. "It feels like I'm cheating to even think about that because I love you so much."

"No, not now," he said. "Give this some time. But you will, and I'll see you again soon."

I'm not sure if he meant he'll see me again soon in a dream, or at home, or in death—but I don't think he meant in death because that's what he always said anytime he left for a while—mostly when he went on a fishing trip.

"I'll see you soon," *he'd say. In fact, those were the last words he said to me face-to-face just two weeks before he died.* "See you soon!"

Next scene ~

We were hanging out in his room again and I looked out the window. The tide was coming in and it sounded like a huge wave was headed our way. *It had rained hard that morning. Maybe the sound from the rain entered my dream?*

I thought that was my cue to leave the dream. I closed my eyes—just like I used to do as a child when I needed to escape a nightmare. I took a deep breath and called out, "Bye, Bart! I love you!" I then found myself sitting on a step, with glass walls or partitions surrounding me. But I was still in his room.

"Why are you leaving so fast?" he asked. He said he'd heard the sound of the water too. "Nope, not a tidal wave. The waves just come in my room sometimes."

We both giggled.

Next scene ~

We walked up the hardwood steps of his room to exit and he opened the large glass door for me. As we stepped through the doorway, I asked if he was hovering around in spirit, watching every move I made and reading my mind. Did he know my thoughts and watch me cry.

He said, "No, Hon. That's a crock of shit."

He was—up there. Up at that level. Wherever it was where I was visiting him—not down on earth, where I lived in pain.

Next scene ~

Bart and I were inside a very large building like a convention center. We held hands and walked. People were everywhere—walking here and there, with more people coming up an escalator. A young man who held a baby walked backward toward us. They were on "the other side"—on earth, where the living reside. Where I had just come from. A young woman—from the side where Bart was—arrived to greet them. The man and the woman embraced. She said, "What a great way to spend my birthday."

We looked at them, but didn't comment.

How sad.

The woman died and her man was left behind on earth to raise their child alone. I was left alone to live my life without Bart. Bart had adult children who were also grieving, but I didn't have children to raise. I felt sad for the man and baby, but I was glad they got to see *her*—on her birthday—during visiting hours. Or whatever that was.

We walked on and Bart was talking, but then it wasn't him anymore—*weird, like dreams can be.* He was suddenly a young, short guy. He said, "You're older than I remember."

I said, "You're a lot younger than I remember—and you don't even look like my Bart!"

I tried to make him grow a beard and get big—something we might be able to do in a dream. Then I looked to the left and Bart was trying to get through a crowd. He had a frantic expression on his face.

This time he was still wearing the Levi 501s and a tan suede button-up shirt that he'd loved—it was the real Bart again. He ran to me and we embraced. He was mad that they had tried to trick me by substituting a fake Bart when I came to visit. Just because I was in a dream didn't mean I wouldn't notice it was no longer Bart by my side.

Dreams are so weird like that.

The real Bart and I went to a place to deal with the imposter. The lady sitting at the table told Bart, "Push the button and let yourselves in. He's waiting for you."

The kid—the imposter—the one who pretended to be Bart, was at the table. I sat between him and an old guy. Bart walked to the other side of the table, reached inside a lower cabinet, and grabbed a bottle of Canadian Club, his drink of choice. "I need a drink before I talk to you," he said. He was angry.

"They let you drink up here?" I asked.

"Yah," the kid said. "We even ate burgers the other day."

"That's crazy," I said.

Bart agreed and then said he'd be flying soon. I didn't know if that meant later that day, or soon, like in an hour....

Bart and the kid each got out their own stack of cards. There was a picture of me on the back of the bottom card of Bart's deck. A picture of another woman was on the bottom card of the kid's deck. Receipts made up the rest of the cards in the decks, but they were more like Taro cards.

Another old guy showed up. His face was pasty and dead looking. He was disoriented. Someone said, "He doesn't know where he is yet."

Final Act ~

I walked out of the glass building, as if visiting hours were over. I must have said goodbye to Bart, but I didn't get to linger in that scene. Dang-it. That was my favorite part... lingering with Bart.

I heard Flavio run up behind me. He laughed at how Bart made guitar sounds with his voice because he had so much to learn about the instrument. I laughed and told him, "You need to come back again soon to teach Bart how to play."

Flavio didn't look exactly like himself either, but he sounded and acted like the Flavio we knew and loved, so it had to have been him.

Flavio and I approached the big glass doors that exited to the outside. We stood on a very steep cliff surrounded by snow and whiteness everywhere. Someone outside told us to be careful. "Not too close," they said. We stepped back from the edge. Everyone wore snow boots, and snow pants, and coats in pale pink or powder blue.

They just stood there and waited. Then a helicopter—or maybe it was a plane—came into view at the top of the high point where we stood. It looked as if it was constructed of brightly colored paper. Flavio thought Bart was piloting that thing. Maybe that's what Bart meant when he said, 'I have to fly soon.'

Then people walked over to the stacks of saucers that lined the building and each took one. The saucers were square with rounded corners, like large Tupperware lids, except they were hard. Some people took a small stack, rather than just one. Then the people sat on the saucers/Tupperware lids and sledded by us really fast on their way back to their homes.

We went over to get our saucer. Obviously, we wouldn't be flying home in the plane (or helicopter). There were still a few saucers available so I separated two that were stuck together. I handed Flavio his sled and I set mine on the ground. We sat down on them and immediately I zoomed toward my home. I knew Flavio was on his own adventure back to his home. We didn't say goodbye as far as I recall.

I landed in someone else's backyard. Not mine. They had a log house. People were there waiting for someone else to return from "up there." It was dusk. I closed my eyes to exit the dream and I woke up in my bed. The time was 6:55 a.m. I sat up and talked to Bart.

"How much was real? Are you really *that* far away? Are you really stuck at that stage, bored, lonely, and unable to reach me? How much was just weird dreaming? I'm more confused now but I'm happy I was able to hug you. I know that part was real. Thank you, my love. I miss you."

Chapter 17:
Pago Pago

I NEVER KNEW HOW MUCH I WOULD APPRECIATE LAND until I was unable to see it, touch it, or stand on it for ninety-eight days in a row. The weight of ninety-six tons of albacore in the *Maverick*'s hull had us sitting low in the water as we approached the entrance to Pago Pago (pronounced Pango Pango) on that November day in 1999. We were in American Samoa, a South Pacific island.

The excitement I felt in my belly when I saw the tropical trees, the endless sandy beach, and small huts tucked among the vegetation on the edge of the shoreline sparked a euphoric feeling of being alive. I'd been missing that feeling.

The rusted-out fishing vessel sitting firm on the bottom of the shallow bay was an ominous sight. A hurricane back in the early 1980s tossed the boat inland and damaged it beyond repair. No one had the finances or the desire to remove it from its final resting place, so there it sat. The boat had become a permanent fixture near the cannery's dock.

Maverick's owner, Miguel, and his friend John flew in to meet us at the cannery where the group had sold their fish for many years. Reggie, the Tahitian-born fish buyer who lived in Samoa for twenty-some years, was there to coordinate the unloading activities. Bart sat with the men at the galley table going over details of the trip. I was busting at the seams to get out and explore the island.

"If you don't need us for a bit, Hon, how 'bout I borrow

Miguel's rental and take the guys for a little drive?" I pleaded.

"I was just going to suggest that. You'll want to go to Tisa's Barefoot Bar. It's a great little spot around the bend there. Go have a drink and enjoy yourselves," he said.

"Awesome, Honey. Thanks!"

I gave him a kiss, grabbed my purse, and bolted out the door to collect the guys. They were more than thrilled to go for an adventure and they both knew Tisa's well, so they could help me find it.

I opened the door to the little blue rental car and saw a cockroach scurry from the floorboard to an unknown location inside the vehicle.

"Oh my God!" I screeched. "There is a cockroach in the car!"

Mario and Brandon laughed and Brandon said, "They are everywhere down here, but don't worry. They will stay hidden as long as we're in the car."

"That is so gross," I said.

"I know, but it's okay," Mario reassured. "We can't get away from them and they only come out in the dark when they can't see us."

"Okay, but it creeps me out," I said.

The guys grinned, but it was clear they didn't like the nasty critters any more than I did.

I drove north along the east side of the island. We passed rundown structures and front yards littered with junk, toys, rusted cars, laundry hanging to dry, and the occasional gravestone. A common Samoan custom is to bury one male family member in the yard of the house they'd lived in.

I observed the poverty-stricken community with awe. The guys had seen it before, but it's always a sobering reminder of how fortunate we are when one sees such a depressed lifestyle.

"Keep your belongings close to you around here," Mario said. "Samoans are the nicest people you'll ever meet, but they have their own unique philosophy."

"Yah, that's right," Brandon chimed in. "What's mine is mine and what's yours is mine."

"Gotcha," I said, understanding the scene.

"They've been known to show up on your boat uninvited and help themselves to anything not nailed down," Brandon explained.

"Wow. That's terrible."

"But it's fine as long as you know that," Mario said.

"There's the bar," Brandon pointed to the right.

We parked in front of a groovy little hut with a straw roof and walked through the open doorway. Tisa welcomed us with delight as if she'd been waiting for our arrival all day. We returned the greeting and chose a table that allowed a great view of the beach, which was any seat in the place.

We ordered our drinks—the guys each ordered a beer and I chose a gin and tonic, something I hadn't had in years, but it sounded refreshing in that hot humid air.

Tiny no-see-ums and crawling sand gnats tickled our limbs (mostly mine), so Tisa surrounded me—and our table—with steel buckets filled with burning citronella. We could then enjoy our drinks and the fact that we were sitting still.

Aaahhhh. I like land.

It was cocktail hour back at the boat, so upon our return, we joined the festivities with Bart, Miguel, and John.

I rummaged through the remaining food in the freezers and found enough chicken to feed all of us. I also located an onion that hadn't gone bad yet, a bag of flour tortillas, grated cheese, and enough salsa to make fajitas. The food helped the fact that we'd been indulging for several hours, but Bart was well beyond his drinking limit for one day and soon lay on our bed.

I was well on my way too but was wound-up like an eight-day clock and wanted to go out. Miguel suggested we go into town for dancing, so I put on a dress and tried to wake Bart to join us. But he was down for the count, so I followed the guys to the car. Everyone but Mario was up for a good time off the boat.

The rest of the evening consisted of more drinking, lots of storytelling and laughing, dancing the night away, and some heavy flirting between Brandon and me. The combination of solid ground under my feet and an unknown amount of gin in my bloodstream made me feel loose, free, and very much alive. Evidently, I danced in a sensual manner because one man came up to me on the dance floor and said, "Will you please dance with my wife like that?"

"Sure!" I said and proceeded to dance with his woman in a way that makes me shake my head when I think about it now. Although the booze and its influence created a strong current that ran through me, my internal compass and love for Bart kept me from doing anything I would regret.

The time came for us to call it a night, so Miguel and John took Brandon and me back to the boat and dropped us off. Brandon went up the steps to his stateroom in the wheelhouse and I entered the master stateroom where Bart was comfortably sawing logs. I smiled to myself, knowing he would probably feel a lot better in the morning than I would. Then I washed my face and crawled into bed beside him.

The sun came up sooner than I wanted. I rose slowly, lifting my thick head off the pillow and slowly entered the galley to find Bart and a strong cup of coffee.

"Good morning," he said. "How are you feeling today?"

"Not so good, Hon. How 'bout you?"

"I feel fine, since I seemed to have missed the fun. How come you didn't wake me?"

"I tried three times but you were out of it. I figured you must really need your sleep, but I still wanted to go. Are you mad at me?"

"No. I didn't know you tried to wake me," he said with a softer tone than when he first spoke.

"Of course I did. You can ask Miguel or Brandon or Mario—they all heard me."

"I believe you. Sorry. I guess I had too much to drink," he said.

"We all did. Good grief! I don't know what got into me. Is that what happens when you spend three months on the ocean? God. It's like I was on a mission to see how much I could consume. I was even dirty dancing with some woman. Disgusting," I said reflecting on my lack of self-control.

"Oh? That's kind of hot," he said and winked at me. "But really... don't worry about it, Hon. Most of us do that after a long trip. Did you have fun?"

"Yes. I'm pretty sure I did," I grinned.

Bart smiled back at me with the twinkle in his eye that made me fall even deeper in love with him.

After my shower, I was ready to go to the store with Bart, but I couldn't find my purse. Evidently, I'd left it somewhere the night before. I was delighted to find my passport in the dresser. Not sure why I removed it from my purse before I went out, but I was grateful that I had.

We went back to the place where I'd spent the evening dancing and I was shocked to see what a dive it was.

"Oh my God—this is where I was last night?"

"Yep," Bart teased. "Fancy, huh?"

"Yikes," I said. "Looks a little different in the daylight."

It was a small building with a simple bar, lined with stools that had torn beige vinyl cushions and black metal frames. The room was square with a tiny wood dance floor and an old-style jukebox, possibly from the 1950s. The rest of the room was covered in a thin puke-colored carpet, with several banquet tables and chairs that matched the bar stools. The room smelled like stale cigarette smoke, and the booze-stained rug that was in desperate need of cleaning... or burning.

I described my purse to the lady who stood behind the bar and I asked if she'd seen it. "Remember me?" I asked. "I was sitting right here with my friends. Three guys. Miguel and his buddy sat to my left and Brandon—the young Kiwi sat here, to my right." I pointed to our places at the bar.

"Hmmmm. Yah, I think I remember seeing you," she said—as if she wasn't sure.

"We were here for hours!" I said, suddenly very angry that she was playing dumb.

"Well I remember your friends and I think I remember seeing you too, but I never saw any purse," she stated matter of fact.

"Here is my phone number," I said, handing her my business card. "If it turns up will you please call me?"

"Sure," she said, grabbing the card without looking at it and tossing it behind the bar.

Bart and I looked at each other, knowing she had my purse and we would never see it again. We walked out of there and back to the car. I was fuming mad. Not because I had lost anything of real value, but because this woman lied to my face and could have given back my purse after she'd taken what she wanted, but she chose not to. I had at most twenty dollars cash in it, a checkbook with a very low balance, some lipstick—my favorite color of course, a nail file, and my wallet that had my driver's license, debit card, and a couple of credit cards.

I spent the next two hours on the phone, locating numbers to the credit card companies, my bank, and my mother. I always felt better when I could talk to my mom. It started to rain hard.

"Can you hear the monsoon rain in the background?" I asked her.

"Yes, I can! Oh, it's so good to hear your voice, Honey," she said. "I can't believe I'm talking to my daughter while listening to the rain in Samoa. That's so cool. I miss you."

"Miss you too, Mom." I laughed at her giddiness. What a cutie.

The rest of the day was eaten up by chores, errands, and boat projects. That afternoon Miguel and Bart sat at the galley table and went through the list of checked off items. Bart and I had been to the travel agent's office earlier that day where we'd made arrangements to fly out the next afternoon. We had secured a room at the Raintree, returning the master stateroom to Miguel since he would be bringing the boat back to the states once we departed.

His neighbor, John, would be his crewman to help with the lines and taking watch, and he would occupy one of the staterooms after the crew vacated the vessel. There wasn't anything significant left to do, so Miguel suggested we go to the yacht club for dinner.

He collected the crew and left the boat a few minutes later. "See you guys over there in a bit," he said over his shoulder.

Bart and I hung back to enjoy the fact that we had the boat to ourselves. It would be the last time for who knows how long, and we were both very much aware of the emotion… and each other.

Bart changed into his brightest aloha shirt, a clean pair of Levi's, and his best loafers. He waited for me in the galley while I put on a dress and freshened up.

"You look real nice, Hon," he said as I entered the galley and sat down to put on my sandals.

"Thanks, Darlin'. So do you. I like that shirt."

"Oh, good," he said just before he kissed me. "You ready to go?"

"Yep. I'm starving!"

Miguel and the crew had a couple hours' head start on us by the time we arrived at the yacht club. They greeted us with excitement, as if they hadn't seen us for months. We chuckled, sat down, and ordered a drink while we looked at the menu. The food was simple fare, which made our choices easy. I chose grilled mahi-mahi with rice pilaf and a salad. Bart ordered a club sandwich with French fries. The guys had already eaten their steaks and hamburgers.

Just as we finished dinner, a large Samoan woman with platinum blonde hair came by to hug Miguel. "You guys are coming to my place next, right?!" she commanded.

"Of course, Evie," Miguel replied. "We wouldn't leave this island without having a drink at your bar."

Bart looked at me with a twinkle in his eye and said, "Well, I guess we're going dancing, Hon."

"Okay," I said. "Sounds fun."

Within fifteen minutes, the tab was paid at the yacht club and we were walking into Evalanie's Cantina, a rectangular building painted a bright chili pepper red. The restaurant section to the right of the entrance was lined with tables, although most were empty. The bar was to the left and decorated with Christmas lights. Smoking was allowed in the building, but there were plenty of fans to keep the place cool, which made the smoke hardly noticeable.

It was 9 p.m., so the music in the jukebox had already been blaring for an hour. The place was set up for karaoke, but no singers were waiting in line to perform. The local DJ was off that night, so we kept the jukebox loaded and Evie kept the volume high to encourage dancing.

Bart and Miguel sat at the bar and told stories, talked about fishing, the boat, and laughed at dirty jokes they didn't want me to hear. The guys and I chose a table nearby to enjoy our drinks. I felt as though they were just being good sports to keep me entertained. Before long, I was dancing in my chair so I boogied over to Bart and tried to get him to dance with me. Miguel was amused by our playfulness and he, too, tried to get Bart to dance with me.

"No, Hon. I'm happy sitting here with Miguel right now, but you go for it," he said, resting his large gentle hand on my ass and pulling me near.

"Oh, man! C'mon, Honey. I wanna dance!" I pleaded.

"Brandon! Dance with Theresa!" he commanded as he lifted his voice toward the table where Brandon and Mario sat.

"Okay!" Brandon said with his flirty little grin, happy to oblige.

Brandon and I danced while Bart and Miguel continued with their conversation. I enjoyed dancing with Brandon and flirting with Bart across the room when he glanced in my direction.

"Don't touch me, Brandon," I said in a teasing way. "I can see the way you're looking at me." I was buzzed and feeling a little dangerous.

"Yes, I want to touch you. You're driving me crazy. Good thing you're leaving and I have enough respect for Bart to keep my hands off you."

"Nice," I said, pleased that he found me attractive. I turned away from him and continued dancing with abandon whenever I felt Bart's eyes on me.

I felt a sense of power knowing that I could be a huge flirt without risk of anything happening. It was a turn on and I knew Bart would benefit from it greatly once we got back to our room.

For the next couple of hours, we danced, laughed, and told more stories—how is it possible that we did not run out of them? We enjoyed the last night we would all be together. Mario would go back to the Philippines, Brandon would go back to New Zealand,

and Bart and I would fly to Seattle the next evening.

By 11:30, we'd put in a solid shift of celebration. The time had come to gather the last of our things from the boat and go to our hotel room.

We walked across the parking lot toward the *Maverick* as Miguel's friend John walked through the door on the bulwarks. He stepped onboard and turned to take my hand. I was happy and felt lighthearted. I hopped onto the thick bumper—almost like a skip—before landing on the deck. But my body fell between the boat and the dock with nothing to stop me except John's quick reflexes and strength to grab my right arm. He kept all 125 pounds of me from falling to my death.

"PUSH!" Bart yelled as the other men lined the dock and pushed with all their might to put more distance between the boat and my dangling body. The tide was coming in and that forced the boat to push hard against the dock. Bart grabbed my other hand and the men pulled me onboard.

My leg hurt and immediately developed a bruise that lasted several months. A knot in my inner right thigh took a year to heal. Thank God I didn't have a stroke from a clot. My ego felt bruised more than anything.

"Are you okay?" everyone asked.

"Holy shit, Hon!" Bart sat next to me on the hold's hatch cover and put his arm around my waist. "That was a close call. I thought I lost you."

"I know. I'm fine. I'm fine. I'm fine. Just super embarrassed," I reassured everyone. The guys looked scared sober and so was I.

John said, "You may need to seriously cut back on your drinking."

"Gee, thanks," I snapped. "You spend a hundred days at sea and we'll see how you do once you get to land. From what I can see, everyone here has been partying like rock stars since we got in. Plus, in case you didn't know, the door was strategically placed directly in front of the bumper earlier today. I know this because I stepped on it when I left to go shopping. Where the hell did the bumper go?"

"I'm sorry, Hon," Bart said with sincere regret. "Leave her alone, man. I moved the boat today when she was gone and didn't tell anyone. I had to pull forward to make room for the boat behind us, but I didn't think to align the door with the next bumper. It's not her fault. It's mine."

"How did I not notice that?" I asked. "I was here with you before we went to dinner."

"I know, but the tide was out and the boat was lower in the water. I think we exited off the stern. I can't believe I didn't move up a little more so you'd have a step to get on the boat. You didn't do anything wrong, Love. It's totally my fault. It's really dark out and you didn't know."

"Thanks, Bart, but I feel really dumb. I'm so embarrassed. God, I could've died."

"You shouldn't feel embarrassed for falling. It was an accident. I'm just glad you're okay. I love you."

"Love you, too. Take me to bed please."

"Gladly! Let me go get our bags and I'll be right back."

Bart kissed me and walked into the house while I waited on the hatch cover and tried to process what had just happened. It was clear that I needed to slow down. Even when the boat is tied up at the dock, it's safer to move slowly and deliberately, always aware of every detail.

I couldn't think about the close call anymore. It made me sick to my stomach.

Bart returned within a minute and took my hand while I stood up off the hatch cover. He guided me to the edge of the vessel and helped me off the boat as if I was his precious cargo and he wouldn't let anything happen to me. I was grateful for his strength, the way he defended me, and his desire to protect me from harm.

Oh, how I love this man.

* * *

My adventure at sea had come to an end. Bart and I were back in Seattle a couple of days later, catching our breath, and making plans. We had worked through some relationship challenges and came to the clear realization that we loved each other desperately and wanted to continue as a team.

During the next two weeks, we met each other's families. We traveled the back roads of Oregon as we went to and from his mom and dad's place in Bend, then to eastern Washington and western Idaho so he could meet my family.

When we arrived in Spokane to see my mom, brother, and nephew, I shared stories of my adventures on the ocean and in another land. I did so with a level of enthusiasm that surprised me. Although I couldn't wait to get off the boat when I was out there, I spoke of it lovingly... with a longing to go back to that unusual world. I was unaware of how I came across until my brother, Bryan, made it clear.

"You're gonna go back and do it again," he said very matter-of-fact.

"No, I don't think so," I said with obvious doubt in my tone.

"You'll do it again. I know you will," he argued.

The weird thing is I could feel it. Bart always told me the ocean is a trip. 'When you're out there, you want nothing more than to get it over with and come home,' he'd said. 'But once you're on the beach, you can't wait to go back.'

He was right. "She" was calling me and I knew there was a good chance I'd be out there again—out there on the high seas and stopping in at faraway ports like Pago Pago, maybe even Tahiti or Rarotonga next time. I knew I would go back.

Me and Bart, Pago Pago, American Samoa, 1999

Ship wrecked, Pago Pago, American Samoa, 1999

Chapter 18:
Moving Forward

BART AND I DECIDED TO MOVE TO FRIDAY HARBOR, Washington, on San Juan Island where he had a small cabin. We would remodel the place to suit our needs and get married there—on our property. Since I was able to work as a recruiter from anywhere, the location wouldn't affect my employment.

Bart wanted to have a *normal life on the beach* with me and he was able to secure a consulting project with Roche Harbor Resort, where he would build out the village they had envisioned. Between the two of us, we were set to make a comfortable living—at home—living together in paradise.

We had a great plan.

We officially relocated to the island in December of 2000. Six weeks later, Bart and his son Skyler had our remodel project underway when stories of the "dot com crash" dominated the daily news. I received a call from my boss who was practically in tears.

"You're going to lay me off, aren't you, Michelle?" I asked her.

"Yes," she said.

I could hear the heart-felt emotion in her voice. "I knew it was coming. Don't feel bad. It's not your fault," I said, reassuring her that I'd be fine.

Honestly, I was scared about losing my job. I'd known that news was coming for two weeks, but I thought I might somehow be safe from a lay-off. Yet, I was nervous that it *could* happen to me.

Theresa Mathews

When I moved to the island, Michelle and her manager made it very clear that they envisioned me being part of the team for many years to come. I had promised them I could go to Seattle to participate in job fairs or events whenever they needed me, and they could count on me to work for them indefinitely. The demise of the company came so fast that none of us expected we would be parting ways that soon.

I had become accustomed to my sizeable paychecks and was immediately aware of the difference between working full-time and collecting unemployment. Work was scarce in Friday Harbor, and since I wasn't able to find remote work in my field, I took a job at the resort's boutique. I would rather go to work for lower wages than sit at home and receive a paycheck from the government.

I sold clothing and accessories to locals, but more to the "yachties" on vacation at the resort. The position was seasonal, but I kept busy through the summer and worked my tail off, which felt good. I actually had a lot of fun!

Shortly after I began my new job at the store, the resort made some changes to their expansion plan. They hired a consultant to take over the entire project, which made Bart's role redundant. His paychecks came to a screeching halt. That meant we had to live off my tiny wages at the clothing store, plus whatever we had left in our savings account to offset the significant reduction in pay. My brother Bryan had come over from Spokane by then to help with remodeling our house. Bart, Skyler, and Bryan worked daily to complete the house in time for our wedding in September.

When the house was finished enough for us to occupy, we moved in—just two weeks before our big day. We decided the finishing touches on the house could wait until later... mostly because we were out of money.

Eleven days prior to tying the knot, the September 11 attacks at the World Trade Center took place. The world stood still. We sat in disbelief like so many Americans, glued to the TV, unable to stop crying. I wasn't sure if we should call off the wedding, or if we held it, would anyone want to attend? We decided to move forward with our lives and we had a spectacular wedding at our new home. The home we created. We celebrated our love and our future together in spite of the world events.

Within a few weeks, my summer job ended and Bart was out of work. That's when Mother Ocean came calling. It wasn't totally *her* fault. We needed money and going to sea was our only hope. I thanked *her* and cursed *her*. *She* always won. And then it was clear. We had to go fishing. Bryan was right. I was going back out there. Again.

Me and Bart—wedding day, September 22, 2001

Dad and Mom at our wedding

Freedom

To go down a road and know
If you find yourself
Going back down that road
It will be because you want to
Not because you have to.

~ Bart Mathews

Chapter 19:
First Watch

IN EARLY APRIL 2002, WE WERE BACK IN HONOLULU, getting the *Maverick* ready for the North Pacific fishing season. In one month's time we had all the repairs done, groceries purchased, and the boat shiny from bow to stern. We even spent a few days on Kauai at Miguel and Aleelat's place for a short vacation before we untied the lines and headed out. We enjoyed a couple of evenings going out to dinner. We danced and soaked up the energy of the Hawaiian air. And then it was time to start the trip.

In May 2002, through sad but eager eyes, and slightly overcast skies, we watched paradise slowly disappear. The shores of Honolulu became smaller and smaller as we steamed toward the fishing grounds, cruising at our full running speed of eight knots.

Our crew was slightly different from my first time, but we were lucky to still have Mario, who had been on the vessel for most of his adult life. Brandon stayed in New Zealand with his girlfriend, and we heard he'd landed a job with a local construction company. Marcello took Brandon's position and was happy to be on such a spectacular boat.

It always amazes me how the removal of one person and/or the addition of another can change the dynamics of a group or family. There's a specialness to the uniqueness of each combination of people.

Everyone was in his own little world as we settled in. We

didn't say much. Each of us adjusted to the motion at our own pace and fixed something quick and simple for ourselves to eat when we were ready. No one was interested in a structured meal or anything too substantial during the first day of our adjustment period.

Within the first hour, a small chop developed and the constant movement from jogging up and down through the three-foot waves gave me a headache and a dizzy sensation. I lay down on our bed and made sure I kept some Saltines and a can of 7-Up nearby.

Before long, it was 10 p.m.—time for the changing of the guards. Bart would be going to sleep and I would start the night watch. I felt nauseous and light-headed as Bart gave me a refresher course on the basics. After all, it had been three years since I'd run that boat.

He started by showing me how to use the radar, the main radio, and the two sidebands. How to check the bilge and the gauges in the engine room, and how often. He showed me how to turn off the alarm on the printer when hurricane warnings for other latitudes and longitudes came over our computer, and how to know when the warning was NOT for us.

He showed me how to play solitaire using the new software program on the computer normally used for tracking our waypoints and fishing progress. He reminded me that when I was watching a movie, to pause the VCR every fifteen minutes or so and look out the window even if I didn't see a single dot on the radar. He also reminded me to go outside and walk around the bridge, and to look for lights on smaller vessels that might not show up on the radar or be seen from the wheelhouse window.

He went through the procedures on when to determine the time to change course and move out of the way of an approaching vessel, and which direction to turn—and why. He explained how many degrees at a time I should make the adjustment, depending on the estimated speed and course of the other vessel. He told me when I should NOT change course, but rather call a fellow seaman on the radio and state our position, call out their position in relation to ours, and suggest a maneuver that would be life-saving. That would, of course, keep us from diverting too far off course for the evening.

Above all, he made it clear that he trusted me and my abilities to run the boat and make good decisions. He made it very clear that if I was uncertain about what to do—no matter what—to wake him.

I secretly hoped for an uneventful evening and kissed Bart goodnight. I settled in and made myself as comfortable as possible. But half-way through my watch my stomach started cramping. When my mouth started to water, my instincts kicked in and without thinking about it, I ran down the steps of the wheelhouse with my lips pinched shut. I prayed that I would reach the head before my dinner came back up. There wasn't a soul on the ocean as far as I could see, so I knew I had a few minutes of privacy in all my misery before I'd have to ask someone to relieve me from my post.

I managed to finish my three-hour watch without further incident, but was relieved to turn the duties over to Mario at 1 a.m.

The next day, after my much-needed shower, I crawled up the aft steps and walked to my favorite bench in front of the bridge. I sat on the bench and placed my feet on the solid steel railing in front of me, which protected me from the cool breeze due to its three and a half-foot height. I breathed in the fresh air and soaked up the sun's rays. I thoroughly enjoyed the mild weather. The bench seat was made of cedar boards that had turned a pale honey color from constant exposure to the weather. Its back, legs, and armrests had ornate iron rails that had rusted out from salt spray.

I sat back and allowed the warmth from the sun to find me behind the barrier and dry my hair as I watched the small rolling swells approach the boat from three directions. The diamonds on the water mesmerized me.

The steady movement made me feel as though I was sitting in a great big rocking chair. A chair that comforted and soothed me while I did my best to accept and embrace this life. Again. I knew within a few days I would be ready to handle a sea fifteen times more intense than the one I was on then, if Mother Ocean was so inclined.

Chapter 20:
Big Day

RIGHT AFTER BART AND I WERE MARRIED and realized we would be going fishing again the following spring, Bart told me I had to become proficient at pulling fish. The pressure was off me for the moment, but being competitive and a pleaser by nature, my new mission was to become proficient—even good—at pulling fish.

I told him, "I may never get any better than I was the last time I fished with you, but you can always count on me to work as hard as I can. And that, my dear, may just have to be good enough!"

* * *

We had been out for five days. We still hadn't caught any fish and everyone was restless as we fought off the intense boredom. The weather was on our side, which made perfect conditions for pulling fish. A light, cool breeze created a small chop in the water, but it was basically smooth sailing.

Still, we sat and waited. Another action movie was in the main VCR securely strapped to a shelf in the corner of the salon. The guys kicked back on the burgundy-colored cushioned benches to admire Steven Seagal while I sat at the galley table and rummaged through a pile of cookbooks searching for new meal ideas.

When Miguel secured a market with a fish buyer in Canada, the *Maverick* no longer delivered fish to the cannery in American Samoa. Captains and crew of the *Maverick* had always maintained proper handling of the fish to ensure the best quality was delivered, but the new market required sashimi-grade tuna, which meant extra measures had to be taken to provide superior results.

Wes (aka Norton) had run the *Maverick* the previous season and installed hooks in the fish hold so the fish could hang by their tails until frozen. This step allowed the fish to freeze in the round before being stacked, as opposed to stacking when the fish were still warm. Stacking fish as they are caught causes them to freeze in large clumps, which was fine for the cannery, but not appropriate for the sashimi market.

The downside to hanging fish was that the fins fell away from their sides. Frozen fins became as sharp as razor blades, so the guys decided that on *this* trip, we would cut off their side fins as the fish were caught. The extra step created a lot more deck work and cramped our hands, but we cut them all—approximately 32,000 fins. Removing the fins caused dry spots if we cut too close and exposed the meat, so the method was used only on that one trip.

Bart chatted back and forth on the radio with the other captains about the sonar's findings. They all had one mission... to get located.

DING! DING! DING! The bells rang short and quick when the force of the fish biting the jigs pulled the lines tight and tripped the lever connected to the bell. DING! DING! DING!

Everyone yelled at once, "Yeah!"

I shut off the movie, turned on the CD player that I'd loaded the night before, and switched the speakers to play on the back deck. Then I followed the guys out the door and stepped into my boots, and made sure my nipper-wrapped gloves and a paring knife were nearby.

"Woo-hoo!" I shouted as I watched the guys plop fifteen-pound albacore on the stainless steel landing tables. With each guy able to pull an average of one fish every thirty seconds, it wouldn't take long to have the landing pin on the bow deck full of fish. All twelve stern lines were loaded. The fish were biting, so there was a good chance the bowlines had fish on too.

I braced my steps by keeping my right hand on the bulwarks as I walked toward the bow. The aggressive splashing on the starboard side of the vessel confirmed we had two fish on and one on the portside line. The landing pin filled up as fish slid out the end of the tube that connected to the stern where the guys pulled them in one after the other.

Oh shit—here we go! I switched myself into high gear.

I grabbed hold of the tag line connected to the pole that extended away from the mast on both sides of the vessel. Tag lines are very similar in diameter to a clothesline, and since they weigh more than the monofilament (mono) line that attaches to the hook (or jig), they don't blow around in the wind.

I secured the blue tagline to the boat by wrapping it around a gripper—a square piece of rubber slightly smaller than a deck of cards—fastened to a metal plate of the same size, then bolted to the inside edge of the bulwarks. Once the tagline was secure, I pulled the mono line in as fast as I could. I leaned over the railing and quickly wrapped my right hand around the mono a couple times. I lifted up on the line to bring the fish out of the water, but my wrap was loose. My hand slipped, which made the mono slide past my nippers and tighten around my fingertips. The fish fell back in the water, still fighting with the jig in its mouth.

"Shit," I yelled. "It shouldn't be this hard!" My frustration mounted.

I tried again. That time I spun the mono around my fists a few times, then reached over the rail with my left hand for assistance. With the strength of both arms and some help from the boat as it rolled over the top of a wave, I lifted the fish out of the water and swung it into the air, then landed it on the bow deck.

In one swift movement, I took the paring knife from my raingear pocket and slit the throat of the albacore, removed the two-pronged metal hook from its mouth, and hurled the jig back into the water. I cussed the whole time because all the lines were loaded and I was already behind.

I untied the tagline from the gripper and set the line free to move away from the boat, allowing us to hook another fish. The lines were barely released before they had fish on again. We were in 'em all right! Careful not to fall in the slimy mess that accumulated on the deck boards, I kept my knees bent to adjust to the boat's movement and walked quickly back and forth from one side of the vessel to the other until all the lines were empty and the fish stopped biting. The landing pin had fish three layers deep by the time I got to it and there were more fish coming out of the chute.

I bent down and grabbed hold of their tails—one or two fish for each hand, and threw them to a larger pin as gently as possible so as not to bruise the meat. Many were still alive and flopped wildly as they flicked blood and scales everywhere and their bodies fought for air, and I still had to cut off the fins. I worked like a mad woman to catch up, and continued to keep my legs bent for balance and to ease the stress on my lower back. I felt the bruising begin on my hands as the little bastards kicked between my thumb and index finger while I wrapped my hands around the base of their tails.

Fish were still coming out of the chute, but at a slower pace. The fish in the larger pin were finally still. They had been rinsed and laid neatly on their sides so they could dry a little more before we sent them to the hold. That kept the ice build-up at the bottom of the steps to a minimum.

I finished hosing off the deck just as Mario and Marcello came forward to help me count the fish. We counted eighty-three as we tossed them in the hold. Bart was standing on the bridge waiting for Mario to jump down onto the steps below.

"How many did we get, Hon?" he asked me.

"Eighty-three big ones!" I shouted up to him, smiling from ear to ear, my heart still pounding from the physical exertion.

"Nice tack! I'm gonna turn us around and see if we can stay with 'em," he said. Then he blew me a kiss and turned away to go back into the wheelhouse.

This is the good stuff.

I smiled and wiped the sweat off my brow.

While we had a break in the action, I decided to go in and potty up, get a drink of water, and put on a dry t-shirt. I heard the bells go off before I could get back outside and into my boots and rain pants. I moved quickly.

Marcello was on the port side doing his best to work the lines on both sides of the boat, while Mario was in the hold stacking fish.

"I'm comin' Boo-boy!" I shouted as I shoved my hands into my gloves and hurried to his aid.

For the same reason the captains in our group give each other nicknames, some of the crewmen have nicknames too. Marcello is known as Boo-boy among the Filipinos, and Mario is just Mario, but pretty much the "lead" with the Filipinos.

"It's okay," he assured me. "Take your time."

He had the lines under control for the time being so I took advantage of the moment. "Hey, Boo-boy?" I asked.

"Yes?"

"I need help with pulling fish. Bart told me I had to get proficient at it and I never did get the hang of things last time I was out. Can you show me your technique?"

"Sure. It's easy... watch me."

He took a short line hanging from the stern to demonstrate.

"Are you right handed or left handed?" he asked.

"Right."

"Take your left hand to tighten the slack on the line," he instructed. "Then put your right hand in front of the line, closer to the end of the hook where the fish is. Keep your thumb down and grab the line from that direction, see?" He showed me how to wrap the line.

"Yeah, I got it," I said, pleased that I could see him move slow enough to watch him make a wrap and understand how he did it. He made a complete circle with his hand around the mono, making the connection secure so the line would not slip from his grip.

"Then you lift up and the fish comes out of the water. Guide him to the landing table with your left hand to keep control of the line. Just like that." Marcello smiled and released the line. "Now you try."

I did the movement just like he showed me. "I got it Boo-boy!" I shouted with delight. "Oh my God! No wonder I had such a hard time... I'd been doing it backwards. This is easy!" I was so proud of myself.

He nodded in agreement and smiled at his accomplished pupil.

DING! DING! DING! The starboard bell rang, signaling there were three fish on. Mario was still in the hold, so it was my turn to show my stuff.

To identify the lines to pull I looked for those without any slack, which suggested there was a fish on. I reached for the tight line closest to me and took hold of the tag line with my left hand and then, hand-over-fist, I pulled it toward me. I made a single wrap around a nearby gripper to steady the line and then took hold of the mono, placing it inside the metal pinch puller as I turned on the hydraulic lever with my right hand. Keeping connection with the lever, I reached down and placed my right hand to rest over the top of the mono as the fish on the other end was reeled in.

When I felt the line move quickly under my fingers, I knew I was protecting myself from a possible pop off that would send the metal hook flying toward my face if the fish wasn't hooked well and he spit it out.

When the fish reached the stern, I turned off the hydraulics and leaned over the railing, which sat much lower in the water than the bow rail. I made a single wrap with my right hand around the mono and lifted the fish out of the water. Guiding the catch with my left hand, I spun around to face the landing table and landed the fish. I steadied the flailing fish by keeping a tight hold on the line close to the hook that was still in its nose, and took a paring knife to slit its throat just under the chin.

Blood immediately squirted onto my face. I sliced off his fins, unhooked the fish, and gave him a hard shove down the tube. The boat took a slight roll that caused my body to jerk to the right. My right foot landed against the bulwarks and my right thigh leaned against the railing as I tossed the jig back into the ocean, released the tag line, and reached for the next closest line. My movements felt more fluid each time I pulled another fish.

U2's "Rattle N' Hum" blasted through the speakers behind us, setting the pace. The adrenaline rushed through my veins while the bright sun warmed my face. My breathing was quick and hard as my body pushed on. Between the bow deck and the hold, Mario was so busy trying to catch up that I never left my post, which was *his* primary workstation that trip. No one cared. We were a team and we were making money.

Marcello realized he could trust me to man the stern, but first he wanted to make sure I was comfortable. "I want to help Mario get caught up since we just caught a bunch of 'em," he said. "Are you okay if I go to the bow for a few minutes?"

"Sure. Go for it," I said. "I'm good."

Marcello smiled and left the area. I pulled a few fish and marveled at my new skill. A bell signaled fish on Marcello's port side so I brought it in on the hydraulic pinch puller. Once I had the fish up toward the boat, I saw how big he was.

Oh my God, he's huge! I'm gonna need to gaff this one. No one is here to help. Okay. I can do this.

I kept the line tight so I wouldn't lose the fish when I reached behind me with my free hand to grab the gaff. I looked around again to see if anyone had emerged from the bow. The guys were still busy elsewhere. That eliminated any stage fright I might have had.

I aimed at the head of that bad boy and lifted the gaff high in the air. I heaved the gaff toward the head of the fish as if I were chopping wood with an axe, and when the gaff hook made contact with the fish it flopped over to its side instead of penetrating the fish's head.

Wow. I didn't expect that. The guys make it look easy. Crap!

I tried again. This time I had a tighter grip on the gaff and BAM—I nailed the fish with a solid force so I could get him onboard.

"Woo-hoo!" I shouted and turned to see if anyone saw that amazing move. I was still alone. I'm the only one who witnessed my talent—or good luck I should say.

I let go of the line so I could use both hands to pull the fish up and make sure I didn't lose the gaff in the drink during the process. Hand over fist, like I'd seen the guys do, I got that fish up and over the railing and into the boat. I had to use all my strength, and that surprised me. But I did it. I gaffed a huge fish.

The guys were amused when I told them what I did and Bart

was proud of me, but I don't think anyone was as impressed as I was.

Just as quick as they started biting, the fish were gone. Bart came down from the bridge to congratulate me on my new skill.

"Nice job," he said with satisfaction. "Looks like you'll have a little break now. They stopped biting for Longline too, but Popeye and Sleepy are still gettin' 'em and they're about twenty miles outside us. We should reach them in about two hours."

"Perfect," I said. "That will give me time to clean up, make dinner, and we can eat by six o'clock."

Bart chuckled. "You've been working your ass off, Hon. You don't have to do anything fancy tonight. We can just heat up a frozen dinner or have a sandwich or something."

"Nope," I said. "We're having shrimp stuffed chicken breasts, oven-roasted potatoes, and steamed vegetables tonight. That's what's on the menu. I have time to make it and we're having it."

He gave me a kiss and went back up the steep steps to the bridge.

"I'm going to cook now," I hollered to the guys.

Relieved to have a break, I got out of my boots and rain pants and stepped into the house. Once in our stateroom, I braced my butt against the wall to keep from falling while I peeled off my wet clothing, then went into the head to wash up. I kept one hand anchored to a wall and then to the dresser to ensure I kept my balance as I walked those few steps. I laughed out loud when I looked into the mirror. Every inch of me was covered in white and gray fish scales, blood, and salt granules.

Yuck!

I washed my face and put on dry clothes. Just outside our stateroom, I grabbed a pair of earmuffs to drown out the intense roar of the engine, then carefully made my way down the steep steps to the engine room where I hung my wet pants and t-shirt on the rails around the main engine. Bart met me in the galley where I greeted him with a cocktail. We clicked glasses and in unison we said, "Cheers!" We were husband and wife for that moment, but we still had a lot more work to do before the day was done.

The oven was quirky and took a long time to heat up. Once the temperature reached 400 degrees, I turned the dial to maintain that temperature, knowing it would drop to the optimum 350 degrees when I opened the door to put in the main dish. I heard the bells outside telling me we were still catching fish at a pace the guys could handle on their own. So I placed the potatoes in the microwave to give them a head start while I prepared the chicken.

The fish started biting again as we finished the scrumptious meal and so we got back to work. We stayed busy for most of the evening and ended up with 673 fish for the day. With a successful catch like that and the fish still biting at sunset, there was no reason to run to a new location. Since albacore are sight feeders and are presumed to drift or sleep at night, we would be able to sustain a close proximity to the school at daybreak. That was the theory anyway.

Bart and the other captains arranged themselves across the ocean's surface with a two-mile separation between each boat before they shut off their main engines. That allowed us to stay together as we drifted during the night.

Mario and Marcello cleaned up the galley from dinner while I enjoyed my shower. I carefully hung onto the large bolt that opened and shut the porthole as I washed my hair with my free hand. I had to massage my hands and fingers to loosen the semi-permanent claw they had formed from tightly squeezing mono and a paring knife all day. My forearms throbbed with fatigue from the constant strain of the day's work. I knew it wouldn't be long before tendonitis began to set in. I took some Motrin for the pain and rubbed lotion into my aching body.

"You impressed a lot of people today, Hon," Bart said in a proud but tired voice as we lay down in our bed. I smiled and moaned quietly—surely I thanked him before I fell asleep. I was unaware of any time lapse between that moment and hearing the alarm that signaled the gray light at 5 a.m. It was time to get up and do it again.

Mario with big fish

Me cutting off fins, spring 2002

Me knee-deep in fish, 2002

Me pulling fish North Pacific, 2002

Me pulling large fish

Bart with fish on *Maverick*

Time

Time is the answer to everything
And the question to all
All that is
Answers to time
Yet time answers to nothing
All time says is be
And you will know.

~ *Bart Mathews*

Chapter 21:
Déjà Vu

TIME WAS BEGINNING TO PUT SOME SPACE between me and the initial blow of losing Bart. Although it had been only nine-and-a-half weeks since his death, some days I found that I was able to peel myself off the floor and put one foot in front of the other.

I had been invited to a birthday luncheon at Downriggers, a restaurant on the waterfront in Friday Harbor. There is just something about getting together with girlfriends that brightens my spirits... and often the positive effects linger for days.

A dozen of us ladies sat at the long table in front of the windows that overlooked the Port. The reflection from the bright October sun on the water looked like sparkling diamonds that lit up the backdrop of sailboats, yachts, and fishing vessels. We filled the room with our voices and laughter as we told each other stories. Several of us had just received our second vodka cosmopolitan when my cell phone rang.

"Oh, jeez, I'm sorry," I told my friends as I grabbed my phone out of my purse. "I thought I'd turned that thing off. Please forgive me." I excused myself from the table and walked toward the lobby where I would not disturb the other patrons. That's when I noticed the caller was Kami.

"Hey, Kami. Hang on a sec. I'm at a restaurant and need to get away from the noise before I can talk."

"Oh, Theresa you don't have to talk to me now. I actually

thought I'd get your voicemail. Why don't you enjoy the party and call me back." Her voice sounded pleading. Troubled. Maybe she was just worried about "bothering" me, but something sounded different.

"No, no, it's okay. I'm in the lobby now and no one else is out here. What's going on?"

"Oh, Theresa, I think you should go back to your friends. You don't want to hear this right now. It's really bad."

"What is it Kami?" I demanded. "Tell me now, please. What's going on?"

"It's Jack Slater. Just like Bart. I can't believe it. It's not even real."

"NO!" I shouted. "What the fuck are you talking about? Ah, Jesus. Kami, how? When? I don't believe it!" My knees buckled and sent me to the floor as the words came out of my mouth. I sat my back against the hostess desk and pulled my knees up close. I listened to the details as my heart raced.

"He brought the boat in with a full load to Astoria and took the crew out to dinner. They went back to the boat and after he got ready for bed, I guess he had a massive heart attack and dropped dead. He fell into the shower, Theresa, and that's where they found him the next morning. It's just like Bart. I can't believe it. This can't be real, but it is. What's happening to our group?" Kami sobbed.

"Fuck. I've got to get to Sue. Does she know yet? I've gotta go to her," I said as I slipped into autopilot mode.

"I'm really sorry to tell you, Theresa, but I thought you'd want to know."

"Yes, Kami. Thank you. I have to go now. I have to pack and get organized and take the next boat off the rock. Shit, Kami! I gotta go! I gotta go!"

"Be careful, and call me when you get to Astoria. Let me know what I can do. Do you want me to take care of your kitty while you're gone? I can feed Sydni for you."

"I think so. I don't know. I'll call you later."

The shock ran through me like a freight train as I steadied my back against the wall and used the hostess desk to pull myself off the floor. The tears couldn't be stopped. I was back in that place of desperation and panic.

How can this be? Why? Why Ultimate of all people. HIM? I don't know if I can start all over again. Oh God help us!

I had been gone long enough that a couple of my friends came to look for me. I was hugging the wall and whimpering. I tried to wrap my brain around what Kami had just told me. I had that dazed look in my wet eyes when Jenny ran to me.

"Shit, Honey, what's going on?"

"We lost another one," I told her.

"Oh, baby, I'm sorry," she said as she pulled me into her arms. "Who is it? What can we do to help? We're here for you. You are strong and you can do this."

A couple more of our friends came out and I told them what happened. I started to cry again. By the look on their faces, I knew they were worried about me.

"C'mon back to the table, T," Debbie said. "There's nothing you can do right this second and you shouldn't drive in this condition. Come sit down and we'll figure things out together. We'll make sure your kitty is taken care of and we'll help you plan your trip. Let's try to stay calm."

"Okay. Good idea. Okay."

We decided I should take the first ferry in the morning. I figured I would need an hour to digest the tragedy before I had the courage to make that dreadful call to Jack's wife, Sue. *Fuck. I know her pain. God. My poor friend. Ouch. My pain. My pain is strong again.*

Oh, Bart I miss you. Take care of Jack, Honey. I'll try to take care of Sue, but I don't know if I can.

I didn't feel like I could linger too long. My mind switched gears and I pulled myself together. Thirty minutes later, I had my cat-care arrangements made and I was on my way home to wrap up the day. My boss—the VP of the sales team of an e-learning company I recruited for—was supportive and encouraged me to go to my friend. He, too, was shocked to hear about the sudden loss, and expressed compassion through the phone. Then it was time to make the dreaded call to Sue.

"Hello?" Sue answered after two rings.

"Oh, Sue," I said with sadness, still in denial as to what I'd heard less than two hours earlier. "Is it true? Is it really true?"

"Yes, Theresa, it's true. I don't believe it. What am I going to do? Now I know your pain and I don't know what to do!" Her voice became louder as she spoke, hysteria wrapped all around it.

"I know, Honey. I'm sorry. Shit. I'm on my way! I'll call Wes and he can meet us too. He rallied for me with you and Jack when Bart died, and we will be there for you. It's unreal. First Wes lost his wife, then I lost my husband, and now you've lost yours. We need to stick together. I'll be on the first boat off the rock tomorrow."

"You don't have to come, Theresa. You are getting stronger and I don't want to bring you down."

"Are you kidding?! You are not doing this by yourself and I wouldn't have it any other way. You've been there for me and I am here for you. You need us and I'm on my way. Drive careful, Sue. I love you and the girls. See you tomorrow."

"Thank you. I do need you. I'm so glad you're coming. Fuck! It hurts so bad I can't believe this!"

"I know. I know. Don't think right now. Just be very careful and I'll be there tomorrow. Hug Megan. Love you."

"Okay. Love you, too."

Wes agreed to meet us at the bar in Astoria around noon.

The next morning, I boarded the boat and made a few phone calls as the ferry transported me to the mainland. Everyone was in disbelief as I spread the bad news. My grief was compounded now. And although Sue, Jaime, and Megan were very sad when Bart died, their grief now was at a whole different level. It was the pain that hits in those early stages. I had to be strong for them.

After a couple of hours on the road, I turned off I-5 onto the Olympic Highway headed westbound. As I approached the 107 turnoff at Montesano, I called Wes. "I should be there in two hours, Wes. Have you arrived yet?"

"I don't know if I can do this again, T."

"Yes, you can! I know it sucks beyond words, but she was there for me and we need to be there for Sue. I can't do it by myself, Wes. I need you too! Please come. I know it's hard—and it must be really hard for you after losing Pam. You keep starting over. Please come," I pleaded.

"Okay. You're right. I'll be there," he assured me.

"Thank you, Wes. Love you. See you soon."

"Love you, too. See you in a bit."

Crossing the bridge brought back feelings. Mostly a sense of panic and sadness. I was also reminded of those feelings of joy that I experienced every *other* time I'd been to Astoria, Oregon.

Astoria had always been a happy place for me. It meant I was able to see Bart during one of his turnarounds. And those were always like being on a mini-honeymoon. Oh, how I loved that overwhelming feeling in anticipation of seeing my husband after being apart for three whole months. The moment my stomach filled with butterflies at the sight of the *Maverick*, as if I were fifteen years old and in love for the first time. That fight for self-control when I walked toward the dock trying to appear cool, instead of running like I wanted to. But my legs would race down the ramp to the boat because I couldn't stand to be out of his arms one more minute. I felt such joy when I saw my husband's smiling face and sparkling eyes as he exited the house and ran to the bulwarks gate to pull me into his arms. Oooohhhh… and the sound of his sexy voice when he purred my name and said things that made me believe I was the most beautiful woman on the planet.

Astoria reminded me of those happy times when the whole world disappeared around us, leaving two lovebirds to get lost in each other—even if just for a few moments. Nothing else mattered. I was exactly where I was supposed to be.

But *this* trip was different. There would be no Bart. No *Maverick*. No joy. This was not a time for celebration. There would be a lot of tears and despair. I drove across the bridge and managed to put my feelings into separate containers. My emotions would have to wait.

As I pulled into the parking lot of Pig 'N Pancake, the sick feeling I'd had ten weeks before returned. It hit me like a ton of bricks but I had to be strong for Sue and the girls, just as Sue and Jack had been strong for me. I pulled myself together and walked toward the building. But then I turned right and walked into the bar across the street instead. Wes was at our table—the same table where we'd sat with Jack only two-and-a-half months earlier.

"Hey, T," he greeted me in his kind voice.

"Hi, Wes," I replied.

He got up and we hugged, giving each other a dose of comfort. "Fuck. Over."

"I know. Jesus, Wes, what's happening to our group? I hope this is it for a while."

"Got that fine." His tone told me he was in shock, disbelief, and pain, just like I was.

"I think Sue and Megan are at the restaurant, but I wanted to come see you first. That's gonna be a tough one. Have you seen her yet?"

"No. I needed a drink to calm my nerves first. But you should call her and let her know you're here."

"Yah, you're right."

I took a sip of my Chardonnay, inhaled a deep breath, and dialed.

"Hi, Theresa," Sue said after one ring.

"Hey, Sue. I'd ask how you are, but I know the answer. I'm across the street with Wes. I wanted to grab a drink right away to get my anxiety under control—I hope you understand."

"Of course I do. I'll be right there. We just ordered our food so I have a few minutes before it gets here."

Less than a minute later, the door swung open wide and Sue charged over. I stood up and we hugged tightly without saying anything. The sobbing came easily. Wes sat quietly and waited his turn to embrace our friend.

The three of us went in and out of silent moments. We were each processing our shock and disbelief. And of course we asked… now what?

"I want to stay here and drink myself into a coma," Sue said. "But I should get back to the restaurant. I've got a seventeen-year-old daughter who just lost her daddy and I need to be with her." Sue started to cry. "The worst part is that I don't know if I can. I'm so broken I can hardly function."

"I'm right behind you, Hon," I said. "Let me finish my wine and I'll be over soon. Two minutes."

"I'll catch up with you guys in a bit if you don't mind," Wes said.

I reached for my purse, but as usual, Wes wouldn't let me pay.

"Thank you," I said, knowing it was a waste of time to argue. "See you in a few?"

"See you in a few, T."

I exited the building and noticed the sky was gray and drizzly. The weather matched our state of mind and broken hearts. I walked into the restaurant and spotted Sue, Megan, Kymberly, and Crocket, who were sitting in a booth by the window. I was glad to see two more members of our Hyena family had dropped everything to help Sue and her daughters. Crocket (whose real name is Dave) and his wife Kymberly are genuine, down-to-earth people who have a way of making others feel as though everything is going to be all right. They bring sunshine with them just by showing up. The gray day spilled into their faces that day. Megan saw me and slid out of the booth.

"Hi, Honey." I wrapped my arms around her tight.

"Hey," was all she could muster. I could feel her pain, but she was unable to let herself cry just then. I knew what that was like. Bart was like an uncle to her and he had died on her birthday, less than three months earlier. And now she had just lost her dad.

The waitress brought their food. I ordered a turkey sandwich. Eating was laborious for me again. I couldn't handle anything with much flavor. We choked down our lunches and did our best to make a plan. Crockett and Wes became our leaders. He and Wes were the captains who would guide us through the awful mess.

Sue, Megan, Kymberly, and I went to Fred Meyer to get a gold chain for Sue. She, too, would wear Jack's wedding ring around her neck.

The lady in the jewelry department who had waited on us in August walked over. "I remember you ladies," she said. "How are you doing?"

Sue and I looked at each other, then back at the lady.

"I'm in the club now," Sue said. "I don't want to be in the club."

"Oh my God," the lady replied. "I'm so sorry." She reached out and touched Sue's hand. All she could do was offer her condolences, but the expression on her face said it all.

By late afternoon, we had congregated at the boat and were waiting for Jaime—Jack and Sue's eldest daughter—to arrive from back east where she was attending her first quarter at college.

The owners of the boat said they would take care of everything. Thank goodness Sue didn't have to deal with the logistics of that. Jack had unloaded the boat's catch two days prior, so all Sue had to do was retrieve his things from the boat. The owners had arrived at the vessel the day before and packed Jack's belongings. Evidently, they thought they were helping Sue, but it was a hasty and insensitive act that left her feeling as if they'd tossed him overboard and dismissed her.

Wes and I were standing on the back deck of the *Delena* when we heard voices and powerful footsteps get louder as they approached from the foredeck. We turned and saw Jaime run past us into the salon where she sobbed in the arms of her mother and sister. The sound that kind of pain makes is different from other cries. It has a distinct guttural roar that is heavy and identifiable. The sound of grief. The sound of a heart breaking. I knew it firsthand.

Wes and I remained outside to give them space. After several minutes, we went in to embrace Jaime. It had been a long day, so we ordered pizza and ate with the crew on the boat before going back to our hotel rooms. Sue and I shared a room since her daughters had each other for the evening. Wes stayed in a room a few doors down.

The next day we all met at the funeral home. Wes and I viewed Jack together. Jack wore a tiny grin on his face, which was how he looked when alive. Jack was always smiling. Wes held me up when my knees buckled. When we said our goodbyes, Wes placed a special note in Jack's pocket, just as Jack had done for Bart.

Sue picked out an urn crafted by the same designer I chose for Bart. It was made of hand-carved wood, making it a one-of-a-kind, but was the "brother" of the only other wooden urn the funeral home had. The first one contained Bart's ashes.

Since several boats unloaded fish that week and had not yet left the area, we were able to get a large group of fishermen together for dinner. Nearly twenty of us sat around tables pushed together at a local restaurant. Captains talked about mechanical, electrical, and refrigeration challenges, along with a wide range of sea tales. The energy was electric. With Bart and Jack out of the picture, however, it just wasn't the same.

Back at the hotel, a handful of us gathered in one of the rooms for a nightcap. The mood was somber as we spoke of the eerie similarities of two men, who even looked like brothers.

How could this happen? How could it happen so soon after Bart's death, in such a similar way? How? Why Ultimate? Is this the last one? Oh please let it be so!

Chapter 22: Power/Powerless

GOING BACK OUT TO SEA FOR THE SECOND TIME in 2002 was very different from my first trip in the late summer of 1999. For one, Brandon and Mario were on that first trip. As I struggled with some of the changes of my new journey, I flashed back to what it was like during my first time out.

* * *

Brandon and I had similar interests in music and we were both relatively new to cooking and the joys that came with creating delicious cuisine. We shared ideas about what to make and how to modify the dish as our own culinary creation. We both tore pages out of magazines that contained recipes we wanted to try. Whenever I needed a friend to talk to, Brandon was a good sport and would converse with me. Or at least listen when I needed to talk. His thrill-seeking stories were entertaining and made me feel young as I vicariously imagined the life he'd led in New Zealand with his buddies. Plus, he was a flirt, which was really good for my ego! Talking about our lives on the beach was fun because I could relate to that a lot more than the life I was experiencing at sea.

Bart didn't let me talk about life on the beach, or dreams, or plans of what we would do when we got home. He said it was negative because I wasn't present and focused on what we needed to do on the boat. Talking about life elsewhere created the impression that I did not want to be there. Then he and everyone else on board would not want to be there either and it would poison the mission.

In the very beginning of that trip, we did talk a little about what we wanted to do for work that would allow us to be together on the beach. But those conversations were limited. I enjoyed dreaming about the future, but for Bart, it made it harder to be in the present. And not being able to talk about anything other than what was going on with the boat was hard for me.

Mario treated me with respect, patience, and grace back then. He was always quick to help with anything I started to do. For instance, if we were going to barbeque dinner and I started to exit the house he would jump to go fetch the hibachi from the fo'c'sle (located in the bow of the vessel) so I wouldn't have to. Whenever he saw me walk towards the fo'c'sle with a basket of laundry, he would quickly take the basket from my hands and offer to carry it for me. When I prepared Bart's breakfast or dinner plate, Mario was often right there to carry it up the steps to him. And Mario seemed amused by my femininity. He said he could tell when I woke up because he could smell my perfume. He wanted to buy that perfume for his wife when he got home. He giggled at me when I sat on the back deck to shave my legs or give myself a pedicure. He had a "big-brother" way of making me feel special and appreciated. When the trip was over and we were at the airport in American Samoa to fly off in different directions, he hugged me and said, "I miss you already—especially your cooking!"

***

So, when I was back on board three years later as Bart's wife, the change in Mario's attitude towards me was surprising and heartbreaking. As the captain's wife, I enjoyed some perks on the boat that other crewmen would never have. When the weather was lousy and fishing wasn't wide open, the guys would sit outside on the stern waiting for fish to bite. They stayed dry and warm in their sweatshirts and raingear, and they kept their minds occupied by reading, or they might prop their bodies in a corner to catch a nap. I usually stayed in the house until they needed me outside.

If I wasn't cooking or cleaning, I wrote in my journal, escaped into a good book, or allowed myself to grab a quick nap. Unfortunately, I felt guilty doing anything that provided too much relaxation or pleasure. Just knowing I was more comfortable than the guys felt wrong, and it seemed Mario had a problem with it too.

I sensed an intensely negative vibe coming from him. I don't claim to be a mind reader, but I've almost always been right whenever I've sensed something. I felt as though he resented me. Maybe my need to be good at everything and please everyone around me intensified my gut feeling, but I was certain I'd nailed it.

After all, Mario was the professional crewman and had spent YEARS of his life out there. On that boat. On that ocean. I was just a girlie girl who was never going to be good enough, but who kept trying to take over. At least that's what I presumed he thought based on how he acted toward me. I also felt out of place. Again. But I was not imagining the heavy fog he cast over me. I did, however, take it personally and let it wreak havoc on my psyche.

I enjoyed taking care of my men, and often asked the guys if they were hungry for lunch, and what they were in the mood for before I began preparing it. The response was usually something like, 'Maybe later.' That always really pissed me off because I was trying to be so accommodating and let them choose, which I thought was respectful and what they would want. But Mario would be in the galley within fifteen minutes to cook something for himself and Marcello anyway, which frustrated me because then it looked as if I wasn't doing my job.

If the bells went off while Mario was cooking, I would go outside to pull fish. I couldn't tell if Mario was just looking for an excuse to get out of pulling fish or if he really wanted a change of pace and preparing lunch offered him that change. Or maybe he resented me even more because then I was outside doing a man's job and he didn't want me to show him up. In any case, I felt as if he was letting me know he was still the one in charge—not me—not at any level—in the galley or on the stern. His silence screamed at me!

The tension grew between us until you could cut it with a knife and finally I'd had enough of that crap. I got up the nerve to confront him.

"Hey, Mario, are you mad at me about something? Did I do something to set you off?" I asked.

He chuckled in a snide passive-aggressive condescending way and said with his Filipino accent, "You are just like my wife. You women have a sixth sense."

What the fuck does that mean? Are you getting off on these mind games or do you have a point?

I bit my lip and kept my reaction to myself. I waited for an explanation but didn't get one. My heart pounded so hard I thought it would jump out my chest or give me a heart attack. *That actually wouldn't be so bad... at least then I could escape the crazy bullshit!*

Nothing from Mario. So I spoke up again. "Mario, I have really been sensing some negative energy from you the last few days and it's killing me. I don't know what I did or why you have a problem with me, but if you just fill me in I'll do whatever I can to fix it because I hate the way this feels!"

"It's nothing, don't worry about it," he replied and blew me off a while longer.

Fine. You can't have any more of my energy then, you fucking crazy bastard. I just won't talk to you, asshole. What a bitch you've become!

Ooooooh, if only I had the guts to say what is running through my mind. Everyone thinks Mario is so wonderful, but he's turned into a spoiled, jealous little prick. If I let him get me to the point where I go off on him, I won't get support from Bart. He'll think it's my fault for not working it out. Allowing myself to lose it on the boat would change the mood for everyone. Right. Good work, you manipulating little fuck. You're making me crazy!

Another day or two went by and he pulled the same crap again about saying they weren't hungry for lunch, only this time he waited a mere five minutes before he was inside preparing food.

That's it. This is going to stop!

I didn't wait for Marcello to leave the room—I wanted to know if they were both in on it.

"I just asked you guys if you were hungry, Mario. You said no, and now you're cooking. Don't you like my cooking? What is it?" I demanded.

He and Marcello ignored me as they sat at the galley table and ate their lunch. Mario looked quite satisfied that he had pushed the right button. He chewed slowly, smirking to his heart's delight. I stormed out of the house in a huff, trying desperately to get a grip on my emotions while I waited for the little jerks to come outside—I was certain I could take them both on at that point.

Finally they appeared. Marcello looked a little scared. He was the sweet one who hated confrontation of any kind. Like me.

Mario spoke for both of them. "It's not that we don't like your cooking," he explained. "But when Aleelat's on the boat... ummm... she's like us, you know. She just always knows what we want."

"But, Mario," I defended, "I watch what you make and that's what I've been serving. Does Aleelat make Filipino food every day?"

"She makes normal things too, like spaghetti and steak, or other American foods. But she just knows," he hummed.

"Well then how is that different than what I'm doing? That doesn't even make sense!"

"IF YOU'RE GONNA COOK, THEN COOK!" he snapped. "JUST COOK THE FOOD. MAKE WHATEVER YOU WANT AND WE'LL EAT IT... JUST COOK IF YOU WANT TO BE THE COOK!"

I wanted to wrap the hook of that gaff around his skinny neck and heave his snotty mouth overboard! The asshole was winning at his game and there was nothing I could do about it. I felt the tears well up, but I fought them off.

"Fine," I said and went inside.

Fuck him. Fuck both of them!

I stomped into my stateroom and sat on the bed.

If that isn't a contradiction, I don't know what is. We like your cooking, but Aleelat just knows? Give me a break. The truth is he's jealous. He doesn't want me to be the cook and he doesn't want me at his station on the stern. I don't need this!

The frustration and anger turned to helplessness at first, then I switched back to being completely enraged. I cried really hard for a while, then threw myself the biggest temper-tantrum I can remember *ever* throwing. My fists pounded the bed and pillows while my teeth strained against each other.

Fuck this, fuck that, fuck them, the little bastards!

With my fists still clenched tight, I continued my tantrum by slamming each foot down as I stomped toward the head where I knew no one would hear me. I locked the door and screamed at the top of my lungs.

"AAAAHHHHH!" I shouted as I slammed my hands down on the sink and stomped my feet on the blue tile floor.

What the fuck am I doing here? I want to go home! I don't belong here! The little prick and his accomplice are destroying me and I have nowhere to run. Am I the only one who can see this? They are wrong and I

KNOW it. I would NEVER treat someone like this. Bart lied to me. He said this would be fun and romantic. It's a fucking prison and I'm the odd man out. Aaaaaahhh!

I caught my breath and tried to calm down.

Okay, okay, okay. Deep breath.

Still unable to shake it off, I pulled myself together the best I could and went upstairs for a little comfort from Bart. I must have been an idiot for thinking I could get that. He was annoyed that I had bothered him with an emotional upset that he could not fix. It only made him feel bad and he told me to talk to Mario and work things out.

"If you don't have a positive attitude," he explained, "then it can ruin the whole trip for everyone."

You've got to be fucking kidding me! Really? Wow. You're supposed to be on my side! Especially when I haven't done anything wrong. The least you can do is offer support and maybe, just maybe, a suggestion on how I might handle things instead of making the problem AND the solution ALL MY RESPONSIBILITY.

Afraid to make things worse by saying those things out loud, I kept my response to myself.

Oh, yes.... The happiness of everyone on this boat is a hundred percent up to me. Why is it always up to me to fix things when the other person is the problem? I'm the goddamn Pollyanna on this boat... forever trying to get these guys to smile, but it's NEVER the responsibility of anyone else to cheer me up! Yah, I get it.

I gave him an—*I give up. You're all full of shit*—look and headed down the steps. I looked up to see him do his usual by kissing the air in my direction, like *that* was supposed to make me feel all warm and fuzzy and loved. It felt more like being kissed off than offering any kind of real support.

Funny. There is barely a day that goes by now when I don't

think of Bart's air-kiss gesture and miss it. My Bart, blowing me kisses. It really was his way of letting me know he loved me, and the thought of it now always brings a smile to my face.

But returning to the boat.... I choked back my feelings, took a deep breath, and stomped back to our stateroom. Gritting my teeth and shaking, I could feel the veins straining in my neck as anger consumed me. And I couldn't *go anywhere*! I couldn't get away from it. From the anger, or my husband who wouldn't stand in my corner and support me, or from the little bastards who turned on me. I was alone out there and nobody cared.

Oh, I want to scream at the top of my lungs!
Choke it back. God-damn-it!

I spun in a world of hate. My angry thoughts took on a life of their own as they had their way with me.

* * *

I could hear the rumble of the stampede as they got closer. Big burly men with long hair and straggly beards roared towards me, wearing layers of ripped leather and heavy fur coats made of bear and wolf. Dirty fists at the end of thick muscular arms held burning clubs high in the air. Anger led the pack, keeping his army of negative thoughts spreading through me like cancer. Hate snuck up from behind and grabbed a hold of my heart, squeezing it so hard, the beat intensified and quickened, allowing hate to win. Resentment joined in when I wasn't looking.

His evil eyes and stinky breath cast a nasty spell over me that forced visions of leaving Bart and this crazy ocean forever! Revenge conquered the others by showing me the many ways I could get even. My heart pounded harder each minute as we plotted the course of despair.

Get me out of here! Get me off this fucking boat!

* * *

When I woke, my eyes were swollen and dried tears felt stiff on my cheeks. I splashed water on my face, which was refreshing, and it brought me back to life. Sort of.

I was tired but relieved that the albacore jambalaya wouldn't take long to prepare. I didn't have the energy to make anything too labor intensive, let alone be mad anymore. I entered the salon and saw the guys sitting at the galley table, each playing a separate game of solitaire.

That's just weird.

Marcello looked at me with compassion. He knew I had been crying. He always seemed to know when I cried. Mario was as chipper as could be and he sang the words to a song different from the one coming out of the speakers.

God he's annoying.

Then almost as quickly as that thought entered my mind, it was replaced with an odd sense of contentment. The strange quirky ways of my dysfunctional little family actually started to comfort me. It was as if my brief detour through Hell allowed me to see things a little clearer. All the emotions, the confusion, the anger, the resentment... all of it had worn me out, and at that moment, I was able to put things in perspective.

The ocean can—and usually does—change people. All of us were adjusting at our own pace. I loved my husband dearly and the other members of my current world were decent people too. I couldn't control how Mario behaved, but I could take back ownership of my job and just cook without debate over the menu. I embraced the power of positive thinking. If you can't fight or flight... float.

Humanity

There is no easy road
Talk is good
But to who?
Anybody who will listen
People are a pain
But can't be lived without
I wonder why.

~ Bart Mathews

Chapter 23:
Typhoon Hagibis

A CATEGORY FIVE SUPER TYPHOON REACHED ITS PEAK in the South Pacific on May 19, 2002, with 110 mph winds. They called it Typhoon Hagibis. That name has been used for three tropical cyclones in the Western North Pacific Ocean. I read that the label was contributed by the Philippines and means "fast" or "swift."

The developing storm dropped enough rainfall on Guam to end the island's wildfire season on May 16 and intensified rapidly to an upgraded typhoon status on May 18. We'd been watching the weather report for days, hoping the storm would turn and miss us completely. Our latitude was 38.07, and our longitude was 172.31, which put us less than a hundred miles north of its center. Hagibis was still gaining power at that point and heading straight for us!

Fortunately, the cooler water we were in had a huge impact on Hagibis by slowing the winds down to 50 to 60 mph by the time it reached us on May 21. We were then in what was categorized as a severe tropical storm. The ocean was still huge, which made it hard to hang on and even harder to fish.

The waves crashed into the starboard side of the boat and continually pounded Mario and me on the back deck. Marcello turned his back to the deck's wall and hunched inward, attempting to shield himself from being drenched when the boats' port side dipped into the bottom of a wave as we rolled with it.

"I'm gonna turn us around, Mario!" Bart shouted from the

bridge above. His voice competed with the thunderous sounds of the howling winds, rain, and the boat laboring through the aggressive waves.

"Okay!" Mario yelled back.

All three of us secured ourselves for the maneuver. The guys grabbed the lines to keep them from wrapping around the boat as Bart turned us 180 degrees. Being in the middle of the ocean without any landmarks or roads with defined edges to indicate your direction, we had to pay attention to the movement of the boat, the wind, and the direction of the swells to know where we were. Bart, of course, had the plotter for an added reference.

We endured the brutal shenanigans for another twenty or thirty minutes, when it became obvious that the conditions were getting worse.

"Pull the gear, Mario!" Bart shouted from the bridge above. "Let's pull down the storm windows and get out of this mess!"

"Okay, Bart!" Mario confirmed.

Mario and Marcello had already secured the longer lines in preparation of a retreat. With their backsides leaned up against the landing tables for support and their legs bent to adjust to sudden thrusts of the vessel, they tightened the remaining short lines and stored the gear. With loose knees and his right hand grabbing hold of the bulwarks, Mario's left hand braced against the starboard side of the house for stabilization as he led the way to the bow, into the brutal winds and crashing waves.

The men moved quickly, yet cautiously around to the port side of the house, where Hagibis was hammering us mercilessly. They locked down the storm windows that were facing the storm, then steadied themselves up and around the front of the house, then back down the starboard side of the vessel to safety. Marcello bolted the storm door to the back deck to keep the massive gusts of water and howling wind away from our stern.

He backed into the house with one hand on the door handle and one hand on the doorway for stability. Marcello was the last one to come inside. He locked the back door behind him, sat on the bench at the galley table for reinforcement, and peeled off his raingear. He then joined Mario down below where they hung their wet clothes in the engine room. Bart kept a close watch from the wheelhouse and was relieved that we all made it inside where we were safe. The only thing to do at that point was to ride it out.

I pushed my butt against the wall for stability and crawled up the steps to the wheelhouse to visit with Bart and check out the view from above. I waited for the moment after we crashed to the bottom of a thirty-foot swell to take the two large steps across the room. I reached for the back of the bench and hung on. We were already climbing up another wave by then, so I spread my feet apart and bent my knees in order to take the fall without being launched across the room.

"How's it going, Honey?" I asked, trying to keep a positive tone.

"Peachy," Bart replied in a semi-sarcastic tone. His feet were firmly pressed next to the plotter on the dashboard in front of him. "This sucks!"

"Yah, it does! It's really hard to hang on. I don't think I can stay up here with you. I'm gonna grab a movie and retreat to our room. Sorry, dear, but everyone's on their own for dinner."

"Good idea, Hon. We're gonna be in this for a while. Hagibis isn't expected to drop speed anytime soon, but it might turn away from us in a few hours."

"See ya later!" I shouted.

Bart kissed the air in my direction and I returned my love the same way, inching my way back down the steps while I hung on for dear life.

Once I reached the last step, I slammed my butt against the wall, bent my knees, and grabbed hold of the bench in the salon near the box where we kept the movies. *Thelma and Louise* jumped out at me, which made my decision-making process quick and painless.

"Perfect," I said out loud.

I carefully made my way to our stateroom and felt my arms getting bruised with each thrust into the walls as the boat's dramatic movement threw me from side to side.

I turned up the volume full-blast to drown out the thundering sounds as the ninety-two-foot steel boat was hurled through the powerful typhoon. Each time a wave hit the vessel's port side, the force shoved us across the ocean's surface with a starboard list that felt like we might do a 360 roll. Although we probably didn't tilt more than forty-five degrees, I was certain we were going full circle.

"Fuck!" I shouted to no one when I ducked the books flying off the shelf above my side of the bed.

I felt the boat stabilize for a moment and took advantage of what I presumed was just a lull before we were hit with another wave. I grabbed the remaining books from the cabinet and stacked them on the floor at the end of the bed between the bunk and the closet. Then quickly returned to my spot in the center of the bed and focused on the Brad Pitt scene in the hotel—right before he robs the poor girls.

After the movie ended, I was tired of lying down. My back hurt from tension and the scissor position my legs had taken in an attempt to stabilize my body. I decided to go watch the storm in a vertical position—if I could. I made my way through the salon to the back door, and with my right hand took hold of the steel handle and stepped up into its frame.

I braced my feet in the doorway and wrapped my left hand

around my right. I was set to look out the window. The winds were blowing so hard they took the deep blue color right out of the water, making the waves pale turquoise, like the bottom of a concrete swimming pool. The tops of the waves were ripped open and sprayed across the length of the swell, resembling what a power washer would do when removing the frothy foam from a latte.

Remarkably, the white plastic lawn chairs the guys usually sat in merely slid back and forth across the deck without being knocked overboard. My red sparkly flip-flops gently floated from one side of the vessel to the other. The deck water didn't wash them overboard through the scupper to the raging waters below.

Refocusing my attention on the massive waves, I realized what a beautiful sight it was... like nothing I'd imagined in my wildest dreams. I wasn't afraid. Not even a little.

The weather was still rough the next morning, but had calmed down enough for the guys to try fishing again.

"Hey, Midnite, ya pick me up?" Popeye's voice came over the radio bright and early.

"Yah, good morning. Okay."

"Fucking Hagibis kicked our butts over here. We've got shit all over the floors from that goddamn storm. I can't believe nothing broke! How'd you guys do?"

"Sorry to hear that, man. We did fine. Had a few books fall out of the shelf and our cupboards are little scrambled, but that's about it. No one got hurt and nothing's broken."

"Good deal. I went in to take a crap this morning and when we took a roll, the goddamn head blasted a shot of air that threw shit all over my back. I hate this fucking weather!"

Bart laughed. "I hear ya, man. It's nasty when that happens. Ha ha ha ha. Theresa experienced the same thing the other day and she threw a fit! I'm lucky she didn't shoot me."

"No kidding! How is she holding up now?"

"She's good, but she doesn't like all this up and down business. She's cooking breakfast right now."

"All right. She's a good sport, man."

"Yah, I know."

"You ready to head east?" Popeye asked.

"Sounds good. We've got our gear in, but haven't caught anything yet. John's starting to see a sign and it looks like there's a tight edge forming just outside them. It will take a little while for the water to get back to normal, but the fish left this crap anyway. We're gonna run over there."

"Copy that. Check ya later."

"Okay. O'er," Bart signed off. "Hey, Mario!" Bart hollered off the back deck to the crew. "There's a sign about twenty miles to the east of us and the *Lady Valerie* has about thirty on board this morning, so I'm gonna kick it up and run over there."

"Okay!" Mario agreed as he jumped up from his seat.

We were anxious to leave that battlefield and start catching fish again. I had breakfast on the table ten minutes later. The guys were already inside and sat down to enjoy the meal. I made scrambled eggs, hash browns, bacon, toast, and of course the rice cooker contained a fresh batch of rice for the crew. I handed a plate up to Bart along with a can of V-8. I gave him a kiss.

"I'd join you, Hon," I said. "But it's still a little bumpy out and I do better eating at the table."

Bart made a sweet purring sound and blew me a kiss. I *felt* him say, 'That's fine, Hon. Love you.' Sometimes words just aren't needed.

I thought about what occurred over those twenty-four hours and how our environment had changed drastically during that time. Hearing Popeye on the radio made me think about what he'd been through out there in his career. He had been on two boats that sunk and yet he still kept going out. He can hardly talk about those events without breaking down. Especially the first one. It could have been in the movie, *The Perfect Storm*, but fortunately, in his case, there were survivors.

Rough seas—view from the wheelhouse

Chapter 24: Senses

THE OCEAN WAS DRY LIKE THE DESERT, with maybe five fish caught all day. It was mid-afternoon on that fine June day back in 2002. The weather was calm, the air was clean and fresh. I decided to take advantage of the perfect opportunity to catch up on laundry while we cruised in a northwesterly direction in search of a more promising block of marine life.

Having a water-maker onboard is essential when you're offshore. Bart kept a close watch on our fresh potable water supply, and at every opportunity, he'd turn on our water maker to ensure we never ran out. With a 500-gallon tank, it didn't take long to make a significant dent it in. Since we could operate the desalination only during decent weather, we had to stay on top of the situation in case we ran into rough seas.

I divided Bart and my clothes and towels into small or medium-sized piles. You never want to turn the dial to "large load" on a boat because when the boat rolls—even just a little—and the water level shifts to the other side of the drum, the machine thinks it needs more water and will continue to fill up each time it gets low on one side. That is a sure way to flood the fo'c'sle.

The day was so gorgeous that I decided to wait outside on the foredeck for my laundry to finish. The deck boards warmed my bare feet as I carefully walked to an open space where I could lie down and feel the sun's rays on my face and exposed limbs. The gentle sound of displaced water splashing against the hull was hypnotic.

I stared up at the sky and marveled at a million different shapes and silhouettes formed by the fluffy white clouds, as if they were drawn on a brilliant Crayola sky blue canvas. The clouds looked like seahorses and dragons—the animated kind that are supposed to be fierce and scary but are cute and cuddly instead. A bunch of faces appeared too, both old and young, oftentimes changing from one to another then back again, or into a whole new figure—the way clouds do. I saw three old bearded fishermen donning rain gear complete with hats and coats. They resembled the guy on the Gorton's Seafood box, only with more character and expression. One of the fishermen had a long string of vertebrae instead of a body, and he was catching a fish in his open mouth through his skeletal head.

The heat of the sun had warmed the deck boards under my body. The warmth felt as if a big down quilt was under me rather than the wood planks that would soon become hard as cement under my aching bones.

I closed my eyes for a moment. The white noise from the hum of the main engine that kept us moving forward, and the slow gentle rippling noises the boat made against the ocean's surface as she rose and fell upon it relaxed me completely, taking my mind on a magical journey. The sky, and all its paternal beings, was like huge arms that held me close, offering up comfort and protection from harm. At the same time, it was as if it merely blew lightly at our stern, providing a soft breeze to cruise freely at our own pace.

The energy that consumed me was a mellow yet powerful force as I went with the flow. I embraced being present and felt as if I was one with the planet. I had a strong desire to see angels for some reason. Then I opened my eyes to witness the performance of my life.

The *Maverick's* butter-yellow bulwarks tucked against my peripheral vision were like curtains pulled back tight to reveal a massive stage. The sky was bursting with beautiful feminine beings in long flowing gowns adorned with bell-shaped sleeves that draped down from their wrists. Their backs were bejeweled with big feathery wings that connected to their shoulder blades. Two were blowing horns, one was strumming a harp, three more reached out to other creatures that shared the sky with them, and another simply looked over us with a loving maternal gaze. There were cherubs everywhere, and more faces, some almost looked familiar.

My guardians were so enchanting, I thought that if they knelt down and reached out in my direction I would certainly be scooped up and they would take me with them to the heavenly world from which they had come.

Am I dead? I don't care. I like it here.

Just then, I noticed the boards of the decking underneath my frame were causing extreme pain to my head and lower back.

Nope, definitely alive!

The foredeck was the only place on the boat where I could sprawl and relax outside, enjoy the beautiful weather (a rare occasion that trip), and not have to share the space with a bunch of blood-splattered fish. It was the only place where I could truly enjoy fresh air. And I was guaranteed to tune in and appreciate the only place on the planet—the wide-open ocean—which is exactly the same now as it was over a billion years ago. Without buildings, trees, and other solid formations to occupy and affect it, the ocean's surface was visibly unchanged.

I slowly rose to my feet and chuckled to myself for choosing such an uncomfortable place to let my imagination run wild. But was it really my imagination?

Whatever the explanation of my trippy visions, I felt that even though my life out there was full of emotional turmoil and mental anguish, this globe on which we live is far more important and huge than anything we could possibly imagine. And my being there to experience the amazing life at sea was a true gift.

Embracing those lingering feelings and unsure what form of entertainment I would choose next, I put another load of wash in and checked my watch. An hour had passed. I glanced back up to applaud the cast of performers, only to see that the show was over.

The sky had returned to an almost shapeless picture with unformed clouds dotted here and there, and a fading streak stretched across it like a brush stroke that had run out of white paint. But the cast had left an impression on me as if the stars of a Broadway play had included me in their most important scene.

* * *

I busied myself with the remaining laundry and chores around the house until it was time to start dinner. I poured Bart a cocktail and a glass of wine for myself. With each hand occupied with a drink, I carefully climbed the shiny teak steps to the wheelhouse where Bart greeted me with as much delight as he could muster. I clicked our glasses together, gave Bart a kiss, then turned to go back down to cook.

I hummed to myself, still enjoying a sense of peace while I worked quickly preparing the twice-baked potatoes. I retrieved the filet mignon that had been marinating in the fridge all afternoon and Mario jumped up from his seat at the galley table to announce he would bring out the barbeque from the fo'c'sle. I smiled and placed the stuffed potatoes in the oven and put the veggies in the steamer. When everything was within ten minutes of being ready, I put the meat on the grill.

After a delicious meal and the galley once again clean, Mario and I sat down at the table to visit. We discussed deep subjects like reincarnation, spirits, intuitiveness, and so on. I felt so tethered to the boat, the ocean, the planet, the universe. My *typically* wrestled spirit was still calm, so I decided to share my experience from earlier that day.

Mario sat and listened quietly, nodding his head. Then a memory I'd tucked away deep inside me came rushing to the surface and I blurted out, "Sometimes I hear voices. Mostly when I'm on watch and everyone else is asleep."

"Yes, that's right," he said. "Do you think you see someone on the stern?"

"Yes! Sometimes I do, but only in my peripheral vision. When I turn to look, no one is there. The other night when the moon was full and I was on watch, I was blown away by how bright everything was. The moon was like a gigantic spotlight on a movie set that lit up a bright pathway toward the horizon and down the other side of the globe. And the phosphorus that sprayed from the sides of the boat when it went up and down the chop resembled sparkling pixy dust as if we were part of an animated film. The whole night seemed unreal. And then I thought I saw someone on the stern but figured I was caught up in the moment and must have been imagining things."

"I remember that moon. You saw Patrick," he said with finality.

"Patrick?"

"Miguel's brother. His ashes were sprinkled at sea in the South Pacific. Right there on the stern."

Mario looked me in the eye and smiled. I knew he was telling me the truth. I knew he believed Patrick was still with us, at least sometimes. I wasn't afraid. In fact, I felt a deeper connection to the boat and to the people on it.

"I want to come back as a porpoise," I told him. "They are peaceful creatures that seem to smile and play all the time," I told him. "It doesn't appear they have many enemies, which makes them high enough on the food chain to live in minimal danger."

"You'll see me then, 'cause I'm coming back as a whale," he said with a serious expression.

We both laughed and continued chatting about the "what-ifs" until we ran out of scenarios. I left him alone at the table to play solitaire and went upstairs to check in with my husband. Feeling totally relaxed and fulfilled, I decided to keep my spiritual explorations to myself. Besides, it wasn't like Bart to leap into a conversation like that, especially when he had so much on his mind. For once, it felt natural to *just be* and not demand dialogue from him.

One of the most beautiful exhibits Mother Nature delivers is the spectacular masterpiece of a sunset in the middle of the ocean. My satisfaction lingered as we sat in silence and watched the brilliant colors change from fire-red, to burnt sienna, and then vibrant orange and peach, to seven shades of purple.

Bart gazed out the wheelhouse window in a trance-like state. His mind was in a different place than mine, which was usually the case anyway, but I didn't care just then. I was delighted to be in my own little world with his body close enough to mine that I could reach out and touch him, yet still be a million miles away.

A great sense of relief consumed me knowing that his focus was most likely on the condition of the boat and our next move. I was glad I didn't have to fill my head with worries about the technical details that must have been spinning around his head, such as—*When had the bilge been checked last? We need to change the oil on the main and turn off the refrigeration tonight. Is our tank full of fresh water, or do I need to turn the water-maker back on while the sea is calm?*

Popeye and Sleepy are less than a block outside us now and they've been fishing wide open—I sure hope they'll stay located long enough for us to catch up. We'll be crossing the dateline around midnight. There'd better be some fish when we get there for all this running! Is the price of fish going to stay up, or drop by the time we get in? Will I be able to fill the boat?

Bart concentrated on our safety and livelihood—all the reasons we were out there. I concentrated on staying sane and keeping everyone else happy with full bellies and satisfied taste buds. With no real work to occupy the nearly twenty hours of daylight, the fact that I was still encountering a bit of euphoria was a major accomplishment. The sun was approaching the horizon when Bart broke the silence.

"We might get lucky and see the green flash tonight," he said staring straight ahead.

"Oh? That would be awesome!" I replied.

"It's pretty flat out here so the waves won't get in the way of the flash," he continued. "You really can't see it on the beach because of all the obstacles like mountains and other land. Be careful to protect your eyes and look to either side of the sun. It happens super-fast, just as the sun hits the horizon, so if you blink you could miss it. I've seen it only a couple of times myself, but it's really cool if you're lucky enough to catch it."

"Okay," I said looking forward with my eyes wide as I tried not to blink. And then I saw it. The green flash appeared and it was spectacular!

"WOW!" I said. "Did you see it too?"

"Yah, I did," he replied grinning wide from my child-like enthusiasm. "Pretty neat, huh?"

"Very cool indeed," I said, satisfied that I was able to witness one of nature's miracles. I had just experienced the most perfect ending to a perfect day.

Chapter 25:
The Turnaround

BY JULY 2, 2002, WE HAD WORKED OUR WAY NORTH and filled the boat with ninety-five tons of albacore. The run to Harbour Marine Products in Vancouver, BC (where we would unload), would take sixteen days. Two weeks of running can seem like an eternity, but with nearly eighty days behind us, the home stretch was nothing in comparison.

The hard work from fishing was done for the time being, but as a working vessel, there was more to do before we could sit back and relax.

Mario and Marcello went to work storing the gear for the next trip. They scrubbed the landing tables, the sides of the steel vessel, the underside of the aft bridge deck, and the ceiling on the stern. They continued cleaning the exterior of the boat while I worked on the interior. I started with our head and master stateroom and made my way into the salon. I wiped down the white Formica walls with Windex as I moved through the house toward the galley.

I cleaned out the refrigerator and cupboards, removed expired food from containers and tossed it overboard, and washed the drawers and shelves so they were ready for new provisions on the next trip.

Bart used Q-tips to clean the electrical equipment on the dashboard of the wheelhouse, ensuring that the build-up of dust, grease, and salt would be gone by the time we docked. He organized the charts, put videos away in their built-in shelf behind the chart table, and tidied the desk piled high with notes, lists, and old Inmarsat email messages. Within a few days, the boat was neat, organized, and sparkling from bow to stern.

The last week of running is always the hardest. Chores are done and there are no fish to catch. It really is just long days of waiting. And staying busy enough to not go stir crazy.

Once we entered the southern tip of the Strait of Georgia (located between Vancouver Island, and the mainland coast of British Columbia, Canada, and extreme northern Washington, United States) we were within twenty-four hours of reaching our destination. The Strait is one of the busiest shipping lanes in the world—more than 10,000 freighters pass through it every year. Oil tankers, naval vessels, fuel barges, cruise ships, fishing boats, ferries, and pleasure craft all share these waters.

Since I didn't like to see boats on my radar in the middle of the ocean, let alone outside the wheelhouse windows, I wasn't much good at the helm. Mario and Marcello were trained seamen and able to take watch, but Bart always took over when we shared the waterways with other vessels.

Once inside the Burrard Inlet (coastal fjord that is shallow on both sides and separates North and South Vancouver, BC) the current was running strong and we were going with it. Our speed increased to nearly ten knots as a result. The narrow twenty-three-mile passage varies from one to four miles wide. That can feel as if you are squeezing through a tight hallway when you share the space with other vessels, especially after being alone in the middle of the ocean for nearly three months.

We marveled at the homes that lined the banks on both sides as we cruised by them. Sometimes we waved at the families in their backyards and on porches on that warm summer day.

I knew we had arrived when I saw stacks of containers piled high. Forklift drivers zipped around the docks and back through huge garage doors that led into a large steel building. A row of workers wearing coveralls stood on the edge of the dock and stared at our vessel.

We slowly approached the dock. With the tide out and our hull packed with ninety-five tons of albacore, we sat low in the water. That made the floor of the wheelhouse almost level with the dock that sat twenty feet above the water line. Mario hopped off the bridge deck at the stern and wrapped the line around a cleat, which stopped the *Maverick* from drifting forward.

"Let's do a spring line, Mario!" Bart shouted from the bridge. "That's good right there."

Meanwhile, Marcello had looped the bowline around a forward cleat and waited for the instruction to tie us off and secure the location. The men squared us away while I watched comfortably from the wheelhouse... out of everyone's way. Keegan was the owner of Harbour Marine and also our fish buyer. He and Miguel (I usually called him Mike) showed up a moment later when Bart exited the wheelhouse and I followed him outside.

"Hey, man," Bart greeted Keegan, firmly shaking his hand.

"Hey, there," Bart said to Miguel, shaking his hand.

"Hi, Bart. Hello, Theresa," Miguel said as he smiled at us both.

"Hi, Mike!" I said, happy to see the boat's owner. Such a nice man with a brilliant mind and gentle spirit.

"Hi, Bart," Keegan said, welcoming us. "How was the run in?"

"It was great. Hey, Keegan, I want you to meet my wife, Theresa," Bart said, reaching his left arm toward me and placing his hand loosely on the small of my back. "This is Keegan," he said to me, completing the introduction.

"Hi, Theresa. It's nice to meet you," Keegan said politely, even though he seemed distracted and did not make eye contact.

"Hi. Nice to meet you also," I said, giving Keegan a firm handshake.

"We're almost ready," Keegan said. "They're getting the totes set up now. Should be about a half-hour and we can start unloading."

"That sounds fine," Bart replied. "Theresa made a pot of coffee. Would you like a cup while we go over some details?"

"Sure."

Keegan and Miguel stepped on board and the men followed me into the wheelhouse and down the teak steps to the salon. I poured three coffees for the men and placed the cups on the galley table. I filled a glass of water for myself. They sat at the table and spaced themselves—Keegan at one end of the bench, Miguel slid in from the other end and scooted to the center, and Bart motioned for me to sit at the other end of the bench. He pulled up a stool to sit next to me.

I sat quietly while the men discussed business, the process to unload the fish, how many dockhands were available to keep things moving quickly, and how we would separate the fish into totes based on the size of the fish.

"Mario will take the first shift," Bart told Keegan.

"Sure, whatever you want to do," Keegan said.

On the way in, Bart and Mario explained to me how important it is to stand watch when fish are being unloaded. Since payment is based on the size of the fish, if someone tossed fifteen-to-twenty pound fish in the ten-to-fifteen pound tote, we would end up shorted on our paycheck. It is also important to keep a good count because the number we ended up with could differ greatly from what the fish buyer's count was if we did not pay attention.

I saw first-hand how that can happen when it was my turn to

oversee the unloading. I had no problem jumping in and barking orders to have someone grab that seventeen-pounder out of the smaller tote and get it into the large tote where it belonged. I received a few looks from the dockhands, but they learned quickly that I meant business.

I also understood how easy it was to become hypnotized and space-off from the repetitive motions of unloading. The people handling the fish often went into autopilot mode and daydreamed once the steel bucket of fish was securely placed on the dock.

The crane operators didn't have that luxury, though. They had to pay attention every single minute. Lifting heavy steel buckets into the air—filled high with frozen albacore—could have been deadly if one of the fish fell out of the bucket and onto someone below, or if the bucket bumped someone. Mishaps can easily occur if safety measures are not followed closely. That is one reason why two or more people typically supervise the process.

Once the unloading was under way, Keegan invited us into the plant to give Miguel, Bart, and me a tour. The workers fed the fish into large stainless steel machines that sliced off the skin. Another machine removed the head and tail, and another machine sliced the meat into loins. The fish then came down a long conveyer belt where workers stood at their stations inspecting the fish. They wore aprons, hairnets, and gloves.

They removed any remaining skin or fins that hadn't come off in the cutting machine, and made sure each sashimi-grade loin looked perfect before sending it on to the final step where the fish were vacuum packed and sent to large freezers for storage. The whole operation was very interesting to watch.

Keegan led us to his quiet office. He offered us coffee and comfortable chairs, and then gave us the news. The price per ton had dropped to $1,300 US dollars.

"What?!" I heard my mouth shout in despair. Bart reached over and placed his hand on my leg to calm me down and let me know it was not a good time to voice my opinion.

"Oh my God," I added, and then decided to keep my mouth shut. Miguel looked at me. He seemed aware that I was about to burst into tears.

That fish buying outfit—and others like it—had been paying fishermen an average of $2,400 US dollars per ton and nearly $3,000 a ton during a few spikes of low supply and high demand. The best sushi bars in the world sought the highest grade tuna and paid top dollar for the product. Similar to the stock market and crude oil, fish markets rise and fall. Unfortunately, they can drop while boats are in the middle of the fishing season and there is nothing fishermen can do about it—unless they could afford to store their load until the price came back up. Most could not.

"I know, I'm sorry," Keegan replied. "We have freezers full that Japan doesn't want right now and we aren't sure when we can unload them. Honestly, we don't even need your fish, but I promised I'd buy them so I'm making an exception for you guys. I know I'll be able to make room, but it could be a few months of me sitting on them, so I just can't give you any more than that."

Bart and Miguel had been in the business a long time and knew that sometimes the price plummets and there is nothing anyone can do about it. They didn't want to do or say anything to jeopardize their relationship with Keegan. If they did, it was likely that we would soon find out the competition offered even less per ton. Or worse, may not want our fish at all.

After Miguel did all the negotiating he could, he and Bart accepted the fact that $1,300 per ton was as good as they would have gotten anywhere else. It was a terrible price for sashimi grade tuna, but like the stock market, the price wouldn't stay low forever.

I took a lot longer to accept the devastating news.

Bart and I had gotten married the previous September after spending a lot more than anticipated for the remodel of our house, and neither of us had received a decent paycheck (or any paycheck for that matter) in nearly a year.

Three months in the middle of the fricking ocean—nearly losing my mind—and we're STILL broke?! WOW. Not part of the plan. Definitely not what we discussed.

The unloading took all day and extended into the evening. Once all the fish had been counted, we compared our tally sheets with those at Harbour Marine for accuracy. We had caught just under 6,000 fish—total weight was 93 tons.

Mario and Marcello hosed off the bow deck covered by a thick layer of fins and fish scales. We would make the deck shiny again during our ride back to the states in the morning, but cleaning up the hold would take a full day. That duty also kept the guys busy while Bart and I shopped for boat parts and coordinated repairs out of Bellingham, Washington.

The grocery list had been growing since we left the fishing grounds. Taking inventory of what was left gave us a good idea of what we ate the most of and which items we could scale back on for the next trip. The Costco run was the most time consuming and labor-intensive. The task required all four of us to participate so we would not miss anything. It was also the most expensive grocery run, averaging $2,500 to $3,000.

Bart didn't need to accompany us to the Asian Market that provided the most fun for the guys and me since the store had everything we could want. The guys loaded up on favorite staples from the Philippines, and all three of us filled the baskets with Thai ingredients. We spent over $600 there and we hadn't even bought produce yet. But we knew one of the highlights of any day at sea would be guaranteed. We would eat well.

The repairs were done, the groceries were on board and put away, and the fuel tanks were loaded.

Before heading back out to sea for the last trip of the season, we decided to swing by Roche Harbor for an overnight and to see our friends on San Juan Island where Bart and I lived. The *Maverick* was a handsome vessel, yet she stood out among the hundreds of shiny white yachts that filled the marina. Our friends greeted us with enthusiasm and the kids who caught our lines (summer help working at the resort) seemed equally thrilled to see a fishing boat like ours.

The weather had been spectacular at home that summer and we were lucky to be there during a long stretch of sunshine. The sky was clear, the temperature was in the mid-70s, and a slight breeze came from the south.

I styled my hair and applied make-up. I put on a necklace, earrings, and my wedding ring to accessorize my outfit: a denim mini-skirt and bright green tank top. I grabbed my purse and stepped into my flip-flops on the way out of the salon, grinning ear-to-ear as I walked down the side of the vessel.

Bart and our next-door neighbor, Dave, sat in lawn chairs on the bow deck enjoying their cocktails and each other's company.

"Hi, Honey," I said to Bart. Both men looked up with big smiles.

"Hey, there," he replied. "You look like you're on a mission."

"I am as a matter of fact. I'm going shopping!"

"Nice! Have a great time, Hon."

"Will do," I said and gave him a kiss.

The boutique at the end of the dock was packed with vacationers and yachties, and I was part of the buzz that filled the room. I was in heaven! As a local who had been gone for a few months, I was somewhat of a celebrity—even among some of the out-of-town shoppers who frequent the resort in summertime. I had a blast as a guest in the store rather than the employee I had been the year before. I had my own personal shoppers to help me pick out the latest styles.... even if I would be able to enjoy them for only a day or two before I had to get back into my work clothes for the rest of the season.

That evening, a handful of our friends gathered on the *Maverick* for a BBQ. We drank, ate, told stories, laughed, and danced until the sun went down. We decided to put a message in an empty bottle of Canadian Club to drop at sea once we got underway. Everyone took turns writing down a message on the yellow paper. Mario secured the bottle for its journey. I soaked up the moment, knowing that in the morning we would have to go back to work.

We untied the lines at 7:30 a.m. I cried as I watched our homeport disappear from sight. Our next—and final stop—in Port Angeles was short, as we needed only fresh produce to top off our provisions.

When we were back in motion, the guys brought out the gear to prepare jigs and lines for the trip. I stored the produce by removing the outer layer from each head of cabbage, then wrapped them in newspaper and placed them in the fo'c'sle. I chopped a few bell peppers of each color and put them in plastic freezer bags, hoping they'd keep for a month or so. Any produce that wouldn't fit in the refrigerator was kept in the fo'c'sle where it would last a little longer. It was cooler there away from the heat of the engine.

I climbed the steel steps on the stern behind the landing tables that led up to the bridge. Reaching for the wheelhouse wall, I steadied myself against the gentle rolling beneath us as I walked to the front of the house. I sat on the bench and rested my feet on the inside wall of the bridge. I looked out at the water and turned my head to the east. I watched the landscape shrink as we moved further away and took a deep breath.

"Three more months," I said out loud to no one but myself. "I can do this."

Chapter 26: Family

A WEEK OR SO INTO THAT FINAL TRIP OF THE SEASON in 2002, I knew it would be my last one. Ever. I made it through the first three-month trip in 2002, but now it was August. In a couple of months, the weather would become real nasty.

I remembered how much I hated that part from my first voyage three years earlier. Spending less than fourteen days on the beach in between two trips of ninety to one hundred days at sea was more than I cared to endure. I just wasn't wired for it. I realized *this* time out how much the ocean had changed me. I didn't think it was good for my marriage, which I treasured deeply. It also was not good for my soul, because I was tormented about being present but constantly wanting to be somewhere else.

I had too much time to be in my head—letting my emotions and imagination run so wild was not healthy. Of course, the experience had also been amazing. I decided to make an honest effort each day to relish in *the now* so I could enjoy the uniqueness about my adventure. Once I'd decided not to continue fishing in the future, I didn't want to miss the craziness once it was over.

A hose broke mid-morning. A few years earlier, the reduction gear had been repaired, but evidently, the fix had worn out. The inner hose that had been placed inside a larger hose as part of the cooling system to the reduction gear had disintegrated because it was not airtight against the outer piece. That caused heat to become trapped inside the smaller hose, which eventually destroyed it.

Fortunately, John—the captain of the *Lady Valerie*—was just a few miles from us and he had an ample supply of spare hose. He was also in need of some whiskey, so the two boats exchanged packages and all was right with the world.

His crew placed more than enough hose in a large black plastic garbage bag, along with magazines, movies, and a couple of candy bars. Three feet of tuna cord had been tied to it with a one-gallon bleach bottle at the other end that was about two-thirds full of water for buoyancy.

We exchanged some of our movies by placing them in a heavy-duty garbage bag, included a fifth of whiskey, a few magazines from our stack, and a bag of chocolate chip cookies from the batch I had baked the day before. Each boat successfully gaffed their package with one pass. Mario and Bart quickly replaced the damaged hose. We were back in business and continued running to the other boats that were catching fish.

Bart relieved me from my watch and I was just about to go down the steps when I stopped at the table behind the bench to see if we had received any Inmarsat satellite email messages.

"Hey, Hon, did you see this one from Faye?" I asked.

"No, I didn't!" he replied with excitement in his voice. "It must have come in while we were replacing the hose."

"She had her baby—it's a boy! They named him Sawyer. Sawyer Jackson. Isn't that cool, Gramps?"

"All right! That's a great name," he said with an ear-to-ear grin.

"Everyone is doing well. Oh, yay! I bet Mason is going to like being a big brother."

"I'm sure he will. I'll have to give her a call in a couple days," Bart replied.

"Faye would love that," I said.

We savored the good news and Bart sat in the chair in front of the computer to send his daughter a note of congratulations. I stepped out of his way and backed down the steps.

It was time for me to prepare spring rolls for lunch. Everyone liked the freshness of steamed spring rolls, but the process is time consuming. Since we weren't catching fish yet, I had lots of time. My hands stayed busy chopping, stirring, steaming and rolling, while my mind wandered.

I wonder if we'll ever have kids. We're not young, but if we can get our finances back up, I think Bart would go for it. Four years. I give myself until 42 to have a child. After that, I think I'll be too close to menopause. Oh, how cool it would be to see Bart's eyes look at me through the innocence of a child. I sure hope we get to be parents together.

Just a little more than an hour after we exchanged packages with the *Lady Valerie*, Bart could barely understand John. "Hey, John, how much of that whiskey have you had, man?"

"The bottle's half gone, buddy" he slurred.

"You're not supposed to drink it all at once! That stuff will sneak up on you. Maybe you should have one of the crew drive for a while. We're just running anyway."

Bart was always the voice of reason.

"Good idea. Over."

We didn't hear from John again until the next day.

All the gear was rigged and ready to go. So the guys kept themselves busy by reading magazines, playing cards, and watching action flicks on the VCR. I escaped into a book for a couple hours and then went back to the galley to start dinner. I stayed with the Asian theme for the day, choosing Chiang Mai noodles as the evening meal. Yum! I had never made that dish before, but promised to make it again before the trip was complete.

After dinner, we still had several hours of daylight and I was restless. The water had gotten bumpy, which reminded me to always keep one hand on the boat as I moved. I pulled myself up the steps to the pilot house by firmly gripping the railing as I took each step, mindful to duck at the third step so as not to smack my head on floor to the upper level like I had done numerous times before.

"Hi, Babe," I greeted Bart when I reached the top step. "What's happening?"

"I was just going to come get you. You got a couple messages from your Mom."

"Oh, goody!" I said.

I took a step toward the computer then sat down to read. Mom always wrote the best letters. I loved getting notes from friends and family, but I especially loved the notes from my parents. There is something special about love we receive from our families. The effect on us when they take the time to write about whatever happened since we last emailed or spoke on the phone is heartwarming. Knowing that they are thinking of us and that they miss us and wonder if we were safe creates a warmth that feels like home. That's what love does. And it lifts my spirits to the moon.

Mom's letter said they wondered what our days were like and when we would be home. They wondered if we were happy, scared, having fun, or in misery. My family enjoyed hearing about the adventures, mostly when the fishing was wide open. They were also amused when I told them what it was like to make brownies when the boat rolled back and forth and I forgot to rotate the pan often enough to keep the dish baking evenly instead of on just one side. We referred to those as "boat brownies."

I could almost see the excitement in my mom's face when she read a recent message from me about finding a glass float. Glass floats had been used around the world by many fisheries to keep their fishing nets, longlines, or droplines afloat. Plastic floats have replaced glass over the years but glass floats can still be found on occasion—primarily in the Pacific—and it's a real treat to spot one.

They loved hearing about the schools of dolphins that played near the bow of the boat, when we saw huge turtles, breaching whales, albatross flying with their enormous wings fully extended. They loved hearing about the board meetings and imagined me pulling fish—especially since I'd always loved being in and around boats but I had never liked fishing. I spared them the details of rough seas and my emotional roller coaster—until I was home of course—because I knew they would have worried more than they already did, and there was nothing they could have done about it.

Hearing from them lit up my mood like a Christmas tree in Times Square. Notes from family carried my happy mood into the next several days with lingering memories of home. My heart was full and my attitude was positive. I had an amazingly good day!

Dolphins playing with the boat

Chapter 27: Dresses and Chain Saws

OUR LAST TRIP IN 2002 STARTED OFF WITH A BANG. Each day was different and yet the same. We were either busy with wide-open fishing or running the boat around the ocean looking for fish. Some days our activity would change on a dime and we'd have a mix of both. Fits and starts. We experienced firsthand the way Wes (aka Norton—the Hyena who rallied for both Sue and me when we lost our husbands even though he had lost his wife that same year) described albacore fishing: "Hours and hours of intense boredom punctuated by moments of sheer terror."

The weather that wrapped up the summer months was decent, with warm days in the 60s, more sun than clouds, and seas that varied from flat calm to ten-foot swells, or seas with no more than a two-foot chop. Just before the second week in September, we landed on a large school—or perhaps several small ones that bumped into each other, which allowed us to fish all day. Because we did not have to run to a new location, we were able to shut down at sunset and drift during the night so everyone on board could sleep at the same time.

The gear went in the water at morning's first gray light, the first bell went off immediately, and we'd keep fishing all day. The fish would stop biting for a while, but we stayed with them and then they'd be back on. Funny how they must have known when we needed a break.

During one long interlude, when it seemed as though the school took a sharp turn and left us for good, I went to the wheelhouse to check in with Bart.

"Hi, Hon," I said when I reached the top of the steps.

"Hey, there," he said with delight. That always made me smile. "It looks like we lost our school but hopefully I can get us located again."

"It's so weird when they just bail like that all at once. It's like they're on timers, or they agreed that at a precise moment they'd all turn ninety degrees and take off," I mused.

"Ha ha, I know! But they do that sometimes. You see this tight edge right here," he said pointing to the plotter.

"Yah," I replied.

"There's a significant temperature change right along here, making a tight edge that follows all the way over there… like that. All these dark colors underneath should be feed and if I'm right, the fish may have gone in that direction."

"Cool," I said. "How long before we get over there?"

"It shouldn't take too long. Maybe an hour or so. Relax for a bit, because if we land on a nice school it's going get busy again."

"Sounds good," I said. I wished the break would last longer, but I also knew it would give us something to do and get us out of there sooner if we filled the boat.

I slid in past Bart on the bench so I could look out the window and kick back next to him. If things became crazy with fishing, the next time I'd see him would likely be at bedtime, so I wanted to enjoy the moment. He kept watching the sonar.

Bart grabbed his binoculars to look for flocks of birds on the feed we were headed towards. I enjoyed listening to his music—the sound track to *The Big Chill*—as I gazed out the window. When the sun shined and the water was just right, the surface sparkled like shiny diamonds on the water. It was hypnotizing.

Bart stood up to look out the window on the port side, so I left the bench and walked out the back door to look at the water below. I immediately saw a couple of albacore swimming alongside the vessel so I quickly re-entered the wheelhouse to tell Bart.

I started to say, "I see f...," but Bart spoke before I could complete the word "fish."

"We're on a school, Hon! Quick! Get the bowlines!" he shouted.

"I'm on it!" I said and retreated below as fast as I could.

Ding! Ding! Ding! Ding! The bells sounded until all lines were loaded. The guys went from zero to sixty in seconds, leaping from their lawn chairs to run the hydraulics.

"Yes!" Mario shouted. "I knew we'd find them again!"

Marcello smiled in agreement and worked quickly. He pulled fish as fast as he could so that he could return the free line back to the water and catch another. His right hand had already brought the next closest line toward the hydraulic pinch-puller to reel in the next fish, while his left hand freed the previous line. We were in 'em and it happened fast!

I had my boots on in seconds. I shoved my hands into my nipper-wrapped gloves and bolted to the bow, still moving carefully so I would not fall. The bowlines were full and fish were already coming out of the chute from the stern. I leaned over the starboard bow and grabbed the line, secured it to the gripper, made a quick wrap of the mono, and yanked that fish out of the water as the boat listed toward the port side. Just as I reached my hand to unhook him, Bart appeared on the bridge above.

"Good one, Hon. Now go get those on the port side. All the lines are full!"

"I know!" I shouted back. "Let me unhook this guy and get the line back in the water first." I looked up and he had already returned to the wheelhouse.

I was too busy to be annoyed. Maybe he didn't know that I was aware of the bowlines.

I'm on deck and he has a birds-eye-view from up there. He's just doing his job. Oh, good. I'm working hard and not mad yet. This might be fun.

I pulled fish as quick as I ever had before. Because the weather was nice, I was able to move around the deck faster than normal, which helped me stay caught up a little better. Even though the fish bit the moment the jig hit the water, I had to toggle between the port lines and starboard lines to get the fish onboard while they were still alive. Since we decided against removing the fins this trip, eliminating that step made it easier for me to stay caught up.

One day when it was super busy, I stayed on one side so long that when the fish finally let up and I went to the other side of the boat, there was a fish just dragging in the water. It made me laugh, but it's not the ideal situation.

Once the bowlines were under control, I jumped in the pen to transfer the fish that had piled up two layers deep. I kept my knees bent to protect my back and reached in with both hands, one fish per hand, and tossed them swiftly—yet gently—to the open deck near the house to be rinsed. Nose first to slide them (not "huck" them), and careful not to bruise the meat. Repeat.

When the pen was down to a single layer with open space for new fish, I hurried over to where the other fish lay. Their bodies had slowed to almost no flopping at all. I rinsed them and laid them out in rows.

Nice tack!

The sun's rays dried the scales in record time, so I was able to get them in the hold and make room for another batch. I opened the door to the hatch and grabbed the closest fish. Nose first, slight angle, down it went. One, two, three, four…. I counted thirty-eight and closed the hatch.

Thirty-eight, thirty-eight, thirty-eight, I chanted in my head so I wouldn't forget the number as I moved more fish from the pen.

Back and forth I went when the bowlines were loaded. The fish started piling up in the chute again, so I reached in to assist and did a double take at one fish that had something odd on its side. Scratched along his big belly was the word, "Hello!"

I laughed out loud. The guys were having fun even though we were slammed. I kept tossing more fish.

"Holy shit!" I shouted, still smiling from the silliness of the guys. I was sweating and breathing hard by then and it looked like we would be at that pace for a while. Within a half-hour, I had another batch of about thirty fish in the hold, and another twenty or thirty waiting to die so we could get them down below.

Mario and Marcello came around the corner just as I was closing the hatch. Both of them were giggling. "Did you see anything unusual on those fish?" Mario asked.

"As a matter of fact I did. Did you do that, Mario?" I asked, laughing.

He laughed for a few seconds before he could answer. He was clearly proud of his cleverness.

"We thought you could use a laugh up here," he said beaming. Marcello was giggling the whole time.

"Well it worked! Nice job, you guys. That was funny. I had to look twice—like, what is on his side? Oh my goodness, Mario!"

We finished that tack and ended up with ninety-six fish. I took a bathroom break, chugged some water, rinsed off the blood, sweat, and scales from my face, and put on a dry t-shirt. Before I could get back outside, I heard the bells go off again.

The day wrapped up with 812 fish. The days that followed

resulted in anywhere from 600, to our biggest day of nearly 1,100 fish. I lost at least eight pounds in that ten-day stretch and felt strong, very tired, and very sore.

We had a good long streak of fishing and the boat was filling up. We were not done yet but everyone felt that we had a chance to leave the grounds with a full load by the time the weather turned too nasty to fish. The days were getting shorter as the summer came to an end. That gave us a little more time to recover since albacore are sight feeders and rarely eat at night.

September 22 arrived. It was our one-year anniversary.

When I said, "I do," I never imagined in my wildest dreams that I'd be out here now.

I had developed "claw hand" from squeezing mono for so many hours every day during those past few weeks. The last run was so intense, it was difficult to recover before we hit it hard again. I was unable to open my hands when I woke in the morning, so I pried my fingers open and stretched them against the sink in the head.

Aaaahhhh that felt good.

Just like the year before, I could not hang onto my toothbrush since the tendons in my fingers and thumbs were so fatigued. My hands just would not cooperate. I weaved my toothbrush in between my fingers, and took a couple swipes until my arm wouldn't stay up any longer.

Wow. How do people live out here and do this all the time?

I completed my morning routine and noticed I hadn't heard bells in a while. I went upstairs to greet Bart with a kiss and wish him a happy anniversary and then the fish were biting again. Down the steps I went, out the back door, and into my boots.

Marcello was either in the hold or on the bow so I took my spot at his station. When the fish reached the vessel, I switched off the hydraulics to retrieve the fish but I struggled with my wrap. My hands weren't working. I pushed through it and kept trying until I got that fish onboard. My forearms were inflamed, which caused me to drop the fish and miss the landing table completely.

"Fuck!" I blurted out.

Bart appeared from nowhere and said, "What's going on, Hon?"

"I don't know! My hands can barely grip this mono and all of a sudden I'm so weak I can't work my arms," I replied, almost in tears with frustration.

"It's okay, Hon, we're just scratching right now. Why don't you take the day off?"

"Are you kidding? That doesn't seem fair. But I'm not much good at the moment. Maybe I'll take some Ibuprofen and rest a bit, then I can help again later."

"Or you could take a day off," he said, beaming at me.

"Thanks, Hon. I love you," I said.

"Love you, too," he said with gusto.

I cleaned myself up and spent the next couple of hours stretching my hands and arms to loosen them. The fishing lightened up quite a bit that day and that helped reduce my level of guilt.

For our anniversary dinner, I made Massaman curry—a new favorite for all of us. The seas were still pretty calm, so I put the candle on the table to make our evening a little more special. We had a bottle of Duck Pond merlot I had been saving, which went really well with the Thai curry.

I even decided to put on a dress and makeup. Bart was thrilled to see me in a dress. He was very flirty and acted as if he'd never seen a girl before. It totally cracked me up.

As if Bart were picking me up for a date, he held out his hand pretending he was presenting something to me in his fist. I smiled wide and reached out to accept the imaginary gift. Bart smiled and said, "If we had a florist out here, this would be a bouquet of flowers."

"I thought that's what it was—thank you—they're beautiful," I said. I loved the gesture and pictured a vase with lilies on the table.

We ate dinner as a family and although I have always loved dresses and being feminine, it felt a little strange since we were still fishing. That may have been the first time in my life I felt awkward when looking nice.

A couple bells went off right after dinner and my instinct was to help even though the guys usually manned the stern unless it got busy and the bow needed attention. Bart told me it was okay, that I shouldn't get my dress dirty.

Funny. I managed to become dirty pulling a single fish and yet Kami had told me that she never got dirty, no matter how many fish she pulled. Thinking of me pulling fish in a dress brought up a memory from fifteen years earlier.

* * *

I showed up at my brother's house for a BBQ in the summertime wearing a dress. He was behind schedule and still cleaning the backyard, so I picked up his chainsaw sitting on the back step and walked over to him.

"You want to put this in the shed, don't you?" I asked, wanting to help before the other guests arrived.

"Yes, thank you," he said laughing. "Watching you walk across the yard in a dress, carrying a chainsaw… that's cool."

* * *

The guys picked away at the few fish we caught in the evening bite and I enjoyed my time off. I sat with Bart in the wheelhouse, enjoyed the sunset, his company, and his love. We didn't dine in a fancy restaurant or go dancing on our anniversary, but we had a wonderful day together. I made the right choice marrying that magnificent man.

Mario balancing on the bow deck; big swell at our stern

Heartbreak

Love is something
That never really leaves
Only goes through withdrawal
Sometimes it doesn't
Come back out
So what
So what?

~ Bart Mathews

Chapter 28:
Another Big Blow

IN JANUARY OF 2007, THE SMALL COMMISSION I had been receiving from my work as a recruiter in a new division of the e-learning company was not enough to pay the bills, let alone eat. So I decided to apply for every full-time position available in the county because remote recruiting opportunities were scarce back then.

Although the pay was incredibly low, the role of Appraiser with the San Juan County Assessor's office looked challenging, interesting, and it came with a steady paycheck and full benefits. I couldn't believe my good fortune when I was chosen for the position and I jumped in with both feet to learn my new trade.

By June 21, I had absorbed a lot about appraising property and was cramming new information into my brain every day. The other members on my team were working outside that day and it was my turn to work in the office. I had just exited the ladies room and started walking back down the hall to my desk when a short, manly-looking woman with long gray hair approached me.

"Theresa Mathews?" she inquired with a big friendly grin on her face.

"Yes?" I replied, not remembering her name although I recognized her from being on the island.

"You've just been served," she said proudly with a sense of defeat while she shoved a summons and complaint into my hands. She walked away, almost skipping, as if she thought I had done something wrong and deserved to be punished.

Bart's sister and her husband had filed a lawsuit against me. I felt the physical punch in my gut as I stood there stunned.

Oh My God — will I ever be able to rebuild my life?

Just three months prior, I had been denied my Petition for Family Allowance by the court. That would have allowed a small amount of the equity in my home to be protected from creditors' claims. The only creditors who had filed a claim, however, were Mary and Kent. That petition had been my only hope for not losing the roof over my head.

But Mary had filed a Declaration in Opposition to my petition with the Superior Court. She listed her reasons why I should not be granted that petition. She felt I should be sent back to the city to start over. Her words were full of inaccuracies, and many things she said were cruel and personally insulting. She wrote that Bart remodeled *his* house long before we were married. She did not mention that I had cashed out my 401K and invested every penny I had to work on that project with him. He and I planned the details together. We did the physical labor together, and co-financed our future home. We had put the finishing details on hold in order to move into the house just one week before we were married there.

Our finances were none of her business, but she made statements about them anyway, without knowing a single detail of our personal situation. From my point of view, she made me sound as if I were nothing more than a gold-digging flavor of the week.

Mary neglected to include the fact that during the eight years we were together before Bart's death, she continuously acknowledged how lucky we were to have such a solid bond and magical love.

She'd often said, "Many people go their whole lives — even spending fifty years together as husband and wife — without experiencing such a gift. You two are so fortunate to have that special thing." She always told me how happy she was for her brother and that she couldn't have handpicked a more perfect partner for him to share his life with.

Those things were left out of her document.

Mary went on to write that we didn't have kids, that we had both been married before, and that we had not been married for very long before his death. She mentioned that I was young and employable and therefore I should be sent packing. Mary implied that somehow she and her husband were more deserving of my 768-square-foot home than I was. Mary and Kent had each other, a double-income, and a multi-million dollar house, but it wasn't enough.

One important detail I need to mention is that only one month after Bart died, I offered to pay them half the amount of money we had borrowed to refurbish the boat. I reminded her that there was only one of me left and I didn't know how I would come up with the rest of the money. But if they could work with me, I would figure it out. She flat-out refused and told me I had to pay the entire debt.

The way I saw it, my only mistake in the financial arrangement was that I trusted Bart, his sister, her husband, and our attorney to work out the logistics. I had no idea that a "what if" clause was not included in the loan. None of them thought it was important or necessary to have me present during the negotiation process or when working out the details. I knew it was difficult on Bart's pride to ask for so much money, so I didn't press the issue. Yet Mary and Kent felt that there was no way I could pay them back except by Bart catching fish on the vessel, and that I was a hundred percent responsible for the loss. Even though I was only one-quarter of the agreement and they represented half the risk.

During the next four months, I worked with my attorneys (yes, plural) to figure out how to save my home and pay back what I was responsible for, which was unclear at that point. The rules seemed to change weekly, leaving me in a state of panic and fear, but I focused on learning my new job and soldiered on.

    I received a call from my main attorney stating that things were looking good and I would be fine. The next week she called to say there were more wrinkles in my case due to all the complications with the boat, debt, and probate, and that the in-laws were fighting me hard. Mary and Kent wanted my house, and it appeared as if they would do all they could to make sure I ended up with nothing.

    The amount of the standard Homestead Allowance within the court system increased during our legal process, which provided me with an opportunity to try again. By that point, I had incurred tens of thousands of dollars in legal fees.

    The thought I absolutely could not fathom was leaving my home, my friends, my support system, and my mom. After living in Spokane for forty years, my mom had moved to the island. She literally saved my life by helping me through the overwhelming grief.

    I reminded the in-laws' attorney that I had tried to negotiate a payment plan with Mary early on, but she had refused. After all the time they spent fighting me and the financial burden I incurred in the process, there was even less money available than what I had initially offered. That argument was hard to deny. We settled out of court and I refinanced my house to pay them off. We haven't spoken since.

Woman

Oh, I want to understand
Oh, I wish that she finds her happiness
Oh, I have traveled many roads
Oh, I have met many people
And I will meet many more
But never another like her
She has a smile like summer
She is soft as light in the morning
And as pretty as a new spring day
Oh, I've known no one else like her.

~ Bart Mathews

Chapter 29:
The Hyena Memorial

THE LOCAL MEMORIAL FOR BART TOOK PLACE eight days after he died. Most of the fishermen were unable to attend since they were finishing up the season. Because of their absence, Kymberly (Crocket's wife—both of whom were there for Sue when Jack died) and Sue worked together to plan Bart's "Hyena Memorial" in November when the guys would be home. With Jack's death just three weeks before the event, the wake became a double memorial.

Uncle Halibut was present for Bart's service in August when he had picked up the boat to finish the season before I returned it to its legal owner and walked away. Jack (Ultimate) was a welcomed partner at sea who showed my uncle the ropes. Jack helped keep him located, and he provided a friendly voice for Uncle Halibut's three weeks on the ocean. Jack made all the difference in the world to Uncle Halibut and, as you can imagine, the shock of Jack's death was tough news to swallow. My uncle came back for the wake in November to honor his new friend, bid final farewell to Bart, and put closure to a series of tragic events.

Mom had barely pulled in the driveway on Friday afternoon when my brother Bryan hopped out of the car, ran to me and gave me a big bear hug. "Hi, Sister," he said, squeezing me tight.

"Hey, Brother. How was the drive?"

"Good. How are you?"

"Okay. Thanks so much for coming. I couldn't do this without you guys."

"I know," he said. "We wouldn't miss it. You've gotta see the albacore. It turned out super cool—you're gonna love it!"

"I can't wait!" I said as we walked toward the back of Mom's white Subaru Outback.

"Hi, Mom," I said as she got out of the car.

"Hi, Precious Love," she said as we embraced. "How ya doin', Honey?"

"Hangin' in there. Really glad you're here."

"Me, too," she said. "The fish turned out beautiful. Check it out!"

We continued the few steps to the hatch where Bryan proudly unveiled the steel replica. Bryan is a natural artist, and a machinist and welder by trade. He paid tribute to Bart by creating a life-sized albacore out of solid steel and a bracket to mount it underneath the bronze plaque I had made to honor Bart. I had given him a few pictures of albacore from my fishing days along with a whole fish we had in the freezer. We always kept a few peanuts (small tuna) for our own consumption.

The real fish turned out to be a perfect template for him to create a statue that represented Bart's work and his last days on earth.

The general manager of Roche Harbor Resort graciously allowed me to place those items on the property at the resort. Bart had been the marina's Harbor Master many years prior and he was a valued member of the community, so having a place to visit him was important to me and I was thankful to have been granted such a request.

"Oh my God," I said, admiring how amazing the albacore looked. "That looks like it might swim away. Nice job, Brother.

Thank you so much for doing this. Wow. That is super cool."

"I know, huh," he said proudly. "It turned out really good. I think his eye could be a little bigger, but by the time I noticed that, I'd finished the rest, so I didn't want to mess it up. Check out his dorsal fin though. It's exactly like the real thing."

"I think it's perfect! I wouldn't change a thing," I told him.

We brought their luggage inside, made sure everyone had a beverage, and gathered around the teak table and chairs on my back deck. Within an hour, Bryan and I had started to prepare dinner. He pulled out the marinated chicken breasts for the BBQ. I chopped vegetables to put on the grill and made a salad. Bryan prepared the sweet potatoes with garlic, butter, and parmesan cheese. We enjoyed our feast and spent the rest of the evening figuring out how to mount the steel albacore before the big event the next day.

Many of The Hyenas arrived at the resort later that evening—most of them took the last two boats of the day to the island.

Uncle Halibut was on the boat that departed Anacortes at 9:35 the next morning, which put him in Roche just after 11 a.m. He went straight over to my neighbor's place across the street to get settled in their guesthouse and say hello, then walked over to my house.

Bryan and Cal—the treasured family friend who lived down the road and the first person who came to my side when I learned of Bart's death—had already scoped out the location where the statue would go and had gathered all the materials needed to mount it. They had two five-gallon plastic buckets, several bags of concrete, three shovels, a rake, and a couple of other items they thought they might need. Cal's truck was loaded with the tools when Uncle Halibut arrived.

"Hey, Bryan… how are you?"

"Hi, Uncle Harold!" Bryan replied with excitement. "I'm good. How are you?"

"Doing fine, thank you."

"I'm really glad you're here."

"I wouldn't miss it. It's just unbelievable. I was just here, but losing Jack... wow. I hope this is it."

"I know. Me too. I never met Jack but I can tell I would've loved the man."

"Well, he sure made a difference for me out there. He was a great guy."

"I've got the albacore in the back of the truck. You can see what it looks like, but you'll get a better view once it's out of there," Bryan said, opening the canopy so he could get a better view. "I dug the hole this morning so we're headed down now to mount it. Wanna come?"

"Wow, that's really neat," Harold said. "I'd love to come help, but I'll walk down if you don't mind. The cab looks pretty small for all three of us."

"Sounds good. I think Mom and Sister are coming too if you want to ride with them."

"Okay. I might do that. I'll be there in a bit either way."

It was a chilly morning with a marine layer that was taking a while to burn off, so we decided to drive down the hill instead of taking the ten-minute walk. I called Wes to invite him to come watch, or help if the guys needed a hand. He was walking out of the hotel just as I parked the car.

"Hi, Wes!" I said wrapping my arms around my friend's neck.

"Hey, T," he said returning the embrace. "How are ya?"

"Doin' okay, thanks. How are you?"

"I'm doin' okay, thanks."

"Hi, Bonnie," Wes said, turning to hug Mom.

"Hi, Wes. It's good to see you."

"Good to see you, too. Wish it was under different circumstances, but this should be a fun party. The guys would appreciate it."

"I'm sure they would," Mom agreed.

I introduced Wes to my uncle and we walked toward the site where Bryan and Cal were almost done mixing the concrete. I made the introductions and Wes marveled at the statue Bryan had made. He grabbed a shovel. Within a short time, the concrete was poured, and the statue mounted and secured. Cal put up a sign to alert people of the wet concrete, which would not take long to set since the hole it was poured into was shallow.

Some people looped up with Kymberly to help prepare for the memorial, others used the time to explore the island and do some sight-seeing. Mom and I were back at the house making sure final details were tended to. Our Hyena friends called throughout the day to let me know they had arrived and were looking forward to seeing us later that afternoon.

As I busied myself with last minute details, I tried to put myself in the mood for another memorial. Aside from the last two Hyena gatherings—when we lost Bart and when we lost Jack—every time I'd met up with that group we were either celebrating something or just having a wonderful time being together.

I felt numb—as if someone else had control of my body as I went through the motions. The constant loss was taking its toll, so I hoped that night's event would bring closure. But that also meant I would never see many of those people ever again.

I wanted to be strong for Sue, but my loss wasn't very far ahead of hers. Wes was our pillar of strength and hadn't asked for support from us when he'd lost his wife Pam earlier that year, so for some reason it didn't register with me how badly he was hurting.

He was his normal flirty self, which brought an enormous amount of comfort and joy at a time when I needed it.

Meanwhile, Mom kept saying, "I need to check my messages from home," as if there was something critical happening that she needed to tend to immediately.

"You should do that now, Mom. It's obviously important to you, so please take care of that. Go in my room and close the door so there aren't any distractions, okay?"

"You're right. I'll do it now. Then I'll relax and help you," she agreed.

"I'm good. Just take care of whatever you need to."

When Mom came out of the room several minutes later she was poker-faced, but had a happier energy, which was nice to see.

"Everything okay?" I asked.

"Yes, everything is great. Thanks, Honey. I just had to clear up some things from home and I got the answers I needed. I'll tell you about it later. Let's focus on today right now—there's a lot going on and it's going to be emotional once we're all together. How are you holding up?"

"I'm okay, but I feel like I'm having an out-of-body experience. And yet, I've been dealing with Bart's death long enough that it's very real, too. I'm looking forward to seeing everyone. But honestly, I'll be glad when this is over."

"I'm sure you will be. What can I do to help?"

"You're doing it, Mom. Thank you."

The time finally came to go to the resort for the event. There were about thirty of us, which I thought was a good turnout. A couple of people came down from Canada, Uncle Halibut came from Montana, Mom brought Bryan over from Spokane, and the rest of the Hyenas were from scattered locations down the coast from Washington State to San Diego, California. The reason for the gathering was heartbreaking, but the group had always been full of life, told great stories, and felt genuine gratitude for each other.

We gathered at one end of the room to officiate the memorial. Bart's brother welcomed everyone and shared some wonderful details about Bart and what the Hyenas meant to him. Wes had been private about his loss when Pam died, but he was finally ready to talk about all the losses our Hyena family had experienced. He honored Bart, Jack, his beloved wife, and Stephano (aka Sleepy aka Pops), who had died the year before Pam. His words were tender, bittersweet, and—true to Wes' style—punctuated with humor. Something we all welcomed.

Sue has always been a fantastic storyteller and she didn't let us down that evening even though it had been only a couple weeks since her husband's death. We laughed through her account of days at sea with Jack, and shed tears as she shared a piece of their love story. Her youngest daughter, Megan, read the poem she wrote on the day her dad died. There wasn't a dry eye in the place.

At that point, still in my own grief, I wasn't able to put together anything creative. I just couldn't do it. I told everyone that very thing, thanked them for coming, and expressed my enormous gratitude for their generosity and continuous love and support throughout the colossal loss. I suggested we get the party started—Hyena style. We all raised our glasses to salute our departed, and then proceeded to drink, eat, and let the fishing stories fly around the room.

The party eventually moved to one of the condos at the resort where Sue and the girls were staying. We carried the night into early morning hours, but then finally crashed. Most of us were stirring and ready to take our fuzzy heads out for some fresh air, breakfast, and Bloody Marys by 10 a.m.

I took flowers from the memorial to Bart's plaque and placed them next to a few bouquets that had already been placed there by the Boogers and the Crocket families. We ate at the Lime Kiln, a little restaurant at the end of the pier, and congregated back at Sue's condo to bid farewell to those who had to catch a ferry off the island. I knew it was the last time I would see many of them, which made the day weigh heavy on my heart.

The next day, after everyone had gone back to their homes, I returned to mine. I did my best to figure things out and move through the day. Mom called to ask how I would feel if she moved to Friday Harbor.

"What? Are you kidding! What's going on? How soon can you get here?" I gasped.

"Remember when I had to go in your room and check my messages?" she replied.

"Yes, of course. You seemed obsessed with that. What happened?"

"Well, you know I've been wanting to get over to the west side of the Cascade mountains for a couple years now. I was following up on a couple of interviews I'd had, and applications I'd put in for jobs over there. I had a message to call back and when I reached the manager, he asked why I would want to move to Bellingham after living in Spokane for forty years. When I told him my daughter lived in Friday Harbor, he became super excited and asked if I'd want to move there, because he had an opening on the island. I accepted, Honey, and I will be moving over there on December 1. Can you help me find a place to live?"

"Yes, of course I can," I said. I helped Mom settle into a wonderful little cabin on the water at the southern end of the island. That house became her sanctuary, and she was mine. I have always been a survivor. A strong woman who others think of as a pillar of strength. But I couldn't have done it without my mom.

When Bart died, I was broken to the core. I kept having to fight to keep my property, and fight against myself to even get up in the morning. Sometimes I rallied, other times I fell back into a bottomless pit. Since Bart couldn't come home, I begged him to come get me. There was a moment when I literally felt myself dying. Like I had the power to give up and let myself go. Just drift away and be with Bart forever. Mom was with me when it happened and I saw the fear in her face.

"Don't let your light go out, Baby," she pleaded. "Your light shines so bright, Honey. Please don't let your light go out."

I felt the power overcome me. I knew I could just let myself die simply by willing it. I wanted to give in, throw in the towel on this life, and let myself die of a broken heart. I wanted to be with Bart so desperately and knew I could just let it happen by wanting it so badly. A voice deep down inside me told the truth.

I'm a survivor and I will get through this. If I die, my parents will never recover. I can't do that to them. I must get through this.

That voice was heard by my soul and I found the strength to soldier on. I can't help but believe that Bart had something to do with it. My sweet man, always looking out for me.

Bart's memorial at Roche Harbor

Hyena memorial left to right: Jaime, Mikey, Megan, and Wes

Hyena memorial group at Roche Harbor

Rants, Rhymes, and Rambles

October 23 started out like any day
I woke up and did my hair in exactly the same way
I left my house for school at exactly 7:38
Little did I know my whole world was about to change
It was 5th period when my teacher came up to me
And a blinding light forbid me to see the pain I didn't want to see
My mom told me that a phone call had confirmed her deepest fears
And the power of the sun would not have been able to dry our tears
I can't believe this could happen to our family or any other
I am absorbed in the pain behind the eyes of my mother
And although her lip is quivering, I can tell she is trying to be strong
And there is nothing right to say to her now that everything feels so wrong
And although I am in her arms, I feel I am completely alone
And the sun and the moon and the stars for the last time have shone
And my life is like the wind, blowing a simple feather
And the feather is my emotions, which have no control over the weather
And the weather is other people's words and actions
And the wind continues to blow without any precautions
And my point is that you should not let time with loved ones go by
Because if your family goes unnoticed you won't have time to say goodbye
And once you have bitten the apple, and felt their love you can't go back
And trying to live without them is more painful than a heart attack
So don't be afraid to love, and be loved and to feel
And do not linger on the fact that you don't always get the fairest deal

Always laugh and dance and sing your favorite songs
Because you won't know how precious something is until it's gone
And thank your family for the lessons they allow you to learn
And do not take for granted the respect that you have earned
And don't let the sun set before resolving your fights
And when you open your eyes, take time to enjoy the sights
And instead of living with regret, cherish life like a piece of art
And like my parents, love your friends and family until death do you part
And although sometimes you don't feel like you will be alright
You MUST wake up each day, and try with all your might
And as I write this it's getting late, the clock says 4:47
And for the first time in a long time, I think I believe in heaven.

~ *Megan Slater*

Chapter 30:
Dead in the Water

IT WAS HALLOWEEN 2002. We had been out for ninety-four days in a row, 174 total days for the season. The price was $2,900 a ton when we made the decision to go fishing nearly eight months earlier. After we'd gone out, the price declined ever further each month. Our payout ended up being less than half of what we expected for our first load in July, and even though the price had come up a little since then, the bottom line would make a significant difference in how we lived for the next six months.

Our buyer agreed to pay us $100 more per ton than what the other coastal buyers were paying, as long as we arrived in Bellingham, Washington, by November 3. If we missed that deadline, we would lose approximately $9,000.

We needed 150 fish to top off the boat, and every fish counted. We had to leave the grounds and cross the line (referring to 200 miles from U.S. soil) no later than 7:30 p.m. in order to stay on course. By 1:30 p.m., we were only two miles away from the 200-mile line when the last fish that could fit on board was neatly tucked in just under the lid to the combing of the fish hold.

We did it. We actually filled the boat!

From the bridge deck, we could hear Bart yell, "YAH! Let's pull the gear and go home!"

Excitement and satisfaction filled the air. The guys were far more stoic than I. Mario gave us his boyish smirk and whistled as he walked to his station on the stern. His little butt wiggled when he waddled down the deck. Marcelo's toothy grin and bright eyes lit up his face as he followed close behind Mario. I wanted to jump up and down and scream and kiss and hug all of them!

One hundred and seventy-four days with those men told me the celebration would be lost on them. I slipped into one of my daydreams as I envisioned land and how it would feel under my feet.

Only three days left. The sun is shining. The midnight blue waters are calm, with not enough chop to even notice. It's the end of this wild adventure and now I can enjoy it. Now that it's over and my real life is in sight, I can reflect on all I've experienced out here and appreciate it.

I went up to the wheelhouse where Bart and I embraced and congratulated each other with zest.

"Nice job, Honey," I said, smacking him on the ass. "The gods do shine on this boat and all who are lucky enough to be aboard her."

He grabbed me quickly, forcing a squeal from my lips. He squeezed me tight and agreed with me.

"Mmmm-hmmm," came from his mouth as he pressed it to mine.

The rest of the day felt more like a cruise… a nice boat ride… allowing us to soak up the deliciousness of a smooth sail on a sparkling ocean that provided the means to sustain four families.

People who want to sail around the world—or at least buy a sailboat and cruise the waters for months on end—must be lured by the same peacefulness I was experiencing at that moment. Surely that is the force enticing sailors to sea. For me, those amazing moments come and go, but the feeling had returned on that afternoon, and I embraced it.

In anticipation of filling the boat, I had taken out the remaining four filet mignon from the chest freezer on the aft deck. I barbequed the meat to a perfect medium-rare, and served it with string beans and fettuccini with Alfredo sauce. We even had a bottle of Cabernet to complete our celebratory meal. Life was good.

My watch had come and gone in no time. I had been in bed about twenty minutes when Mario was at our stateroom.

"Bart? Hey, Bart! The engine stopped!" Mario yelled through our stateroom curtain.

"What? What happened?" Bart yelled back in a panic. He was still half-asleep as he bolted out of bed and threw on his clothes.

"We are dead in the water. The low oil pressure alarm went off just before the engine stopped," Mario said as he followed Bart to the engine room.

"Oh, shit," was all I heard out of Bart's mouth as they both ran down the narrow stairs.

I sat up in disbelief. *How could this be? With all the things that could go wrong out here. Our MAIN ENGINE? God help us.*

Bart checked the pressure gauges and the fluids. The switches appeared to be in the right position, so why did the engine freeze? He made a few adjustments, tightened connections, and he cranked it. Bart and the guys stood by helplessly as they heard clunking sounds from the engine parts being sucked through the main when it died for the last time.

I got dressed and was sitting on the bench in the wheelhouse when Bart came up the steps. His expression told me it was very serious and he might not have the magic touch this time.

Very calmly he said, "We're not going anywhere for a while. I just heard the engine suck in parts and it's completely locked up."

"Oh shit, Honey," I said as my heart sank to my toes, missing a few beats on the way down. I knew better than to allow fear into my psyche. Complacent is one of the worst things you can be out there. That's when people make stupid mistakes. But letting fear take over? That could paralyze you—or worse yet, make you panic. Then you definitely end up being more of a liability than an asset.

"What do you want me to do?" I asked.

"Nothing right now. Thanks. I'm gonna call Miguel."

When Miguel answered, Bart said cheerfully, "Hey, there. What's goin' on, man?"

"We're havin' a party. There's a dozen little nine-year-old girls runnin' around here in costumes. They're so cute, Bart. You should see J.D. She's dressed as Pocahontas. I'm a pirate and Aleelat is a maiden."

"All right! That sounds like fun. Wish we were there. Do you have a stiff cocktail in your hand?"

"Of course, Bart. What is it?"

"The main died. We're dead in the water."

"Oh," Miguel said.

After Bart explained the situation to Miguel, they decided to rig the main to run on five cylinders instead of six. That didn't work. I sat in the wheelhouse in case Miguel called back with a fabulous plan that would get us moving again. Meanwhile the guys worked in the engine room. They decided to hook up the "get home" system, a backup unit that runs on hydraulics. All fingers and toes were crossed.

Bart sat down with a sigh and leaned his head into mine. The smell of morning mouth from both of us, and diesel on his clothes and hands permeated the air.

"I don't know what else to do," he said with a defeated tone. "We're not going to make the deadline for that price now. The guys are tired and we've tried everything. I give up. I need you."

"Oh, Honey, I'm so sorry. What can I do to help?" I asked Bart again as I looked at his weary face.

"Nothing, you're doing it. Just keep being supportive. I don't know what to do," he said as he buried his face in my chest and let me comfort him. He looked like he would cry.

"I'm so proud of you," I said. "You are being such a trooper. We'll get out of here, darlin'. I'm not worried in the least. Look how far you've gotten us already—and with a full load of fish! You are my hero."

"Thank you," he said. "I love you."

"I know, Babe," I said.

I wrapped my arms around him and placed my hand gently on his cheek. "We're gonna be okay. Miguel is going to call back as soon as he has a solution. He'll find someone to come tow us home if the get-home doesn't work. And the fish are already sold, so they have to honor the price based on these circumstances. Don't worry. I'm hungry. I don't think anyone is going back to bed anytime soon so I'm going to make a pizza."

"Oh, that'd be great, Hon," he said. "I'm so glad you're here."

"Me, too," I replied, and meant it.

Captain Bart was still running the show, but he took his captain-hat off and my sweet husband stepped in. It was my turn to be the pillar of strength and keep the positive attitude alive. I fell in love all over again at that exact moment. I was honored that Bart actually needed me to help him during the crisis—even if it was only for moral support.

By then it was 2:30 in the morning. The guys continued to work in the engine room while I made a couple of pizzas. We sat in disbelief as we ate. Bart talked with the guys about possible solutions. It was decided that the "get home" system was the only hope we had. Once we were underway, I went back to bed.

My poor husband. What's next?

When I got up mid-morning, we had been underway for a few

hours. The sea was flat calm and we were only traveling at 1.5 knots. There was a low coming in, just days behind us, and the currents could change at any moment. It seemed likely we would be pushed back out to sea and get stuck in the storm that was on its way. Even if the weather stayed good, at that rate it would have taken us two weeks to arrive in Bellingham. Bart was exhausted, but didn't want to give up his watch until he heard from Miguel.

"We need to get towed in and Miguel is checking on it," he told me. "He has to check with the insurance company and the nearest Coast Guard station to see if we qualify for a free tow. We still might make it."

Since our lives were not in danger, the Coast Guard would not tow us. Miguel found a local tug company that had a boat not too far from our location and could be there within a few hours to bring us home. The mood on *Maverick* was once again full of excitement and happiness because we were almost there—and because we had a full load. Bart went down below to get some rest while I took over. The sun was shining, the sky was blue, there were diamonds on the water.

Gorgeous! *I will miss this part.*

The tug arrived on November 2. The first attempt to secure a towline was unsuccessful. The tug's captain earned his nickname immediately—"Cowboy Bob." He rammed us twice before getting the line on and then he took off with such force that he yanked the cleat right off our starboard bow like it was made of cheap plastic.

"STOP!" Bart hollered. He threw his hand up in the air to signal his command. "NOW GO SLOW," he demanded. "That's it. STOP THERE."

Cowboy Bob didn't seem to have a clue what he was doing and Bart didn't want him to break our boat any more than he had already. The guys rigged the towline by going through the hawse pipe (the hole in the hull through which the anchor rode passes). The 100-feet of thirteen-inch cable put so much pressure on the boat that we were listing hard to one side and the bulwarks were getting bent out of shape.

Bart stopped us again to re-rig the line. That's when we learned that Cowboy Bob had been only First Mate before, and he'd been on that tug for only five days. He had never brought a boat in from offshore.

Great.

Bart was tempted to have me run the *Maverick* so he could show the guy how to run his boat. Cowboy Bob was panicked by that point and suggested that the tow wouldn't work and he would leave the area. That's when Bart totally took control and asked the captain to follow his instructions very carefully. The weather was still pretty calm and we would be successful only if the guy would slow down. He agreed.

To help support the bulwarks, the guys wrapped the cable around the anchor spool and placed fire hose inside the inner tube of the hawse pipe to prevent chaffing. Unfortunately, the cable burned right through the hose.

Bart decided to go through the bow pull and around the anchor spool, but the anchor would have to be removed first. Fog was setting in and it was almost dark by then. It started to rain and the temperature was dropping so they had to act fast.

I had a birds-eye view from the wheelhouse window where I watched the hydraulic lines pop and spray oil all over the deck and men. The anchor winch was no good, so they had to use the come-along to bring the anchor around to the side of the vessel and onto the deck. They pulled our cable through the bow pull and attached it to the tug's towlines.

Third time's a charm! It was nearly twelve hours from the time the tug first arrived, but we were finally underway and able to get ahead of the storm that was nipping at our heels. We arrived in Bellingham the evening of November 4. Miguel greeted us with whiskey, wine, flowers, and a cake. We celebrated many accomplishments that night. Mostly, we knew how lucky we were to have survived without injury, damage to the boat, or worse. That *knowing* didn't need to be spelled out. You could feel it. And you could see it on everyone's faces.

Mario, me, Marcelo, fall 2002

Restlessness

The smell, the fragrance, the energy
Does it hover?
Is it close enough to touch?
How long can it be resisted?
As long as a leaf can fall
As long as frost can melt
When the cold morning sun hits
As fast as a cloud of breath can disappear
There are sounds that tell about it
A far away train at night
A coyote talking to the moon
Bare branches rubbing against each other
The old college bell in the evening
Irresistible
To move, to travel, to be on the lam
To explore the crispness
To run with the wind
The fall, the autumn, the restlessness

~ Bart Mathews

Chapter 31: Wes (aka Norton)

WES REMINDED ME OF A CROSS BETWEEN Sam Elliot and Richard Dreyfus. He stands five-foot-nine, has medium-fair skin, thick gray hair that he keeps short around his neck and ears, a neatly-trimmed mustache above smiling lips, and wears wire-rimmed glasses that frame hazel eyes. One can always rely on his quick wit, and easy-going energy. His gentle voice is comforting and friendly, with a deep tone I find sexy and mysterious—as if he's got something up his sleeve and always ready for adventure.

He grew up in New Jersey with loving parents and an older brother who left the house when Wes was a boy. As a free spirit who danced to the beat of his own drum, Wes followed his heart and headed west when it was time to make grown-up decisions about what to do with his life. He ended up a commercial fisherman out of Newport, Oregon, where he happened to drop anchor.

Wes became instant friends with Bart when they met in port during a turnaround in 1973. The men fished together a few years later on Wes' boat, the *Sea Breeze II*, which was a sweet vessel that offered plenty of options to earn a living. Depending on the season and the price fish buyers were paying, Wes would rig his boat to catch shrimp, crab, bottom fish, or albacore.

In the summer of 1981, albacore was said to have moved closer to the coastline, so the guys went jigging. During a break in the action one day when the ocean was glassy slick, the fish nowhere to be found, and the other boats in the fleet had moved out of sight in search of larger schools, the *Sea Breeze II* trolled slowly across its private pool of salt water. With nothing more than a slight, gradual list, conditions were calm and hypnotic. It was so mellow, the guys were bored. In the wheelhouse, Wes kept his eye out for schools to work on and fought off the intense distraction of a toothache.

"Hey, man, how ya doin'?" Bart asked as he stepped into the wheelhouse.

"This toothache is killing me," Wes replied, grabbing the side of his jaw.

"I may have a remedy for that. Come outside for a minute, I want to show you something."

"Yah, okay," Wes agreed and followed Bart to the back deck.

"Check it out, man," Bart said, pointing to his invention.

He had made a swing by taking an old tractor tire, which is typically used as a bumper when fastened to the side of a commercial dock. He had tied twenty feet of half-inch rope around it, then secured the line to a rung on the mast.

"Ha ha, cool," Wes said in admiration of their new toy.

"Go ahead, man, give it a try."

"Sure—looks like fun." Wes climbed a few steps up the steel ladder to the mast.

Bart reached up and grabbed hold of the tire after Wes was sitting in the center of the swing. "Ready?"

"Ready," Wes replied, tightened his grip on the rope, and leaned his body in towards the tire.

Bart pulled back and gave Wes a strong push, just as the ocean rolled under the vessel and tipped it slightly to its port side. That sent Wes sailing out across the deep blue ocean at what he said felt like 200 miles per hour. He soared over the outriggers, giving him a birds-eye view of the bright rubber skirts that covered the steel jigs in the water below.

"Whoa! Holy shiiiiiiiiiit!" he screamed as the boat gently rolled back the other way, sending him flying toward the vessel.

Bart watched in disbelief, then grabbed his sides as he doubled over in hysterical laughter.

Wes's feet grazed the tops of the blue barrels on the deck. He moved so fast, he didn't have time to plan his exit. The boat reached the top of that gradual ripple and tipped port side again, sending Wes back over the ocean at the speed of sound. His eyes widened, his grip tightened, and his mouth opened to scream, but he was moving so fast no one heard him.

This went on a half a dozen times before the innocent bend in the water's surface stabilized, allowing the momentum to cease. Still laughing, but trying to control himself, Bart helped Wes out of the tire.

"What the fuck, Bart? That scared the shit of me!" Wes said once he was back onboard.

"Sorry, man, I had no idea it would do that. Bet ya forgot about that toothache though."

"Well, that's true. Asshole." They both laughed and Bart untied the rope and removed the tire for good.

Wes had experienced dozens of adventures throughout his fishing career—both exciting and frightening. Many of those trips were shared with his wife, Pam, who also had a love for the sea. He became a Hyena (nicknamed Norton) in the late 1980s after he sold the *Sea Breeze II*.

In the spring of 2005, the North Pacific season had just begun and Wes was running the *Maverick* that year. Mikey (G-man aka Guitar Man) was running the *Wendy Seaa*, Jack (Ultimate) still ran the *Dalena*, and Steve (aka Stephano, Pops, or Sleepy) was running the *America*. Stephano had been ill that year, but downplayed the severity of his condition and headed out for another season as if it were like any other. About sixty hours into the journey, he lay down in his bunk, began spitting up blood and gasping for breath.

Jack placed calls to several on-shore doctors. They arranged to have three Navy Seals bring medical gear and plasma to Stephano by parachuting out of a C-130 overhead. But Stephano died in his bunk the night before the planned jump. The boat was 400 miles out of Honolulu, Hawaii.

As U.S. captains on the nearest vessels, Wes and Mikey ran their boats over to the *America* to help the foreign crew with the details of the tragedy. They wrapped their friend's six-foot body in a blanket and placed him in the walk-in freezer to prepare for the three day run back in. Once Stephano's crew was equipped with clear directions and a plotted course, they ran the *America* into Honolulu to meet the boat's owner. Stephano's family had his body cremated and his ashes dispersed at sea later that year.

Wes and Mikey steered their boats toward the Emperor Sea Mount, a mountain range that is mostly undersea and extends from the "Big Island" of Hawaii to the Aleutian Trench off Alaska. That spot typically marked the beginning of the fishing season in the North Pacific and the guys were ready to get on with it.

Three months without the friendly banter on the radio from his friend and mentor made the trip difficult, but Wes filled the boat and went in. He returned home to his loving wife, Pam, who mentioned she felt like she was standing in a bucket of sand. An MRI revealed a brain tumor. She fought a grueling battle for eight months, but the cancer took her life in April 2006.

Even through the sadness he experienced after losing the love of his life and three of his best friends—all within a year-and-a-half—Wes maintained his gentle spirit and amazing sense of humor. Talking to Wes was like taking a mini-vacation. The sound of his voice still makes me feel as if everything is going to be okay.

He lets me know he cares, and I can nearly always count on a good laugh that cleanses my soul.

Wes continued running the *Maverick* for the next six years, jigging for albacore in the North and South Pacific Oceans. But the overwhelming amount of debris in the waters that followed Japan's tsunami in 2011 made running at night nearly impossible. He told me the most interesting item out there was an entire house. The kitchen cabinets were visible through the open window frames, and the roof was still intact as it floated by, approximately two thousand miles from land. The eerie sight reminded everyone at sea just how fragile life is and how powerful Mother Nature can be.

After threatening to retire for several years, Wes threw in the towel of his fishing career in the fall of 2012. He had been unable to shake the flu for more than six months, so he finally saw his doctor. Test results revealed Stage 4 lung cancer.

True to form, Wes accepted his fate with grace and his wonderful sense of humor. He continued to offer his many friends and the Newport locals a great smile, a friendly greeting, and a twinkle in his eye that brightened the day no matter how gray it seemed. Wes lost his life in March of 2013, but his spirit lives in all of us who were lucky enough to have known him.

Sea Breeze II

Wes and his daughter, Lindsey, on her wedding day

Chapter 32:
The Scattering

THE DAY HAD FINALLY COME. It was early November 2007. Sue and I were going to send our boys home where they would join Stephano in the deep waters of the Pacific Ocean.

My dad and stepmom Carol flew from Idaho to San Diego, California. My dad's first cousin, Duke, and his wife, Esther, live in San Diego, which made their drive to the marina a short one. Mom and I flew down from Friday Harbor, Washington. Many of the Hyenas came for the event. Some were local to the San Diego area, and some made the trek from Oregon. Jaime and Megan arrived in their usual style, wearing the latest trends and looking amazing! Sue's family was there, as well as many of Jack and Sue's friends who lived in and around San Diego.

Sue and I started our day with Bloody Marys and then went to Safeway where we chose two beautiful red roses. We bought a pint of Bacardi Rum for Jack, and a pint of Canadian Club for Bart. All the plans had been made well in advance. Everything was set.

Sue bought a gorgeous gray silk sweater to wear with her indigo denim jeans. The shimmer in the fabric took on a silvery green color, almost a pale charcoal, which made the sparkle in her blue eyes brighter than normal. I wore faded blue jeans and an off-white silk camisole, with the sheer white lace duster I had worn on my wedding day. Both of us wore our wedding rings and the long gold chains around our necks that held our husbands' thick gold wedding bands. Sue also wore the pink pendent she bought when Bart died. I added the St. Christopher medallion I'd purchased when I sent Uncle Halibut and the guys off to finish the season the year before. San Diego is usually still warm in November, so Sue and I wore sandals, displaying our perfectly manicured toes.

The coolers were loaded with beer, wine, water, soda, and ice. Crocket and Popeye assisted the crew in wheeling the provisions down the steep ramp to *The Premiere,* the sport boat Sue ran. Booger and Mrs. Booger, who had just lost their home to the fire that ripped through Southern California, arrived with high energy and good spirits.

"Theresa, you look beautiful!" Andi (Mrs. Booger) declared. "I LOVE your duster!"

"Thank you—it's part of my wedding dress," I told her. "I had it made to go with a satin tank dress. It was gorgeous, and so cool that I get to wear part of it again."

"What a great idea. I lost my wedding dress in the fire. Ha ha ha ha ha ha!" she busted out laughing.

"God, Andi... I'm so sorry. I can't even imagine losing everything like that."

"Hey, darlin', it's just stuff. The pictures we can't replace, but we have our memories. And I still have Bobby and my family. That's all that matters. Plus, I get to start over and not have all the clutter."

"You are by far the most positive person I know. Touch me. I want that attitude to rub off." We enjoyed a good hug and more laughs as we made our way around the boat, greeting everyone as they arrived.

Sue and I were ready for that day. It was time. Yet it felt odd. Wrong even, that Bart and Jack weren't part of our adventure on the water. So many Hyenas were there, but not our husbands.

The sun was shining brightly and it warmed our faces. *The Premiere* cruised swiftly at about fifteen knots toward our waypoint. A breeze from the west kept the water to a light chop, but added a chill to the air in contrast to the warmth from the sun.

"You see that lighthouse, Hon?" Dad asked as he pointed north.

"Yah," I said.

"There's a cemetery on that hill right there where *my* dad is buried. This trip has a lot of sentimental value to me. Brings up a lot of emotions. It's nice to be here, Honey."

"I didn't know that. Very cool, Dad. I sure am glad you guys are here. It absolutely means the world to me. Salute to Grandpa!" Looking at the lighthouse, I raised my water bottle and Dad put his arm around my waist and gave me a squeeze.

"That's right, Sister," Duke confirmed in his raspy voice. Duke is Dad's first cousin and a fellow-marine. "A lot of marines were buried up there and a few of them are your relatives."

I stood in the comfort of my dad's arms, listening to Duke share a brief history lesson of life as a marine and the significance of that area. There are many historical memorials nearby honoring fallen marines, navy men, army soldiers and, of course, fishermen.

"Look!" someone shouted. "The *Star of India*!"

Our boat slowed to a stop as we all looked to the south in amazement. One of the largest tall ships in the world, the *Star of India* is breathtaking. It sails only once a year, and there she was. Out there with us on that special day.

* * *

We had reached our waypoint. It was time to release their ashes.

"Are you ready?" Sue asked me.

"Yes. Let's do it."

We went up to the wheelhouse where our husband's hand-carved wooden urns sat. They were almost identical. Just like the spirits of the two men who once occupied the bodies, now ashes.

"We better make sure we grab the right one," we said in unison, laughing.

"Yah, I think we should scatter our own husbands' ashes."

"Can you imagine? Jack and Bart would shake their heads and laugh at us!"

"I know."

We loosened the underside of the urns with a screwdriver and took out the plastic bags inside.

"Fuck," I said.

"I know," Sue replied.

"I need a minute."

"Me, too."

We held our husbands' ashes for a moment. Unbelievable. So many thoughts. So many feelings. We looked at each other. It was time.

Sue, Jaime, Megan, and I walked to the stern with the ashes, a rose for each man, and their bottles of whiskey. Everyone else on board found a comfortable place to lean, sit, or stand. Silence echoed across the deck of the vessel.

The four of us stood close, made eye contact, and said a prayer bidding farewell to our Bart and Jack. I struggled getting the bag open, making Sue wait. We had to do it at exactly the same time.

"Okay?" she said.

"Okay."

We gently poured their remains into the water. We watched the ocean turn from deep blue to white. Jaime cried hard. Sue quickly wrapped her arm around Jamie while Megan and I secured our arms around each other. Sue and I were aware of nothing except where we were at that exact moment. The roses went in next.

With wet eyes, we watched them drift away from the boat.

"Time for the toast," Sue commanded.

"Time for the toast," I agreed.

We turned to face our guests. "To Bart and Jack!" we shouted, raising the bottles.

"To Bart and Jack!" everyone roared back, raising their glasses.

We poured the whiskey into the ocean, clicked the bottles together before dropping them in the water. Then we hugged each other and the girls. We pulled ourselves together to celebrate, to honor, and to enjoy the wonderful friends and family who shared that day with us.

We followed our guests inside the galley to indulge in the buffet lunch. I sat inside next to Paul and Rita, a Hyena couple I'd met a couple years prior when Bart worked for the American Albacore Fishing Association. Rita stayed home while Paul fished off the coast. Their son, Scott, ran the *Jody H*, named after his wife.

We took our time getting *The Premiere* back to the marina. The mood was mellow, and the wind had picked up, making the run back in cool and a little bumpy. Sue and I hugged everyone tightly as they left the boat. Dad, Carol, Duke, and Esther embraced Mom and me before going back to Duke and Esther's place for the night.

"Thank you so much for being here," I said. "It means the world to me."

"We wouldn't have missed it, Honey," Dad said.

"Thank you for including us," Duke and Esther replied. "So you'll join us for dinner tomorrow night before you and your mom fly back?"

"That would be lovely, thank you."

"See you tomorrow, Babe," Dad said.

"See you tomorrow!" Carol echoed, choking back tears.

Popeye and Crocket helped us haul a few of our personal

things back to the car while the crew finished cleaning the boat.

"Thank you, Sue," I said. "It's so cool that your boss let us use the boat AND the crew. It would have cost us a fortune if we had to hire a vessel and the people to run it."

"Absolutely! Yah, he's wonderful and it made this whole thing complete. Feels weird, doesn't it? It's so final now."

"Yah. I know."

Sue, Jaime, Megan, Mom, and I piled in Sue's car and went back to our hotel. Moments after we got there one of Sue's brothers arrived, along with a handful of Hyenas and a few of Jack and Sue's buddies. We continued the party in our suite for a couple of hours, sharing stories—fishing and otherwise—talking about nautical tattoos, and trying to accept the next chapter in our lives.

All the future chapters would be without Bart and Jack. We would be okay, but the unknown was huge. Having each other and our kin around us created a softness in that gigantic abyss of the unknown. *It* was almost as big as the will and determination to survive and enjoy life no matter what. But *it*—the unknown—the big empty hole—the feeling of that important limb removed from my body—was still there. I tried to keep *it* in the background, which was easier by then, but I could still feel *it*.

The love between Bart and I would continue forever and would allow me to love again. He showed me how to love and be loved. He empowered me, and my strength increased due to his support in everything I chose to do thereafter. He taught me to be present, keep things in perspective, and to let go of anger as quickly as possible in order to be free and settle back into peace and real living. He was the voice of reason and to this day I sometimes find myself wondering—*What would Bart do?*

Living *in the now* has always been a struggle for me, but it's gotten easier over the years. Maybe it's maturity. Maybe it's life's experiences and the influences of the wonderful people who have enriched my life along the way. Since the worry of losing my home at such a fragile time in my life has passed, I've gradually let go of the tight grip I had on trying to control the future. Reliving the past is something we all do, but I now recognize how far I've come in surviving mine.

Loss is something we all experience if we live long enough, but it's unique and special for everyone. Our own pain is truly our own. How we walk through the hurt, recover from the emptiness and solider on as we find new joy, is up to each of us and cannot be outlined in a manual.

For me, I'm thankful that I'm able to celebrate Bart every time I call up a memory of him, rather than let myself curl up in a ball and go down the deep hole of sadness and grief. He made my life better. He made the world better because he was here. He is gone, but his essence lives on and I continue to embrace the life I'm living, with the excitement of not knowing what lies ahead.

Star of India

Sue Slater and me—the scattering

Epilogue: Near Extinction

NOTHING STAYS THE SAME. I was fortunate to be part of a special group. An elite fishing fleet. A fun pod of people who would do anything for one another. The stories I heard about those folks kept me on the edge of my seat wanting more. When I had the pleasure of meeting them, I formed my own opinions, but knowing what so many had gone through—near death experiences for many of them—gave me a different perspective and real respect.

If they judged me, it didn't show. They treated me with grace from the get-go, as if they'd been waiting all day to meet me and were happy to have me join their world, a world unknown to the masses.

Once I had gone commercial fishing myself, I was initiated so to speak, and had experiences of my own to share. When we gathered and the stories flew, I understood what they were talking about. I could relate. I was one of them.

The year after my last trip at sea (in 2002), when a handful of the fishermen and their wives decided to start the American Albacore Fishing Association (AAFA), Bart wanted to be part of the action. He had also stated very clearly to me that he wanted to live on the beach with me and stop going to sea. He was voted in unanimously to manage the organization, and so began his desk job.

In that position, he worked tirelessly with board members, government officials on the West Coast and in Canada, Japanese fish buyers, and fellow fishermen. He learned much more about the fishery and the politics of what made it work—and what was wrong with the system.

He stayed in touch with the guys on the fishing grounds, sent fishing gear to coastal destinations to help with their turnarounds, and kept me updated on the gossip in the fleet. But his buddies on the water missed him terribly and Bart was miserable. The torment of wanting to be home with me and that intense tug at his heart by Mother Ocean was evident.

In 2004, when *Lady Barbara* was in need of a captain, he learned she was also available for purchase. This was the opposite course we had set as a couple, but we needed Bart to be happy. Acquiring the boat seemed like a reasonably low-risk endeavor with the potential for a high return on investment, which would help make a great life for both of us.

When Bart worked out a deal with the owner to charter the boat with the option to buy, he was back on the water. He was in his zone. All was right with the world. The fact that the boat was in need of a lot more work than we initially knew created an extreme financial burden and high-stress. Yet, Bart was happy to be on the water with the Hyenas again.

Bart's excitement was electric, like a lightning bolt had shot through my soul. Everything became clear. And, Mother Ocean's pull was tugging at my heart. *Lady Barbara* was able to fish inside the 200-mile limit, so I could possibly spend up to four weeks on the boat and then take a break to tend to business at home. A shorter run would avert my internal agony. I could do it! I wanted to go back! I held off telling Bart because I knew once I said the words I had to be ready to go. Still, he knew. Jack and Sue were set to buy the *Dalena* and we were buying the *Lady Barbara*. We would be first-time boat owners together. The three of them talked about the adventures we would share in the South Pacific while I held my secret close. Or so I thought. Bart knew my heart. He knew I would tell him when I was ready, but I did not get the chance.

The following year was the beginning of the end. Stephano's death was hard on everyone, but no one had any idea how many deaths would follow, nor how soon they would leave us. After Bart and Jack died, a heavy fog rolled in over the group and never left. It wasn't fun anymore for those who remained at sea, but they kept at it and tried to create their new normal.

Wes and Popeye fought like cats and dogs, but they maintained a level of respect for one another in spite of their differences. New members joined the group, but they were not the same as the original Hyenas. They didn't follow the same rules and they weren't voted in the way it used to be done.

In January 2013, just two months before Wes died, he told me the Hyenas were no more. The guys who were the glue of the fleet were gone, and those who remained were outnumbered by the new guys, who just weren't Hyena quality.

Only a few of the original Hyenas still fish. Most of them run bait boats close to shore, or they manage their boats from land with hired captains who take the boats fishing. The kids who fished with their parents are grown and have their own lives on the beach. The days when the Hyenas fished together are memories now. And the memories of those we've lost are bittersweet, which brings us both joy and sadness as we reminisce about the good ol' days.

In Memoriam

Eddie Diehl (the father of Barry aka Popeye)

Steve Anderson (Stephano aka Pops aka Sleepy)

Pam Wickham (the wife of Wes aka Norton)

Bart Mathews (Midnite, my husband)

Jack Slater (Ultimate, Sue's husband)

Stan Lambert (Sandbar)

JD Needham (daughter of Mike aka Miguel and Aleelat)

Wes Wickham (Norton)

Don Knottingham (Longline aka Dirty Don)

Special Tribute

*Jaime, the daughter of Jack (Ultimate) and Sue
welcomed her first child in 2014.
She named him Jack.*

*Lindsey, the daughter of Wes (Norton)
welcomed her first child in 2015.
She named him Wesley.*

About the Author

Theresa Mathews lives on an island in the Pacific Northwest where she works from her home office as a Corporate Recruiter. She loves to travel, spend time on or near the water, hike, enjoy music, feel the rumble of a Harley Davidson motorcycle, and cook for family and friends. She is working on her second book, a novel. You can learn more about her at www.theresa-mathews.com.

FISHING WITH HYENAS won the following awards:

2018 Best Memoir by Pacific Book Awards

First in Category for the 2017 Journey Awards in Narrative Non-Fiction by Chanticleer International Book Awards

2017 Distinguished Favorite Award by Independent Press Awards

> To access blog updates from the author,
> press information,
> or to order signed copies of this book,
> go to
> www.theresa-mathews.com
>
> Both eBook and print versions are available through Amazon.com

Made in the USA
Monee, IL
13 July 2020